Study Guide

for use with

Financial Accounting
Information for Decisions

Fourth Edition

John J. Wild
University of Wisconsin at Madison

Prepared by
April Mohr
Jefferson Community and Technical College

**McGraw-Hill
Irwin**

*Boston   Burr Ridge, IL   Dubuque, IA   Madison, WI   New York   San Francisco   St. Louis
Bangkok   Bogotá   Caracas   Kuala Lumpur   Lisbon   London   Madrid   Mexico City
Milan   Montreal   New Delhi   Santiago   Seoul   Singapore   Sydney   Taipei   Toronto*

Study Guide for use with
FINANCIAL ACCOUNTING: INFORMATION FOR DECISIONS
John J. Wild

Published by McGraw-Hill/Irwin, an imprint of The McGraw-Hill Companies, Inc., 1221 Avenue of the Americas, New York, NY 10020. Copyright © 2008 by The McGraw-Hill Companies, Inc. All rights reserved.

2 3 4 5 6 7 8 9 0 BKM/BKM 0 9 8 7

ISBN   978-0-07-304379-1
MHID   0-07-304379-6

www.mhhe.com

The McGraw-Hill Companies

TO THE STUDENT

This study guide was prepared as a learning tool for your study of *Financial Accounting: Information for Decisions*, 4e by John J. Wild. The materials provided in this study guide are not a substitute for your textbook. Rather, the objectives of this study guide are to:

▶ Summarize important information that is explained in the textbook. For example, the **chapter outline** of each chapter identifies important topics in the chapter. While you are reading each chapter's outline, you should ask yourself whether or not you clearly understand the listed topics that are set forth in the outline. If not, you should return to the appropriate chapter in your *Financial Accounting: Information for Decisions*, 4e textbook and carefully reread the sections that explain the topics about which you are unclear.

▶ Provide you with copies of **visuals** that your instructor may use in class to introduce selected topics.

▶ Provide you with copies of **alternative demonstration problems** that your instructor may use in class to review selected topics.

▶ Provide you with a quick means of testing your knowledge of the chapter. The **problems** included for each chapter include true-false and multiple-choice questions, matching of key terms and definitions, fill-in-the-blank questions, and a variety of exercises requiring application and analysis of many of the concepts covered in the chapter. If you are unable to correctly answer the problems, you should again return to the appropriate chapter in your *Financial Accounting: Information for Decisions*, 4e textbook and review the sections about which you are unclear.

How can you get the most out of this study guide? The best approach may be summarized as follows:

▶ **First**, read the learning objectives and the related summary paragraphs. Then, ask whether your understanding of the chapter seems adequate for you to accomplish the objectives. If not, return to and reread the relevant sections of the related chapter in your *Financial Accounting: Information for Decisions*, 4e textbook.

▶ **Second**, review the chapter outline, taking time to think through (describing to yourself) any explanations that would be required to expand the outline. Use the notes column to make note of questions that arise or concepts that seem particularly difficult. Return to your *Financial Accounting: Information for Decisions*, 4e textbook to locate the answers to your questions and review the difficult concepts.

▶ **Third**, review the visuals. The visuals reinforce major concepts of the chapter.

▶ **Fourth**, read and then complete the requirements of each of the problems. Check your answers against the solutions that are provided after the problems. Return to your *Financial Accounting: Information for Decisions*, 4e textbook for additional review of any material that you haven't fully mastered.

▶ **Fifth,** raise any unanswered questions that you may have in class and/or see your Instructor for help.

You may also find it helpful to **bring the chapter outlines, visuals and alternative demonstration problems to class** as explained below.

► You can highlight the sections of the chapter outline and/or visuals that your instructor emphasizes.

► You may use the notes column of the chapter outline to record additional information that is provided by your instructor. In this regard, don't forget to note whether or not your Instructor will hold you responsible for the information covered in the appendices, if any, that conclude each chapter. (The outlines of the appendices always appear at the end of the chapter outline.)

► Instructors often use the alternative demonstration problem(s) in class to illustrate key concepts in the chapter. You can use your copy of the alternative demonstration problem as a starting point for solving the problem in class. (If a given alternative demonstration problem in not covered in class, you may wish to solve it anyway; see your instructor for the solution.)

► Often, in addition to assigning various quick study questions, exercises and problems from the end-of-chapter textbook materials as homework, instructors select additional questions, exercises and/or problems for use in class. You can make note of those questions, exercises and/or problems in the notes column of the chapter outline. Later, as you study the chapter outline, you will have a list of quick study questions, exercises and/or problems that were covered by your instructor during class in addition to those that were assigned as homework (which are typically listed on your class syllabus).

The next two pages are provided to recommend an **overall approach to succeeding** in your accounting course.

I would truly appreciate your feedback as to the usefulness of this study guide and any ideas you would like to share.

April Mohr
april.mohr@kctcs.edu

HOW TO SUCCEED IN YOUR ACCOUNTING COURSE

A. **Stay Up-To-Date**

Accounting is a unique discipline in that learning takes place in "building blocks." The best analogy is that it is almost impossible to learn to read without learning the sounds of the letters in the alphabet. In is almost impossible for you to learn topics in accounting without having a level of understanding of the previously addressed topic. Accounting is the language of business, and like any language, it is learned through a developmental process.

Staying up-to-date includes completing all assignments on a timely basis. This allows you to take full advantage of classroom assignment check. The best insurance for staying up-to-date is to use good time management skills. This means that you need to commit to a regular weekly study schedule—and stick to it! Staying up-to-date will give you the foundations to learn and *succeed!*

B. **Make Effective Use of Your Textbook**

1. Overview the chapter.

    a. Preview the learning objectives and mark those that the instructor has listed in the course outline or mentioned in class.

    b. Read the opening page of each chapter, which provides a very brief look at contents, as well as a look back and ahead. This allows you to see the links or building blocks you will put in place.

    c. Read the Summary of Learning Objectives found at the end of the chapter. This first pass on summaries is just to get a broad perspective of the contents. Do not expect to understand all that you read at this point.

2. Read the chapter.

    a. Use a highlighter or take notes as you read to keep you mentally alert and focused.

    b. Writing is a proven vehicle for learning. Use the wide text margins to note key concepts as well as questions that arise. This will clarify your thoughts as you read.

    c. Use the Quick Check feature. The Quick Check sections are interspersed throughout each chapter. The brief Quick Check questions are designed to help you assess whether you are grasping the essential concepts. Guidance Answers to Quick Checks are found at the end of each chapter.

    d. Reread the Summary of Learning Objectives. Make sure you thoroughly understand those specified by the instructor.

3. Solve the demonstration problem(s) at the end of each chapter. *Don't overlook these!* Students find these most helpful in learning how to solve accounting problems. They address all major topics of the chapter. If you need help getting started, refer to the approach to planning the solution that is provided. Compare your answers to the complete solution that follows each demonstration problem.

C. Get Involved and Stay Involved

1. The more actively involved you are in the learning process, the more you will understand and retain the course materials. Don't hesitate to ask questions that arise while you were reading the chapter, completing homework assignments, or otherwise studying.

2. Participate fully in each and every classroom activity.

3. Form a study group or a learning team. Meet regularly outside of class. Support each other's learning. Teaching others is proven to be the most effective way of reinforcing learning and increasing your retention. Every student will benefit.

TABLE OF CONTENTS

CHAPTER 1
INTRODUCING ACCOUNTING IN BUSINESS

Learning Objective C1:

Explain the purpose and importance of accounting in the information age.

Accounting is an information and measurement system that identifies, records, and communicates relevant, reliable, and comparable information about an organization's business activities. It helps assess opportunities, products, investments, and social and community responsibilities.

Learning Objective C2:

Identify users and uses of accounting.

Users of accounting are both internal and external. Some users and uses of accounting include (a) managers in controlling, monitoring, and planning; (b) lenders for measuring the risk and return of loans; (c) shareholders for assessing the return and risk of stock; (d) directors for overseeing management; and (e) employees for judging employment opportunities.

Learning Objective C3:

Identify opportunities in accounting and related fields.

Opportunities in accounting include financial, managerial, and tax accounting. They also include accounting-related fields such as lending, consulting, managing, and planning.

Learning Objective C4:

Explain why ethics are crucial to accounting.

The goal of accounting is to provide useful information for decision making. For information to be useful, it must be trusted. This demands ethical behavior in accounting.

Learning Objective C5:

Explain the meaning of generally accepted accounting principles, and define and apply several key accounting principles.

Generally accepted accounting principles are a common set of standards applied by accountants. Accounting principles aid in producing relevant, reliable, and comparable information. The business entity principle means that a business is accounted for separately from its owner(s). The objectivity principle means independent, objective evidence supports the information. The cost principle means financial statements are based on actual costs incurred. The monetary unit principle assumes transactions can be reflected in money terms. The going-concern principle means financial statements assume the business will continue. The revenue recognition principle means revenue is recognized when earned.

Learning Objective C6 (Appendix 1B):

Identify and describe the three major activities in organizations.

Organizations carry out three major activities: financing, investing, and operating. Financing is the means used to pay for resources such as land, buildings, and machines. Investing refers to the buying and selling of resources used in acquiring and selling products and services. Operating activities are those necessary for carrying out the organization's plans.

Learning Objective A1:

Define and interpret the accounting equation and each of its components.

The accounting equation is: Assets = Liabilities + Equity. Assets are resources owned by a company. Liabilities are creditors' claims on assets. Equity is the owner's claim on assets (the residual). The expanded accounting equation is: Assets = Liabilities + [Common Stock – Dividends + Revenues – Expenses].

Learning Objective A2:

Analyze business transactions using the accounting equation.

A transaction is an exchange of economic consideration between two parties. Examples include exchanges of products, services, money, and rights to collect money. Transactions always have at least two effects on one or more components of the accounting equation. This equation is always in balance.

Learning Objective A3:

Compute and interpret return on assets.

Return on assets is computed as net income divided by average assets. For example, if we have an average balance of $100 in a savings account and it earns $5 interest for the year, the return on assets is $5/$100, or 5%.

Learning Objective A4 (Appendix 1A):

Explain the relation between return and risk.

Return refers to income, and risk is the uncertainty about the return we hope to make. All investments involve risk. The lower the risk of an investment, the lower its expected return. Higher risk implies higher, but riskier, expected return.

Learning Objective P1:

Identify and prepare basic financial statements and explain how they interrelate.

Four financial statements report on an organization's activities: balance sheet, income statement, statement of retained earnings, and statement of cash flows.

I. Importance of Accounting

Providing information about what businesses own, what they owe, and how they perform is an important aim of accounting. **Accounting** is an information and measurement system that identifies, records and communicates relevant, reliable, and comparable information about an organization's business activities. **Recordkeeping**, or **bookkeeping**, which includes just one function of accounting, is the recording of transactions and events, either manually or electronically. Technology is a key part of modern business and has changed the way we store, process, and summarize large masses of data. Technology has allowed accounting to expand to include consulting, planning and other financial services.

A. Users of Accounting Information

Accounting is the *language of business* because all organizations set up an accounting information system to communicate data to help people make better decisions.

1. **External information users** are not directly involved in running the organization; they include shareholders, lenders, directors, customers, suppliers, regulators, lawyers, brokers, and the press. External users have limited access to an organization's information but they must receive information that is relevant, reliable and comparable. **Financial accounting** is the area of accounting aimed at serving external users by providing them with *general-purpose financial statements*.

2. **Internal information users** are those directly involved in managing and operating an organization. They use the information to help improve the efficiency and effectiveness of an organization. **Managerial accounting** is the area of accounting that serves the decision-making needs of internal users. Internal users and the information they require include:

   a. Research and development managers need data on current and projected costs and revenues to decide whether to pursue or continue research and development projects.

   b. Purchasing managers need data on quality and quantity of merchandise and materials purchases.

   c. Human resource managers need data on current payroll costs, employee benefits, performance and compensation.

   d. Production managers need data on costs and quality of production processes.

   e. Distribution managers need data on quantity and delivery schedules.

   f. Marketing managers need data on sales and costs to effectively target consumers and set prices.

      g. Servicing managers need data on warranties and maintenance information to provide a valuable product to its customers.

   3. Both internal and external users rely on internal controls to monitor and control company activities. **Internal controls** are procedures designed to protect company property, ensure reliable reports, promote efficiency, and encourage adherence to company policies.

B. **Opportunities in Accounting**

   1. The four broad areas of opportunities in accounting include financial accounting, managerial accounting, taxation, and accounting-related careers.

   2. The majority of accounting opportunities are in *private accounting. Public accounting* offers the next largest number of opportunities while still other opportunities exist in government (and not-for-profit) agencies, including business regulation and investigation of law violations.

   3. The professional standing of accounting specialists are denoted by a certificate such as certified public accountant (CPA), certified management accountant (CMA), certified internal auditor (CIA), certified bookkeeper (CB), certified payroll professional (CPP) and personal financial specialist (PFS).

II.   **Fundamentals of Accounting**

A. **Ethics – A Key Concept**

   Ethics are beliefs that distinguish right from wrong; they are accepted standards of good and bad behavior.

   1. Ethical behavior is important in all successful organizations. Users must be able to trust accounting information. Good ethics are good business.

   2. The AICPA and IMA have set up ethical codes of conduct to be followed.

B. **Generally Accepted Accounting Principles**

   Financial accounting is governed by rules known as **generally accepted accounting principles, GAAP.** GAAP aims to make accounting information relevant, reliable and comparable. Two main groups establish GAAP.

   1. **Setting Accounting Principles**

      a. The Financial Accounting Standards Board (FASB) is the private group that sets both broad and specific principles.

      b. The **Securities and Exchange Commission** (SEC) is the government group that establishes reporting requirements for companies that issue stock to the public.

c. The **International Accounting Standards Board** (IASB) issues *International Financial Reporting Standards* (IFRS) that identify preferred accounting practices. The IASC hopes to create more harmony among accounting practices of different countries; however, it does not have authority to impose its standards on companies.

2. **Principles of Accounting**
   Accounting principles are both general (basic assumptions, concepts and guidelines for preparing financial statements) and specific (detailed rules used in reporting transactions). The principles discussed in this chapter are:

   a. **Objectivity principle**—accounting information is supported by independent, unbiased evidence.

   b. **Cost principle**—accounting information is based on actual costs incurred in business transactions. Cost is measured on a cash or equal-to-cash basis.

   c. **Going-concern principle**—accounting information reflects the assumption that the business will continue operating instead of being closed or sold

   d. **Monetary unit**—transactions and events are expressed in monetary, or money, units (generally the currency of the country in which the business operates).

   e. **Revenue recognition principle**—provides guidance on when a company must recognize revenue; to *recognize* means to record it.

   f. **Business entity principle**—a business is accounted for separately and distinctly from its owner(s). A business entity can take one of three legal forms:

      i. *Sole proprietorship* is a business owned by one person that has unlimited liability. Requires no special legal requirements. The business is not subject to an income tax but the owner is responsible for personal income tax on the net income of the entity.

      ii. *Partnership* is a business owned by two or more people, called partners, who are subject to unlimited liability. No special legal requirements must be met. The only requirement is an oral or written agreement between the partners which usually outlines how profits and losses are to be shard. The business is not subject to an income tax, but the owners are responsible for personal income tax on their individual share of the net income of the entity.

iii. *Corporation* is a business that is a separate legal entity whose owners are called shareholders or stockholders. These owners have limited liability because the business is legally responsible for its own actions and debts. The entity is responsible for a business income tax and the owners are responsible for personal income tax on profits that are distributed to them in the form of dividends. **Sarbanes-Oxley** is an act which requires extensive documentation and verification of internal controls. The goal of this act is to provide more transparency, accountability and truthfulness in reporting transactions.

III. **Transaction Analysis and the Accounting Equation**

A. **Accounting Equation**

The accounting system reflects two basic aspects of a company: what it owns and what it owes. Together, liabilities and equity are the source of funds to acquire assets. The relation of assets, liabilities and equity is reflected in the **accounting equation**: **Assets = Liabilities + Owner's Equity (A = L + OE)**

1. **Assets** are resources owned or controlled by a company; these resources are expected to yield future benefits.

2. **Liabilities** are creditors' claims on assets.

3. **Owner's Equity** is the owner's claim on assets; equity is also called *net assets* or *residual equity (interest)*.

A corporation's equity—often called stockholders' or shareholders' equity—has two parts: contributed capital and retained earnings:

a. **Contributed capital**, refers to the amount that stockholders invest in the company—included under the title **common stock**.

b. **Retained earnings** refer to income (revenues less expenses) that is not distributed to stockholders. The distribution of assets to stockholders is called **dividends**, which reduce retained earnings. **Revenues** increase retained earnings and are the assets earned from a company's earnings activities. **Expenses** decrease retained earnings and are the cost of assets or services used to earn revenues.

4. The above breakdown of equity yields the expanded accounting equation:
A= L + Contributed Capital + Retained Earnings
A = L + Common Stock – Dividends + Revenues – Expenses

5. **Net income** occurs when revenues exceed expenses. A **net loss** occurs when expenses exceed revenues, which decreases equity.

B. **Transaction Analysis**

Business activities can be described in terms of transactions and events. **External transactions** are exchanges of value between two entities, which yield changes in the accounting equation. **Internal transactions** are exchanges within an entity; they can also affect the accounting equation. **Events** refer to those happenings that affect an entity's accounting equation and can be reliably measured. The following section uses the accounting equation to analyze eleven selected transactions and events. Remember that each transaction leaves the accounting equation in balance and assets always equal the sum of liabilities and equity.

Transaction 1: Investment by Owner

+ Assets (Cash) = + Equity (Common Stock)

After this transaction, the cash (an asset) and the stockholders' equity each equal the amount invested. The source of the increase in equity is the owner's investment (stock issuance), which is included in the column titled Common Stock.

Transaction 2: Purchase supplies for cash

+Assets (Supplies) = – Assets (Cash)

This transaction merely changes the form of assets from cash to supplies; the decrease in cash is exactly equal to the increase in supplies.

Transaction 3: Purchase Equipment for Cash

+ Assets (Equipment) = – Assets (Cash)

Like Transaction 2, this transaction is an exchange of one asset, cash, for another asset, equipment; the equipment is an asset because of its expected future benefits.

Transaction 4: Purchase Supplies on Credit

+Assets (Supplies) = + Liability (Account Payable)

The supplies are acquired in exchange for a promise to pay for them later; the liability created is referred to as *accounts payable*.

Transaction 5: Provide Services for Cash

+ Assets (Cash) = + Equity (Revenues)

The company earns revenues by providing services to its clients; the increase in equity is included in revenues because the cash received from clients is earned by providing services.

Transactions 6 and 7: Payment of Expenses in Cash

- Assets (Cash) = – Equity (Expenses)

These two transactions involve the payment of cash for this month's rent and employee salary; the costs of both rent and salary are expenses, as opposed to assets, because their benefits are used in the current month (they have no further benefits after the current month). Both transactions decrease equity which is included in the column titled Expenses.

Transaction 8: Provide Services and Facilities for Credit

+ Assets (Accts Receivable) = + Equity (Revenues)

The company earns revenues by providing services to its clients; the clients are billed for the services. This transaction results in an asset, called *accounts receivable*, which is the amount owed by this client, and also yields an increase in equity reflected in the column titled Revenues.

Transaction 9: Receipt of Cash from Accounts Receivable

+ Assets (Cash) = – Assets (Accounts Receivable)

The client pays the company the amount that it was billed for the services provided in Transaction 8. This transaction does not change the total amount of assets and does not affect liabilities or equity; it converts the receivable (an asset) to cash (an asset). It does not create new revenue. The revenue was recognized in Transaction 8.

Transaction 10: Payment of accounts payable

– Assets (Cash) = – Liability (Accounts Payable)

The company made a partial payment to the vendor for the supplies acquired in Transaction 4. This transaction decreases cash and decreases its liability to the vendor. Equity does not change; this event does not create an expense. The expense will be recorded in the future when the company derives the benefits from these supplies by using them.

Transaction 11: Payment of cash dividend

– Assets (Cash) = – Equity (Dividends)

The company declared and paid a dividend to its owner. Dividends (decreases in equity) are not reported as expenses because they are not part of the company's earnings process, and they are not used in computing net income.

IV. **Financial Statements**

A *Income Statement*

Reports on operating revenue and expense activities *over a period of time.* Net income (or loss) is computed as sales less all costs and expenses. Revenues are reported first followed by expenses. Expenses reflect the costs to generate the revenue reported.

B. *Statement of Retained Earnings*

Reports changes in retained earnings of the business over a period of time. Changes result from net income, which increases retained earnings. A net loss and dividends decrease retained earnings. Ending retained earnings is reported on the balance sheet.

C. *Balance Sheet*

Reports a listing of amounts for assets, liabilities, and equity *at a point in time.*

D. *Statement of Cash Flows*

Reports on cash flows for operating, investing, and financing activities over a period of time.

V. Decision Analysis—Return on Assets (ROA)

   A. Return on assets, also called return on investment (ROI), is a profitability measure; useful in evaluating management, analyzing and forecasting profits, and planning activities.

   B. It is calculated by dividing net income by average total assets.

VI. Return and Risk Analysis (Appendix 1A)

   A. Net income is often linked to return. Return on assts (ROA) is stated in ratio form as income divided by assets invested.

   B. **Risk** is the uncertainty about the return we will earn. All business investments involve risk, but some involve more risk than others.

   C. The lower the risk of an investment, the lower is our expected return. Higher risk implies higher, but riskier, expected returns.

   D. The trade-off between risk and return is a normal part of business. We use accounting information to assess both return and risk.

VII. Business Activities and the Accounting Equation (Appendix 1B)

   There are three major types of business activities:

   A. Financing Activities—provide the means organizations use to pay for resources such as land, buildings, and equipment to carry out plans.

   B. Investing Activities—the acquiring and disposing of resources (assets) that an organization uses to acquire and sell its products or services.

   C. Operating Activities—involve using resources to research, develop, purchase, produce, distribute, and market products and services.

WARNING: <u>NO MATTER WHAT HAPPENS</u> ALWAYS KEEP THIS SCALE IN BALANCE

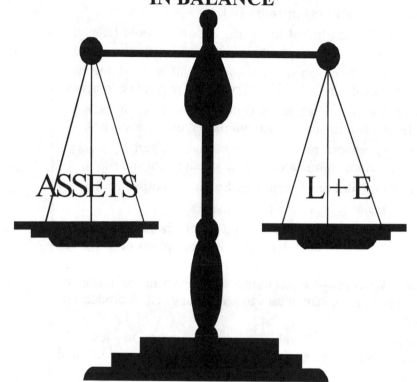

Basic Accounting Equation

ASSETS = LIABILITIES + EQUITY

<u>TRANSACTION ANALYSIS RULES</u>

1) Every transaction affects at least two items.

2) Every transaction must result in a balanced equation.

<u>TRANSACTION ANALYSIS POSSIBILITIES:</u>					
A		=	L	+	E
(1)	+	and		+	
or (2)	-	and		-	
or (3)	+ and -	and		No change	
or (4)	No change	and		+ and -	

Chapter One – Alternate Demonstration Problem #1

One spring, Jane Smith decided to earn money as a lawn service professional. After discussions with neighbors, she obtained enough commitments for lawn servicing jobs that she thought she could be successful at it. On June 1, 20X8, on the basis of these commitments, Jane started her business under the name of Ultimate Lawn Care, Inc.

On August 31, 20X8, Jane noted the following events which occurred during the first three months of business:

- On June 1, Jane personally invested $2,000 in the business by depositing the $2,000 in the business's bank account.

- Deposits during the first three months, all from customer collections, totaled $11,400.

- Checks written during the 3-month period included the following:

  - Truck and equipment rental, $1,800
  - Gas, oil, and lubrication, $880
  - Miscellaneous supplies used, $90
  - Helpers, $4,700; including payroll taxes, $500;
  - Insurance, $175;
  - Telephone, $100
  - Dividend (transferred to personal bank account), $2,000.

At the end of August:

- Customers still owed $600 for services that were performed.
- The business owed another $100 to a vendor for gas and oil.

Required:

1. Show the effect of each transaction on the accounting equation.

2. Prepare an income statement for Ultimate Lawn Care, Inc. for the three months ended August 31, 20X8.

3. Prepare a balance sheet for Ultimate Lawn Care, Inc. at August 31, 20X8.

4. Explain why the company's cash balance at the end of the summer does not agree with the amount of net income earned during the summer.

(If this alternative demonstration problem is not covered in class, see your instructor for the solution.)

Problem I

The following statements are either true or false. Place a (T) in the parentheses before each true statement and an (F) before each false statement.

1. ( ) Two businesses with the same owner must have separate accounting records.

2. ( ) Land appraised at $40,000 and worth that much to its purchaser should be recorded at its worth ($40,000), even though it was purchased through hard bargaining for $35,000.

Problem II

You are given several words, phrases, or numbers to choose from in completing each of the following statements or in answering the following questions. In each case select the one that best completes the statement, or answers the question, and place its letter in the answer space provided.

_____ 1. The board that currently has the primary authority to identify generally accepted accounting principles is the:

     a. APB.

     b. FASB.

     c. FEI.

     d. ASB.

     e. AICPA.

_____ 2. If Kay Bee Company rendered services for a customer in exchange for $175 cash, what would be the effects on the accounting equation?

     a. Assets, $175 increase; Liabilities, no effect; Owner's Equity, $175 increase.

     b. Assets, no effect; Liabilities, $175 decrease; Owner's Equity, $175 increase.

     c. Assets, $175 increase; Liabilities, $175 increase; Owner's Equity, no effect.

     d. Assets, $175 increase; Liabilities, $175 decrease; Owner's Equity, $350 increase.

     e. There is no effect on the accounting equation.

Problem III

Many of the important ideas and concepts discussed in Chapter 1 are reflected in the following list of key terms. Test your understanding of these terms by matching the appropriate definitions with the terms. Record the number identifying the most appropriate definition in the blank space next to each term.

_____ Accounting
_____ Accounting equation
_____ Assets
_____ Audit
_____ Balance sheet
_____ Bookkeeping
_____ Business entity principle
_____ Common stock
_____ Contributed capital
_____ Corporation
_____ Cost principle
_____ Dividends
_____ Equity
_____ Ethics
_____ Events
_____ Expanded accounting equation
_____ Expenses
_____ External transactions
_____ External users
_____ Financial accounting
_____ Financial Accounting Standards
      Board (FASB)
_____ Generally Accepted Accounting
      Principles (GAAP)
_____ Going-concern principle
_____ Income
_____ Income statement
_____ Internal transactions

_____ Internal users
_____ International Accounting Standards
      Board (IASB)
_____ Liabilities
_____ Managerial accounting
_____ Monetary unit principle
_____ Net assets
_____ Net income
_____ Net loss
_____ Objectivity principle
_____ Partnership
_____ Proprietorship
_____ Recordkeeping
_____ Retained earnings
_____ Return*
_____ Return on assets
_____ Revenues
_____ Revenue recognition principle
_____ Risk*
_____ Securities and Exchange Commission
      (SEC)
_____ Shareholders
_____ Shares
_____ Sole proprietorship
_____ Statement of cash flows
_____ Statement of retained earnings
_____ Stock
_____ Stockholders

* *Key term discussed in Appendix 1A.*

1. An information and measurement system that identifies, records, and communicates relevant information about a company's business activities.

2. Rules that specify acceptable accounting practice.

3. Persons using accounting information who are not directly involved in running the organization.

4. A business owned by two or more people that is not organized as a corporation.

5. The federal agency charged by Congress to set reporting rules for organizations that sell ownership shares to the public.

6. Part of accounting that involves recording transactions and events, either manually or electronically (also called bookkeeping).

7. An analysis and report of an organization's accounting system and its records using various tests.

8. Assets = Liabilities + [Common Stock – Dividends + Revenues – Expenses].

9. Activities within an organization that can affect the accounting equation.

10. Business owned by one person that is not organized as a corporation; also called a *sole proprietorship*.

11. Area of accounting mainly aimed at serving external users.

12. Codes of conduct by which actions are judged as right or wrong, fair or unfair, honest or dishonest.

13. Owners of a corporation (also called shareholders).

14. A business owned by one person that is not organized as a corporation (also called a proprietorship).

15. A business that is a separate legal entity under state or federal laws with owners called shareholders or stockholders.

16. Refers to the amount that stockholders invest in the company; included under the title common stock.

17. A principle that requires financial statement information to be supported by independent, unbiased evidence.

18. A report of changes in retained earnings over a period of time; adjusted for increases (owner investment and net income) and for decreases (dividends and net loss).

19. Resources expected to produce current and future benefits.

20. Creditor's claims on an organization's assets.

21. Group that identifies preferred accounting practices and encourages global acceptance; issues International Financial Reporting Standards.

22. The income from an investment.

23. Owner's (shareholders') claims on an organization's assets.

24. The equality where Assets = Liabilities + Owner's Equity.

25. The amount of uncertainty about an expected return.

26. Equity of a corporation divided into units (also called shares).

27. A corporation's basic ownership share (also called capital stock).

28. The principle that requires a business be accounted for separately from its owner(s).

29. Persons using accounting information who are directly involved in managing the organization.

30. Financial statement that lists the types and amounts of assets, liabilities, and equity at a specific date; also called the statement of financial position.

31. Amount earned after subtracting all expenses necessary for its sales (also called earnings, income or profit).

32. Exchanges of economic consideration between one entity and another entity.

33. A ratio reflecting operating efficiency; defined as net income divided by average total assets (also called return on investment).

34. The accounting principle that requires financial statement information to be based on actual costs incurred in business transactions.

35. Area of accounting aimed at serving the decision-making needs of internal users.

36. Equity of a corporation divided into units (also called stock).

37. The costs incurred to earn sales.

38. A corporation's distributions of assets to its owners.

39. A part of accounting that involves recording transactions and events, either manually or electronically (also called recordkeeping).

40. Happenings that both affect an organization's financial position and can be reliably measured.

41. Amounts earned from selling products or services (also called sales).

42. A principle that requires financial statements to reflect the assumption that the business will continue operating.

43. An independent group of seven full-time members who are responsible for setting accounting rules.

44. Owners of a corporation (also called stockholders).

45. Amount earned after subtracting all expenses necessary for sales (also called earnings, net income or profit).

46. Financial statement that subtracts expenses from revenues to yield a net income or loss over a specified period of time.

47. A principle that assumes transactions and events can be expressed in money units.

48. Another name for equity.

49. The excess of expenses over revenues for a period.

50. A corporation's accumulated net income and losses that have not been distributed (in dividends) to shareholders.

51. The principle that requires that revenue is recognized when earned.

52. A financial statement that lists cash inflows (receipts) and cash outflows (payments) during a period; arranged by operating, investing, and financing activities.

Problem IV

Complete the following by filling in the blanks.

1. The cost principle requires financial statement information to be based on _____ incurred in business transactions. The _____ principle requires financial statements to reflect the assumption that the business will continue operating instead of being closed or sold. The _____ principle requires financial statement information to be supported by evidence other than someone's opinion or imagination.

2. The balance sheet equation is _____ equals _____ plus _____. It is also called the _____ equation.

3. The statement of cash flows shows the events that caused _____ to change. It classifies the cash flow into three major categories: _____, _____, and _____ activities.

Problem V

The following are eight transactions completed by Cornell, Inc., a law firm.

1. Paid the rent for three months in advance on the law office, $3,000.
2. Paid cash to purchase a new computer for the office, $900.
3. Completed legal work for Ray Holland and immediately collected the full payment of $2,500 in cash.
4. Purchased law books on credit, $700.
5. Completed $1,500 of legal work for Julie Landon on credit, and immediately entered in the accounting records both the right to collect and the revenue earned.
6. Paid for the law books purchased in Transaction 4.
7. Received $1,500 from Julie Landon for the legal work in Transaction 5.
8. Paid the weekly salary of the office secretary, $575.

The assets, liabilities, and owner's equity of Linda Cornell's law practice prior to the above eight transactions are shown on the next page. In the spaces provided, show (by additions and subtractions) the effects of each transaction on the company's assets, liabilities, and equity. Include new totals after each transaction as in Exhibit 1.9 in the text.

		Assets				= Liabilities +		Equity		
Cash	+ Accounts Receivable +	Prepaid Rent +	Law Library +	Office Equipment =	Accounts Payable +	Common Stock	+ Revenues	− Expenses
$4,000			$12,000	$3,250		$19,250		
1.								
2.								
3.								
4.								
5.								
6.								
7.								
8.								

Refer to the above and complete the following by filling in the blanks.

a. Did each transaction affect two items of the equation? _____

b. Did the equation remain in balance after the effects of each transaction were entered? _____

c. If the equation had not remained in balance after the effects of each transaction were entered, this would have indicated that _____.

d. Cornell, Inc. earned $2,500 of revenue upon the completion of Transaction 3, and the asset that flowed into the business as a result of this transaction was in the form of _____.

e. Cornell, Inc. earned $1,500 of revenue upon the completion of Transaction 5, and the asset that flowed into the business upon the completion of this transaction was _____.

f. The right to collect $1,500 from Julie Landon was converted into _____ in Transaction 7. Nevertheless, the revenue was earned upon the completion of the _____ in Transaction 5.

g. The $1,500 collected in Transaction 7 was recognized as revenue in Transaction 5 because of the _____ principle, which states that (1) revenue should be recognized at the time it is _____, (2) the inflow of assets associated with revenue may be in a form other than _____, and (3) the amount of revenue should be measured as the cash plus the cash equivalent value of any _____ received from customers in exchange for goods or services.

Solutions for Chapter 1

Problem I

1. T
2. F

Problem II

1. B
2. A

Problem III

1	Accounting	29	Internal users
24	Accounting equation	21	International Accounting Standards Board (IASB)
19	Assets		
7	Audit	20	Liabilities
30	Balance sheet	35	Managerial accounting
39	Bookkeeping	47	Monetary unit principle
28	Business entity principle	48	Net assets
27	Common stock	31	Net income
16	Contributed capital	49	Net loss
15	Corporation	17	Objectivity principle
34	Cost principle	4	Partnership
38	Dividends	10	Proprietorship
23	Equity	6	Recordkeeping
12	Ethics	50	Retained earnings
40	Events	22	Return*
8	Expanded accounting equation	33	Return on assets
37	Expenses	41	Revenues
32	External transactions	51	Revenue recognition principle
3	External users	25	Risk*
11	Financial accounting	5	Securities and Exchange Commission (SEC)
43	Financial Accounting Standards Board (FASB)		
2	Generally Accepted Accounting Principles (GAAP)	44	Shareholders
		36	Shares
		14	Sole proprietorship
42	Going-concern principle	52	Statement of cash flows
45	Income	18	Statement of retained earnings
46	Income statement	26	Stock
9	Internal transactions	13	Stockholders

* *Key term discussed in Appendix 1A.*

Problem IV

1. costs; going-concern; objectivity
2. assets; liabilities; equity; accounting
3. cash; operating; investing; financing

Problem V

	Cash	+ Receivable +	Prepaid Rent	+ Library +	Office Equipment =	Accounts Payable +	Common Stock	+ Revenues	− Expenses
	$4,000			$12,000	$3,250		$19,250		
1. −	3,000	+ $3,000							
	1,000		3,000	12,000	3,250		19,250		
2. −	900				+ 900				
	100		3,000	12,000	4,150		19,250		
3. +	2,500							+ $2,500	
	2,600		3,000	12,000	4,150		19,250	2,500	
4.				+ 700		+ $700			
	2,600		3,000	12,700	4,150	700	19,250	2,500	
5.	+	$1,500						+ 1,500	
	2,600	1,500	3,000	12,700	4,150	700	19,250	4,000	
6. −	700					− 700			
	1,900	1,500	3,000	12,700	4,150	0	19,250	4,000	
7. +	1,500 −	1,500							
	3,400	0	3,000	12,700	4,150	0	19,250	4,000	
8. −	575								− $575
	$2,825 +	$0 +	$3,000 +	$12,700 +	$4,150 =	$0 +	$19,250 +	$4,000 −	$575

a. Yes
b. Yes
c. an error had been made
d. cash
e. an account receivable
f. cash; legal work
g. revenue recognition; earned; cash; noncash assets

CHAPTER 2
ANALYZING AND RECORDING TRANSACTIONS

Learning Objective C1:

Explain the steps in processing transactions.

The accounting process identifies business transactions and events, analyzes and records their effects, and summarizes and presents information useful in making decisions. Transactions and events are the starting points in the accounting process. Source documents help in their analysis. The effects of transactions and events are recorded in journals. Posting along with a trial balance helps summarize and classify these effects.

Learning Objective C2:

Describe source documents and their purpose.

Source documents identify and describe transactions and events. Examples are sales tickets, checks, purchase orders, bills, and bank statements. Source documents provide objective and reliable evidence, making information more useful.

Learning Objective C3:

Describe an account and its use in recording transactions.

An account is a detailed record of increases and decreases in a specific asset, liability, equity, revenue, or expense item. Information from accounts is analyzed, summarized, and presented in reports and financial statements for decision makers.

Learning Objective C4:

Describe a ledger and a chart of accounts.

A ledger (or general ledger) is a record containing all accounts used by a company and their balances. It is referred to as the *books*. The chart of accounts is a list of all accounts and usually includes an identification number assigned to each account.

Learning Objective C5:

Define *debits* and *credits* and explain their role in double-entry accounting.

Debit refers to left, and *credit* refers to right. Debits increase assets, expenses, and dividends, while credits decrease them. Credits increase liabilities, common stock, and revenues; debits decrease them. Double-entry accounting means each transaction affects at least two accounts and has at least one debit and one credit. The system for recording debits and credits follows from the accounting equation. The left side of an account is the normal balance for assets, dividends, and expenses, and the right side is the normal balance for liabilities, common stock, and revenues.

Learning Objective A1:

Analyze the impact of transactions on accounts and financial statements.

We analyze transactions using the concepts of double-entry accounting. This analysis is performed by determining a transaction's effects on accounts. These effects are recorded in journals and posted to ledgers. We also identify the financial statements affected by each transaction.

Learning Objective A2:

Compute the debt ratio and describe its use in analyzing company performance.

A company's debt ratio is computed as total liabilities divided by total assets. It reveals how much of the assets are financed by creditor (nonowner) financing. The higher this ratio, the more risk a company faces because liabilities must be repaid at specific dates.

Learning Objective P1:

Record transactions in a journal and post entries to a ledger.

Transactions are recorded in a journal. Each entry in a journal is posted to the accounts in the ledger. This provides information that is used to produce financial statements. Balance column accounts are widely used and include columns for debits, credits, and the account balance.

Learning Objective P2:

Prepare and explain the use of a trial balance.

A trial balance is a list of accounts from the ledger showing their debit or credit balances in separate columns. The trial balance is a summary of the ledger's contents and is useful in preparing financial statements and in revealing recordkeeping errors.

Learning Objective P3:

Prepare financial statements from business transactions.

The balance sheet, the statement of retained earnings, the income statement, and the statement of cash flows use data from the trial balance (and other financial statements) for their preparation.

I. Analyzing and Recording Process

A. The accounting process identifies business transactions and events, analyzes and records their effects, and summarizes and presents information in reports and financial statements. The steps in the accounting process that focus on *analyzing and recording* transactions and events are: (1) record relevant transactions and events in a journal, (2) post journal information to ledger accounts, and (3) prepare and analyze the trial balance. Accounting records are informally referred as the *accounting books*, or simply the *books*.

B. **Source documents** identify and describe transactions and events. Source documents are sources of accounting information and can be in either hard copy or electronic form. Examples are sales tickets, checks, purchase orders, bills from suppliers, employee earnings records, and bank statements. Source documents provide objective and reliable evidence about transactions and events.

C. An **account** is a record of increases and decreases in a specific asset, liability, equity, revenue, or expense item. The **general ledger**, or **ledger**, is a record containing all accounts used by a company.

D. Accounts are arranged in three basic categories based on the accounting equation. A separate account is kept for each of the following:

1. **Asset Accounts**—resources owned or controlled by a company that have expected future benefits; examples include Cash, Accounts Receivable, Note Receivable, Prepaid Accounts, Supplies, Equipment, Buildings, and Land.

2. **Liability Accounts**—claims by creditors against assets; obligations to transfer assets or provide products or services to other entities; examples include Accounts Payable, Note Payable, Unearned Revenue, and Accrued Liabilities.

3. **Equity Accounts**—owner's residual interest in the assets of the business after deducting liabilities; examples include Common Stock, Dividends, Revenues, and Expenses.

II. Analyzing and Processing Transactions

A. Ledger and Chart of Accounts

1. A ledger (or general ledger) is the sum of all the accounts a company uses.

2. The **chart of accounts** is a list of all the accounts in the ledger with their identification numbers.

B. Debits and Credits

1. A **T-account** represents a ledger account and is used to understand the effects of one or more transactions.

2. The *left* side of an account is called the **debit** side. A debit is an entry on the left side of an account.

3. The *right* side of an account is called the **credit** side. A credit is an entry on the right side of an account.

4. Whether a debit or a credit is an increase or decrease depends on the account.

5. In an account where a debit is an increase, the credit is a decrease. In an account where a credit is an increase, the debit is a decrease.

6. The **account balance** is the difference between the total debits and the total credits recorded in an account.

C. Double-Entry Accounting

1. The total amount that is debited to accounts must equal the total amount credited to accounts for each transaction. The sum of debit account balances in the ledger must equal the sum of credit account balances.

2. Assets are on the left side of the equation; therefore, the left, or debit, side is the *normal balance* side for assets.

3. Liabilities and equities are on the right side; therefore, the right, or credit, side is the *normal balance* side for liabilities and equity.

4. Equity increases from revenues and stock issuances and it decreases from expenses and dividends. Increases (credits) to common stock and revenues *increase* equity; increases (debits) to dividends and expenses *decrease* equity.

5. The normal balance of each account (assets, liability, common stock, dividends, revenue, or expense) refers to the left or right (debit or credit) side where *increases* are recorded.

D. Journalizing and Posting Transactions

1. A **journal** gives a complete record of each transaction in one place; it shows the debits and credits for each transaction. The process of recording each transaction in a journal is called **journalizing**. The process of transferring journal entry information to the ledger is called **posting**.

2. The **general journal** can be used to record any type of transaction. Steps for recording entries in a general journal include:

   a. Date the transaction; enter the year at the top of the first column and the month and day on the first line of each journal entry.

   b. Enter titles of accounts debited (account titles are taken from the chart of accounts and aligned with the left margin of the column), and then enter amounts in the Debit column on the same line.

   c. Enter titles of accounts credited (account titles are taken from the chart of accounts and indented from the left margin of the column to distinguish them from debited accounts), and then enter amounts in the Credit column on the same line.

   d. Enter a brief explanation of the transaction on the line below the entry.

3. A blank line is left between each journal entry for clarity.

4. When a transaction is first recorded, the **posting reference (PR) column** is left blank (in a manual system); later, when posting entries to the ledger, the identification numbers of the individual ledger accounts are entered in the PR column.

5. T-accounts are simple and direct means to show how the accounting process works; however, actual accounting systems need more structure and therefore use **balance column accounts.** The balance column account format is similar to a T-account in having columns for debits and credits; it is different in including date and explanation columns.

6. The heading of the Balance column does not show whether it is a debit or credit balance; instead, an account is assumed to have a *normal balance* (that is, the side where increases are recorded). Unusual events can temporarily give an account an *abnormal balance* (that is, the side where decreases are recorded).

7. To ensure the ledger is up-to-date, entries are posted as soon as possible using the following steps:

   a. First, identify the ledger account that is debited in the entry; then, in the ledger, enter the date, the journal and page in its PR column, the debit amount, and the new balance of the ledger accounts.

   b. Second, enter the ledger account number in the PR column of the journal.

   c. Repeat the first two steps for credit entries and amounts.

©The McGraw-Hill Companies, Inc., 2008

E. **Analyzing Transactions – An Illustration**

The illustrations below follow the four steps in processing transactions. Each transaction is analyzed in terms of its effect on the accounting equation. Double-entry accounting is used to record the transaction in journal entry form, and the financial statements affected by each transaction are identified. (The following abbreviations are used for the financial statements: IS for income statement, BLS for balance sheet, SCF for statement of cash flows, and SRE for statement of retained earning.) The first eleven transactions are from Chapter 1; five additional transactions are included.

Transaction 1: Investment by owner
Analysis:
+ Assets (Cash) = + Equity (Common Stock)
Double entry:
Debit Cash and credit Common Stock
Statements affected:
BLS and SCF

Transaction 2: Purchase supplies for cash
Analysis:
+Assets (Supplies) = – Assets (Cash)
Double entry:
Debit Supplies and credit Cash
Statements affected:
BLS and SCF

Transaction 3: Purchase equipment for cash
Analysis:
+ Assets (Equipment) = – Assets (Cash)
Double entry:
Debit Equipment and credit Cash
Statements affected:
BLS and SCF

Transaction 4: Purchase supplies on credit
Analysis:
+Assets (Supplies) = + Liability (Account Payable)
Double entry:
Debit Supplies and credit Accounts Payable
Statements affected:
BLS

Transaction 5: Provide services for cash
Analysis:
+ Assets (Cash) = + Equity (Revenues)
Double entry:
Debit Cash and credit Revenue (type of revenue would be identified in account name)
Statements affected:
BLS, IS, SCF, and SRE

Transactions 6 and 7: Payment of expenses in cash

Analysis:
- Assets (Cash) = – Equity (Expenses)
Double entry:
Debit Expenses (type of expense would be identified in account name) and credit Cash
Statements affected:
BLS, IS, SCF, and SRE

Transaction 8: Provide consulting and rental services on credit

Analysis:
+ Assets (Accts Receivable) = + Equity (Revenues)
Double entry:
Debit Accounts Receivable and credit Revenue (type of revenue would be identified in account name)
Statements affected:
BLS, IS, SCF, and SRE

Transaction 9: Receipt of cash on account

Analysis:
+ Assets (Cash) = – Assets (Accounts Receivable)
Double entry:
Debit Cash and credit Accounts Receivable
Statements affected:
BLS and SCF

Transaction 10: Partial payment of accounts payable

Analysis:
– Assets (Cash) = – Liability (Accounts Payable)
Double entry:
Debit Accounts Payable and credit Cash
Statements affected:
BLS and SCF

Transaction 11: Payment of cash dividend

Analysis:
– Assets (Cash) = – Equity (Dividends)
Double entry:
Debit Dividends and credit Cash
Statements affected:
BLS, SCF, and SRE

Transaction 12: Receipt of cash for future services

Analysis:
+ Assets (Cash) = + Liabilities (Unearned Revenue)
Double entry:
Debit Cash and credit Unearned Revenue (type of unearned revenue is often identified in account name)
Statements affected:
BLS and SCF

Transaction 13: Pay cash for future insurance coverage
Analysis:
– Assets (Cash) = + Assets (Prepaid Insurance)
Double entry:
Debit Prepaid Insurance and credit Cash
Statements affected:
BLS and SCF

Transaction 14: Purchase supplies for cash
Analysis:
+ Assets (Supplies) = - Assets (Cash)
Double entry:
Debit Supplies and credit Cash
Statements affected:
BLS and SCF

Transactions 15 and 16: Payment of expenses in cash
Analysis:
– Assets (Cash) = – Equity (Expenses)
Double entry:
Debit Expense (type of expense would be identified in account name) and credit Cash
Statements affected:
BLS, IS, SCR, and SRE

III.   **Trial Balance**

A. Preparing a Trial Balance

1. A **trial balance** is a list of accounts and their balances at a point in time.

2. The three steps to preparing a trial balance are as follows:

    a. List each account and its amount (from the ledger),

    b. Compute the total debit balances and the total credit balances, and

    c. Verify (prove) total debit balances equal total credit balances.

B. Searching for and Correcting Errors

1. If a trial balance does not balance (the columns are not equal), the error(s) must be found and corrected. Find the errors by checking the following:

    a. Verify that the trial balance columns are correctly added.

    b. Verify that the account balances are accurately entered from the ledger.

    c. See whether a debit (or credit) balance is mistakenly listed in the trial balance as a credit (or debit).

    d. Recompute each account balance in the ledger.

      e.   Verify that each journal entry is properly posted.

      f.   Verify that the original journal entry has equal debits and credits.

2.   If an error in a journal entry is discovered before the entry is posted, it can be corrected in a manual system by drawing a line through the incorrect information and writing in the correct information.

3.   If an error in a journal entry is not discovered until after it is posted, a *correcting entry* that removes the amount from the wrong account and records it to the correct account should be journalized and posted.

C. Using a Trial Balance to Prepare Financial Statements

The statements prepared in this chapter are called *unadjusted statements* because further account adjustments need to be made (as described in chapter 3).

1.   A balance sheet reports on an organization's financial position at a *point in time*. The income statement, statement of retained earnings, and statement of cash flows report on financial performance over a *period of time*.

2.   A one-year, or annual, reporting period is known as the *accounting*, or *fiscal*, *year*. A business whose accounting year begins on January 1 and ends on December 31 is known as a *calendar-year* company. A company that chooses a fiscal year ending on a date other than December 31 is known as a *noncalendar-year* company.

3.   Income Statement—reports the revenues earned less the expenses incurred by a business over a period of time.

4.   Statement of Retained Earnings—reports information about how retained earnings changes over the accounting period.

5.   Balance Sheet—reports the financial position of a company at a point in time, usually at the end of a month, quarter, or year. The *account form* of the balance sheet reports assets on the left and liabilities and equity on the right. The *report form* of the balance sheet reports assets on the top and liabilities and equity on the bottom.

6.   Presentation Issues:

      a.   Dollar signs are not used in journals and ledgers; they do appear in financial statements and other reports such as the trial balance. The usual practice is to put dollar signs beside only the first and last numbers in a column.

      b.   Companies commonly round amounts in reports to the nearest dollar, or even to a higher level.

IV. **Decision Analysis—Debt Ratio**

    A. A company that finances a relatively large portion of its assets with liabilities has a high degree of *financial leverage*. Higher financial leverage involves greater risk because liabilities must be repaid and often require regular interest payments (equity financing does not). The risk that a company might not be able to meet such required payments is higher if it has more liabilities (is more highly leveraged).

    B. One way to assess the risk associated with a company's use of liabilities is to compute the **debt ratio**.

        1. It is calculated as total liabilities divided by total assets.

        2. It tells us how much (what percentage) of the assets are financed by creditors (non-owners) or liability financing; the higher the debt ratio, the more risk a company faces from its financial leverage.

THREE PARTS OF AN ACCOUNT

(1) ACCOUNT TITLE	
Left Side called (2) DEBIT	Right Side called (3) CREDIT

RULES FOR USING ACCOUNTS

Accounts are assigned balance sides (debit or credit).

To increase any account, use the balance side.

To decrease any account, use the side opposite the balance side.

FINDING ACCOUNT BALANCES

If total debits equals total credits, the account balance is zero.

If total debits are greater than total credits, the account has a debit balance equal to the difference of the two totals.

If total credits are greater than total debits, the account has a credit balance equal to the difference of the two totals.

BALANCE SIDES

ALL ACCOUNTS ARE ASSIGNED BALANCE SIDES.

| ASSETS | = | LIABILITIES + EQUITY |

are on the left side of the
accounting equation
therefore
they increase using the
debit or left side.

are on the right side of the
accounting equation
therefore
they increase using the
credit or right side.

| DEBIT BALANCE | | CREDIT BALANCE |

Asset Accounts

Debit	Credit
+ side	– side
Normal	
Balance	

Liability Accounts

Debit	Credit
– side	+ side
	Normal
	Balance

Equity Accounts

Debit	Credit
– side	+ side
	Normal
	Balance

Financial Accounting, 4e

EQUITY ACCOUNTS

Common Stock
(increases equity, which is on the right
side of the accounting equation,
equity increases with credits)

Debit	*Credit*
– side	+ side
	Normal
	Balance

Dividends
(decreases equity,
equity decreases with debits)

Debit	*Credit*
+ side	– side
Normal	
Balance	

> Each time assets are
> distributed to
> stockholders,
> the dividends account
> balance increases.
> As such, its normal
> balance is a debit.

All Revenue Accounts
(increases equity,
equity increases with credits)

Debit	*Credit*
– side	+ side
	Normal
	Balance

All Expense Accounts
(decreases equity,
equity decreases with debits)

Debit	*Credit*
+ side	– side
Normal	
Balance	

> Each time
> an expense
> is incurred,
> the expense account
> balance increases.
> As such, its normal
> balance is a debit.

USING ACCOUNTS – SUMMARY

$$Assets = Liabilities + Equity$$

Asset Accounts
Debit +
Balance

Liability Accounts
Credit +
Balance

Equity Accounts
Credit +
Balance

Equity Accounts

Common Stock
Credit +
Balance

Dividends
Debit +
Balance

Revenue Accounts
Credit +
Balance

Expense Accounts
Debit +
Balance

RULE REVIEW

Transaction analysis rules:
- Each transaction affects at least two accounts.
- Each transaction must have equal debits and credits.

General account use rules:
- To increase any account, use balance side.
- To decrease any account, use side opposite the balance.

Chapter Two – Alternate Demonstration Problem #1

Wigor Inc. completed the following transactions during the year ended December 31, 20X8, its first year of operations:

a. Bill Wiggins personally invests $30,000 In the new business in exchange for common stock and deposits the cash in a bank account opened under the name of Wigor Inc.

b. Equipment for use in the business was purchased for $9,000. Two-thirds of the price was paid in cash; the rest was due in a year.

c. Service fees earned were $60,000; $6,000 of this was on credit.

d. Operating expenses incurred were $35,000; $4,000 was on credit.

e. Wigor Inc. collected half the money owed to it.

f. Wigor Inc. paid off $2,000 it owed.

g. Wiggins bought a car for $12,000 for his personal use, half paid for now from his personal savings and half to be paid in a year.

Required:

1. Prepare journal entries for each of the events.

2. Prepare a trial balance at the end of the year for Wigor Inc.

(If this alternative demonstration problem is not covered in class, see your instructor for the solution.)

Problem I

The following statements are either true or false. Place a (T) in the parentheses before each true statement and an (F) before each false statement.

1. ( ) Debits are used to record increases in assets, withdrawals, and expenses.

2. ( ) The process of recording transactions in a journal is called posting.

3. ( ) The debt ratio is used to assess a company's risk of failing to pay its debts when they are due.

Problem II

You are given several words, phrases, or numbers to choose from in completing each of the following statements or in answering the following questions. In each case select the one that best completes the statement, or answers the question, and place its letter in the answer space provided.

_____ 1. Properties or economic resources owned by a business, or probable future economic benefits obtained or controlled by a particular entity as a result of past transactions or events, are called:

    a. Dividends.

    b. Assets.

    c. Retained earnings.

    d. Revenues.

    e. Owner's equity.

_____ 2. The journal entry to record the completion of legal work for a client on credit and billing the client $1,700 for the services rendered would be:

    a. Accounts Receivable 1,700
           Unearned Legal Fees   1,700

    b. Legal Fees Earned 1,700
           Accounts Receivable   1,700

    c. Accounts Payable 1,700
           Legal Fees Earned   1,700

    d. Legal Fees Earned 1,700
           Sales   1,700

    e. Accounts Receivable 1,700
           Legal Fees Earned   1,700

_____ 3. A ledger is:

  a. A book of original entry in which the effects of transactions are first recorded.

  b. The collection of all accounts used by a business.

  c. A book of original entry in which any type of transaction can be recorded.

  d. A book of special journals.

  e. An account with debit and credit columns and a third column for showing the balance of the account.

Problem III

Many of the important ideas and concepts discussed in Chapter 2 are reflected in the following list of key terms. Test your understanding of these terms by matching the appropriate definitions with the terms. Record the number identifying the most appropriate definition in the blank space next to each term.

_____ Account   _____ Double-entry accounting
_____ Account balance   _____ General journal
_____ Balance column account   _____ Journal
_____ Chart of accounts   _____ Journalizing
_____ Common stock   _____ Ledger
_____ Compound journal entry   _____ Posting
_____ Credit   _____ Posting reference (PR) column
_____ Creditors   _____ Source documents
_____ Debit   _____ T-account
_____ Debt ratio   _____ Trial balance
_____ Dividends   _____ Unearned revenue

1. A liability created when customers pay in advance for products or services; earned when the products or services are delivered in the future.

2. A corporation's distributions of assets to its owners.

3. List of accounts and their balances at a point in time; total debt balances equal total credit balances.

4. An account with debit and credit columns for recording entries and another column for showing the balance of the account after each entry.

5. The source of information for accounting entries and can be in either paper or electronic form; also called *business papers*.

6. Individuals or organizations entitled to receive payments.

7. A record where transactions are recorded before they are posted to ledger accounts.

8. Process of transferring journal entry information to the ledger.

9. Record within an accounting system where increases and decreases in a specific asset, liability, equity, revenue, or expense are entered and stored.

10. Tool used to show the effects of transactions and events on individual accounts.

11. Process of recording transactions in a journal.

12. Recorded on the left side; an entry that increases asset and expense accounts, and decreases liability, equity, and revenue accounts; abbreviated Dr.

©The McGraw-Hill Companies, Inc., 2008

13. The difference between the total debits and total credits (including the beginning balance) for an account.

14. A list of accounts used by a company, includes an identification number for each account.

15. A journal entry that affects at least three accounts.

16. An all-purpose journal for recording transactions and events.

17. A ratio of total liabilities to total assets; used to describe risk associated with a company's debts.

18. Recorded on the right side; an entry that decreases asset and expense accounts, or increases liability, equity, and revenue accounts; abbreviated Cr.

19. Record containing all accounts (with amounts) for a business.

20. An accounting system in which each transaction affects at least two accounts and has at least one debit and one credit.

21. A column in journals where account numbers are entered when entries are posted to ledger accounts.

22. Corporation's basic ownership share; also generically called *capital stock*.

Problem IV

Complete the following by filling in the blanks.

1. Assets created by selling goods and services on credit are called _____. Liabilities created by buying goods and services on credit are called _____

2. Probable future sacrifices of economic benefits arising from present obligations of a particular entity to transfer assets or provide services to other entities in the future as a result of past transactions or events are called _____.

3. An excess of revenues over expenses for a period results in a _____. An excess of expenses over revenues results in a _____. The financial statement that lists revenues and expenses is the _____.

4. The process of recording transactions in a journal is called _____. The process of transferring journal entry information to the ledger is called _____.

5. The _____ creates a link between a journal entry and the ledger accounts by providing a cross-reference for tracing the entry from one record to the other.

6. A trial balance that fails to balance is proof that _____ either in journalizing, in posting, or in preparing the trial balance.

7. A trial balance that balances is not absolute proof that no errors were made because _____.

8. The steps in preparing a trial balance are:

_____.

_____.

_____.

_____.

_____.

9. a. The normal balance of an asset account is a _____.

   b. The normal balance of a liability account is a _____.

   c. The normal balance of the common stock account is a _____.

   d. The normal balance of the retained earnings account is a _____.

   e. The normal balance of a revenue account is a _____.

   f. The normal balance of an expense account is a _____.

Problem V

Following are the first 10 transactions completed by P. L. Wheeler's new business called Wheeler's Repair Shop, Inc.:

   a. Started the business by issuing common stock to P. L. Wheeler in exchange for $1,800 cash, which was deposited in a bank account in the name of the business.

   b. Paid three months' rent in advance on the shop space, $675.

   c. Purchased repair equipment for cash, $700.

   d. Completed repair work for customers and collected cash, $1,005.50.

   e. Purchased additional repair equipment on credit from Comet Company, $415.50.

   f. Completed repair work on credit for Fred Baca, $175.

   g. Paid Comet Company $290.50 of the amount owed from transaction (e).

   h. Paid the local radio station $75 for an announcement of the shop opening.

   i. Fred Baca paid for the work completed in transaction (f).

   j. Paid $350 cash dividend to P. L. Wheeler.

Required:

1. Record the transactions directly in the T-accounts that follow. Use the transaction letters to identify the amounts in the accounts.

2. Prepare a trial balance as of the current date using the form that follows.

©The McGraw-Hill Companies, Inc., 2008

Cash   Accounts Payable
_____   _____
              | |
              | |
              |
              | Common Stock
              | _____
              | |
              | |

Accounts Receivable   Retained Earnings
_____   _____
              | |
              | |

Prepaid Rent   Repair Services Revenue
_____   _____
              | |
              | |

Repair Equipment   Advertising Expense
_____   _____
              |
              |

WHEELER'S REPAIR SHOP, INC.

Trial Balance

_____, 20____

Financial Accounting, 4e

Problem VI

Journalize the following transactions and post to the accounts that follow.

a. On November 5 of the current year, started business by issuing common stock to Sherry Dale for $2,450 cash, which was deposited in a bank account in the name of a new business named Dale Real Estate Inc.

b. On November 6, the business purchased office equipment for $425 cash.

GENERAL JOURNAL

DATE	ACCOUNT TITLES AND EXPLANATION	P.R.	DEBIT	CREDIT

GENERAL LEDGER

Cash — Account No. 101

DATE	EXPLANATION	P.R.	DEBIT	CREDIT	BALANCE

Office Equipment — Account No. 163

DATE	EXPLANATION	P.R.	DEBIT	CREDIT	BALANCE

Sherry Dale, Capital — Account No. 301

DATE	EXPLANATION	P.R.	DEBIT	CREDIT	BALANCE

Solutions for Chapter 2

Problem I

1. T
2. F
3. T

Problem II

1. B
2. E
3. B

Problem III

9	Account	20	Double-entry accounting
13	Account balance	16	General journal
4	Balance column account	7	Journal
14	Chart of accounts	11	Journalizing
22	Common stock	19	Ledger
15	Compound journal entry	8	Posting
18	Credit	21	Posting reference (PR) column
6	Creditors	5	Source documents
12	Debit	10	T-account
17	Debt ratio	3	Trial balance
2	Dividends	1	Unearned revenue

Problem IV

1. accounts receivable; accounts payable
2. liabilities
3. net income (profit); net loss; income statement
4. journalizing; posting
5. Posting reference (PR) column
6. at least one error has been made
7. some types of errors do not create unequal debits and credits
8. (1) Determine the balance of each account;
   (2) List in their ledger order the accounts having balances, with the debit balances in one column and the credit balances in another;
   (3) Add the debit balances;
   (4) Add the credit balances;
   (5) Compare the two totals for equality.
9. (a) debit; (b) credit; (c) credit; (d) credit; (e) credit; (f) debit

Problem V

Cash			
(a)	1,800.00	(b)	675.00
(d)	1,005.50	(c)	700.00
(i)	175.00	(g)	290.50
		(h)	75.00
		(j)	350.00

Repair Equipment	
(c)	700.00
(e)	415.50

Retained Earnings	
(j)	350.00

Accounts Receivable			
(f)	175.00	(i)	175.00

Accounts Payable			
(g)	290.50	(e)	415.50

Repair Services Revenue		
	(d)	1,005.50
	(f)	175.00

Prepaid Rent	
(b)	675.00

Common Stock		
	(a)	1,800.00

Advertising Expense	
(h)	75.00

WHEELER'S REPAIR SHOP, INC.
Trial Balance
(Current Date)

Cash	$ 890.00	
Prepaid rent	675.00	
Repair equipment	1,115.50	
Accounts payable		$ 125.00
Common stock		1,800.00
Retained earnings	350.00	
Repair services revenue		1,180.50
Advertising expense	75.00	
Totals	$3,105.50	$3,105.50

Problem VI

GENERAL JOURNAL

DATE	ACCOUNT TITLES AND EXPLANATION	P.R.	DEBIT				CREDIT			
20— Nov. 5	Cash	101	2	4 5 0		00				
	Common Stock	301					2	4 5 0		00
	Owner's initial investment.									
6	Office Equipment	163		4 2 5		00				
	Cash	101						4 2 5		00
	Purchased office equipment									

GENERAL LEDGER

Cash — Account No. 101

DATE	EXPLANATION	P.R.	DEBIT			CREDIT			BALANCE		
20— Nov. 5		G-1	2	4 5 0	00				2	4 5 0	00
6		G-1				4 2 5		00	2	0 2 5	00

Office Equipment — Account No. 163

DATE	EXPLANATION	P.R.	DEBIT			CREDIT			BALANCE		
20— Nov. 6		G-1		4 2 5	00					4 2 5	00

Common Stock — Account No. 301

DATE	EXPLANATION	P.R.	DEBIT			CREDIT			BALANCE		
20— Nov. 5		G-1				2	4 5 0	00	2	4 5 0	00

CHAPTER 3
ADJUSTING ACCOUNTS AND
PREPARING FINANCIAL STATEMENTS

Learning Objective C1:

Explain the importance of periodic reporting and the time period principle.

The value of information is often linked to its timeliness. To provide timely information, accounting systems prepare periodic reports at regular intervals. The time period principle assumes that an organization's activities can be divided into specific time periods for periodic reporting.

Learning Objective C2:

Explain accrual accounting and how it improves financial statements.

Accrual accounting recognizes revenue when earned and expenses when incurred—not necessarily when cash inflows and outflows occur. This information is valuable in assessing a company's financial position and performance.

Learning Objective C3:

Identify the types of adjustments and their purpose.

Adjustments can be grouped according to the timing of cash receipts and cash payments relative to when they are recognized as revenues or expenses as follows: prepaid expenses, unearned revenues, accrued expenses, and accrued revenues. Adjusting entries are necessary so that revenues, expenses, assets, and liabilities are correctly reported.

Learning Objective C4:

Explain why temporary accounts are closed each period.

Temporary accounts are closed at the end of each accounting period for two main reasons. First, the closing process updates the retained earnings account to include the effects of all transactions and events recorded for the period. Second, it prepares revenue, expense, and dividends accounts for the next reporting period by giving them zero balances.

Learning Objective C5:

Identify steps in the accounting cycle.

The accounting cycle consists of 10 steps: (1) analyze transactions, (2) journalize, (3) post, (4) prepare an unadjusted trial balance, (5) adjust accounts, (6) prepare an adjusted trial balance, (7) prepare statements, (8) close, (9) prepare a post-closing trial balance, and (10) prepare (optional) reversing entries.

Learning Objective C6:

Explain and prepare a classified balance sheet.

Classified balance sheets report assets and liabilities in two categories: current and noncurrent. Noncurrent assets often include long-term investments, plant assets, and intangible assets. A corporation separates equity into common stock and retained earnings.

Learning Objective A1:

Explain how accounting adjustments link to financial statements.

Accounting adjustments bring an asset or liability account balance to its correct amount. They also update related expense or revenue accounts. Every adjusting entry affects one or more income statement accounts *and* one or more balance sheet accounts. An adjusting entry never affects cash.

Learning Objective A2:

Compute profit margin and describe its use in analyzing company performance.

Profit margin is defined as the reporting period's net income divided by its net sales. Profit margin reflects on a company's earnings activities by showing how much income is in each dollar of sales.

Learning Objective A3:

Compute the current ratio and describe what it reveals about a company's financial condition.

A company's current ratio is defined as current assets divided by current liabilities. We use it to evaluate a company's ability to pay its current liabilities out of current assets.

Learning Objective P1:

Prepare and explain adjusting entries.

Prepaid expenses refer to items paid for in advance of receiving their benefits. Prepaid expenses are assets. Adjusting entries for prepaids involve increasing (debiting) expenses and decreasing (crediting) assets. *Unearned* (or *prepaid*) *revenues* refer to cash received in advance of providing products and services. Unearned revenues are liabilities. Adjusting entries for unearned revenues involves increasing (crediting) revenues and decreasing (debiting) unearned revenues. *Accrued expenses* refer to costs incurred in a period that are both unpaid and unrecorded. Adjusting entries for recording accrued expenses involve increasing (debiting) expenses and increasing (crediting) liabilities. *Accrued revenues* refer to revenues earned in a period that are both unrecorded and not yet received in cash. Adjusting entries for recording accrued revenues involve increasing (debiting) assets and increasing (crediting) revenues.

Learning Objective P2:

Explain and prepare an adjusted trial balance.

An adjusted trial balance is a list of accounts and balances prepared after recording and posting adjusting entries. Financial statements are often prepared from the adjusted trial balance.

Learning Objective P3:

Prepare financial statements from an adjusted trial balance.

Revenue and expense balances are reported on the income statement. Asset, liability, and equity balances are reported on the balance sheet. We usually prepare statements in the following order: income statement, statement of retained earnings, balance sheet, and statement of cash flows.

Learning Objective P4:

Describe and prepare closing entries.

Closing entries involve four steps: (1) close credit balances in revenue (and gain) accounts to Income Summary, (2) close debit balances in expense (and loss) accounts to Income Summary, (3) close Income Summary to Retained Earnings, and (4) close Dividends account to Retained Earnings.

Learning Objective P5:

Explain and prepare a post-closing trial balance.

A post-closing trial balance is a list of permanent accounts and their balances after all closing entries have been journalized and posted. Its purpose is to verify that (1) total debits equal total credits for permanent accounts and (2) all temporary accounts have zero balances.

Learning Objective P6 (Appendix 3A):

Explain the alternatives in accounting for prepaids.

Charging all prepaid expenses to expense accounts when they are purchased is acceptable. When this is done, adjusting entries must transfer any unexpired amounts from expense accounts to asset accounts. Crediting all unearned revenues to revenue accounts when cash is received is also acceptable. In this case, the adjusting entries must transfer any unearned amounts from revenue accounts to unearned revenue accounts.

Learning Objective P7 (Appendix 3B):

Prepare a work sheet and explain its usefulness.

A work sheet can be a useful tool in preparing and analyzing financial statements. It is helpful at the end of a period in preparing adjusting entries, an adjusted trial balance, and financial statements. A work sheet usually contains five pairs of columns: Unadjusted Trial Balance, Adjustments, Adjusted Trial Balance, Income Statement, and Balance Sheet.

Learning Objective P8 (Appendix 3C):

Prepare reversing entries and explain their purpose.

Reversing entries are an optional step. They are applied to accrued expenses and revenues. The purpose of reversing entries is to simplify subsequent journal entries. Financial statements are unaffected by the choice to use or not use reversing entries.

Chapter Outline

I. **Timing and Reporting**

  A. The Accounting Period

    To provide timely information, accounting systems prepare periodic reports at regular intervals.

    1. The **time-period principle** assumes that an organization's activities can be divided into specific time periods such as a month, a three-month quarter, a six-month interval, or a year. Reports covering a one-year period are known as **annual financial statements**. **Interim financial statements** cover one, three, or six months of activity.

    2. Annual reporting period:

      a. Calendar year—January 1 to December 31.

      b. **Fiscal year**—Any twelve consecutive months used to base annual financial reports on.

      c. **Natural business year**—a fiscal year that ends when a company's sales activities are at their lowest level for the year.

  B. Accrual Basis versus Cash Basis

    1. Accounts are adjusted at the end of a period to record internal transactions and events that are not yet recorded.

    2. **Accrual basis accounting**—uses the adjusting process to recognize revenue when earned and to match expenses with revenues. This means the economic effects of revenues and expenses are recorded when earned or incurred, not when cash is received or paid. Accrual basis is consistent with GAAP.

    2. **Cash basis accounting**—revenues are recognized when cash is received and expenses are recognized when cash is paid. The cash basis is not consistent with GAAP.

    3. Accrual accounting also increases the **comparability** of financial statements from one period to another.

  C. Recognizing Revenues and Expenses

    1. The **revenue recognition principle** requires revenue be recorded when earned, not before and not after.

    2. The **matching principle** requires expenses be recorded in the same period as the revenues earned as a result of these expenses.

II.   Adjusting Accounts

The process of adjusting accounts involves analyzing each account balance and the transactions and events that affect it to determine any needed adjustments. An **adjusting entry** is recorded to bring an asset or liability account balance to its proper amount. This entry also updates a related expense or revenue account.

A. Framework for Adjustments

Adjustments are necessary for transactions and events that extend over more than one period. Adjusting entries are necessary so that revenues, expenses, assets and liabilities are correctly reported. Each adjusting entry affects one or more income statement accounts and one or more balance sheet accounts (but not the cash account).

B. Prepaid (Deferred) Expenses

1. **Prepaid Expenses** are items *paid for* in advance of receiving their benefits. Prepaid expenses are assets. When the assets are used, their costs become expenses.

2. Common prepaid items are prepaid insurance, supplies, and other prepaid expenses.

3. Adjusting entries for prepaids involve increasing (debiting) expenses and decreasing (crediting) assets (with the exception of depreciation on plant and equipment assets).

4. A special category of prepaid expenses is plant assets. **Plant assets** are long-term tangible assets used to produce and sell products and services; they are expected to provide benefits for more than one period.

5. **Depreciation** is the process of allocating the cost of plant and equipment assets over their expected useful lives. **Straight-line depreciation** allocates equal amounts of an assets' net cost to depreciation during its useful life.

6. Adjusting entries for depreciation expense involve increasing (debiting) expenses and increasing (crediting) a special account called Accumulated Depreciation. Accumulated depreciation is a contra asset account. A **contra account** is an account linked with another account, and having an opposite normal balance.

7. Accumulated depreciation is reported as a subtraction from the related plant asset account balance in the balance sheet.

8. **Book value** is a term used to describe the asset less its contra-asset (accumulated depreciation).

C. Unearned (Deferred) Revenues

1. **Unearned Revenues** are liabilities created by cash received in advance of providing products or services. The company has an obligation to provide the service or product. As they are provided unearned revenues (liabilities) become *earned* revenues (revenues).

2. Adjusting entries for unearned revenues involve increasing (crediting) revenues and decreasing (debiting) unearned revenues.

D. Accrued Expenses

1. **Accrued expenses** refer to costs that are incurred in a period but are both unpaid and unrecorded.

2. Common accrued expenses are salaries, interest, rent, and taxes.

3. Adjusting entries for recording accrued expenses involve increasing (debiting) expenses and increasing (crediting) liabilities. (The liability is a payable.)

4. Future payment of accrued expenses generally results in cash payments in the next period. Debit the payable for amount accrued and credit cash for the full amount paid. If the amount paid exceeds the amount accrued, the difference is an expense in the current period.

E. Accrued Revenues

1. **Accrued revenues** refer to revenues earned in a period that are both unrecorded and not yet received in cash (or other assets).

2. Accrued revenues commonly result from services, products, interest, and rent.

3. Adjusting entries for recording accrued revenues involve increasing (debit) assets and increasing (credit) revenues. (The asset is a receivable.)

4. Accrued revenues at the end of one accounting period result in cash receipts in a future period. Debit cash for the full amount received and credit the receivable for the amount accrued.

5. If the amount received exceeds the amount accrued, the difference is an additional amount earned to be credited to revenue.

F. Links to Financial Statements

The process of adjusting accounts is intended to bring an asset or liability account balance to its correct amount. It also updates a related expense or revenue account. Each adjusting entry affects one or more income statement accounts *and* one or more balance sheet accounts. Failure to make a necessary adjustment will result in misstatements of amounts on each of the financial statements. (See Exhibit 3-12 for a summary of adjustments.)

G. Adjusted Trial Balance

An **unadjusted trial balance** is a list of accounts and balances prepared *before* adjustments are recorded. An **adjusted trial balance** is a list of accounts and balances prepared *after* adjusting entries have been recorded and posted to the ledger.

III. Preparing Financial Statements

Financial statements are prepared directly from information in the *adjusted* trial balance:

A. Revenue and expense balances are transferred from the adjusted trial balance to the income statement.

B. The net income, retained earnings, and dividends are then used to prepare the statement of retained earnings.

C. Asset, liability, and common stock balances on the adjusted trial balance are transferred to the balance sheet; the ending retained earnings is determined on the statement of retained earnings and transferred to the balance sheet.

D. Financial statements are usually prepared in the following order: income statement, statement of retained earnings, balance sheet, and statement of cash flows.

IV. Closing Process

The **closing process** is an important step at the end of the accounting period *after* financial statements have been completed. It prepares accounts for recording the transactions and the events of the *next* period.

A. Steps in closing process:

1. Identify accounts for closing.

2. Record and post closing entries.

3. Prepare a post-closing trial balance.

B. Purpose of closing process:

1. Resets revenue, expense, and dividend account balances to zero at the end of each period so that these accounts can properly measure income and dividends for the next period.

2. Helps in summarizing a period's revenues and expenses.

C. Temporary and Permanent Accounts

1. **Temporary** (or nominal) **accounts** accumulate data related to one accounting period; they include all income statement accounts, the dividends account, and the Income Summary account. The closing process applies only to temporary accounts.

2. **Permanent** (or real) **accounts** report on activities related to one or more future accounting periods. They carry their ending balances into the next period and generally consist of all balance sheet accounts. Real accounts are not closed.

D. Recording Closing Entries

1. To record and post **closing entries** is to transfer the end-of-period balances in revenue, expense, and dividends accounts to retained earnings.

2. To close these accounts, transfer their balances first to a temporary account (used only for the closing process) called **Income Summary**. Its balance equals net income or net loss and is transferred to Retained Earnings.

3. The four steps necessary to close temporary accounts are:

    a. Close credit balances in revenue (and gain) accounts to Income Summary; bring accounts with credit balances to zero by debiting them.

    b. Close debit balances in expense (and loss) accounts to Income Summary; bring accounts with debit balances to zero by crediting them.

    c. Close the Income Summary account to the Retained Earnings account; after the first two steps, the balance of the Income Summary account is equal to the period's net income. If a net loss occurred, the third entry is reversed: debit Retained Earnings and credit Income Summary.

    d. Close the Dividends account to the Retained Earnings account; bring the Dividends account, which has a debit balance, to zero by crediting it.

E. Post-Closing Trial Balance.

1. A **post-closing trial balance** is a list of permanent accounts and their balances from the ledger after all closing entries have been journalized and posted.

2. The aim is to verify that (1) total debits equal total credits for permanent accounts, and (2) all temporary accounts have zero balances.

F. Accounting Cycle Summary

The term **accounting cycle** refers to the steps in preparing financial statements; it is a cycle because all steps are repeated each reporting period. Exhibit 3.19 shows the ten steps in the cycle:

1. Analyze transactions
2. Journalize
3. Post
4. Prepare unadjusted trial balance
5. Adjust
6. Prepare adjusted trial balance
7. Prepare statements

8. Close

9. Prepare post-closing trial balance

10. Reverse (optional; explained in Appendix 3C).

V. **Classified Balance Sheet**—organizes assets and liabilities into subgroups that provide more useful information to decision makers:

A. Classification Structure

1. One of the more important classifications is the separation between current and noncurrent assets and liabilities.

2. Current items are expected to come due (both collected and owed) within one year or the company's *operating cycle*, whichever is longer.

3. The **operating cycle** is the time span from when cash is used to acquire goods and services until cash is received from the sale of those goods and services. Most operating cycles are less than one year; a few companies have an operating cycle *longer* than one year.

B. Classification Categories

1. **Current Assets**—cash or other assets that are expected to be sold, collected, or used within one year or the company's operating cycle, whichever is longer. Examples: cash, short-term investments, accounts receivable, short-term notes receivable, goods for sale (called *merchandise* or *inventory*), and prepaid expenses.

2. **Long-Term Investments**—assets that are expected to be held for more than the longer of one year or the operating cycle. Examples: notes receivable, investments in stocks, and land held for future expansion.

3. **Plant Assets**—tangible, long-lived assets that are both *long-lived* and *used to produce or sell products and services*. Examples: equipment, machinery, buildings, and land that are used to produce or sell products and services.

4. **Intangible Assets**—long-term resources that benefit business operations. They usually lack physical form and have uncertain benefits. Examples: patents, trademarks, copyrights, franchises, and goodwill.

5. **Current Liabilities**—obligations due to be paid or settled within one year or the operating cycle, whichever is longer. Examples: accounts payable, notes payable, wages payable, taxes payable, interest payable, and unearned revenues. Any portion of a long-term liability due to be paid within one year or the operating cycle, whichever is longer, is a current liability.

      6. **Long-Term Liabilities**—obligations *not* due within one year or the operating cycle, whichever is longer. Examples: notes payable, mortgages payable, bonds payable, and lease obligations.

      7. **Equity**—owners' claim on assets; divided into two main subsections: common stock and retained earnings.

VI.   Decision Analysis—Profit Margin and Current Ratio

  A. Profit Margin

      1. **Profit margin** (also called *return on sales*) is a useful measure of a company's operating results.

      2. It is calculated as net income divided by net sales.

      3. It is interpreted as reflecting the portion of profit in each dollar of sales.

  B. Current Ratio

      1. The **current ratio** is an important measure of a company's ability to pay its short-term obligations.

      2. It is calculated as total current assets divided by total current liabilities.

VII. Alternative Accounting for Prepayments (Appendix 3A)

  A. Recording the Prepayment of Expenses in Expense Accounts Prepaid expenses may originally be recorded with debits to expense accounts (instead of to asset accounts). If so, then adjusting entries must transfer the cost of the unused portions from expense accounts to prepaid expense (asset) accounts.

  B. Recording the Prepayment of Revenues in Revenue Accounts Unearned revenues may originally be recorded with credits to revenue accounts (instead of to liability accounts). If so, then adjusting entries must transfer the unearned portions from revenue accounts to unearned revenue (liability) accounts.

  C. Note that the financial statements are identical under either procedure, but the adjusting entries are different.

VIII. Work Sheet as a Tool (Appendix 3B)

  A. Working papers are internal documents. One widely used working paper is the work sheet, which is a useful tool for preparers in working with accounting information. It is usually not available to external decision makers.

    B. Use of a Work Sheet

        Preparing a work sheet has five important steps:

        1. Enter the unadjusted trial balance in the first two columns.

        2. Enter the adjustments in the third and fourth columns. Total columns to verify debit adjustments equal credit adjustments.

        3. Prepare the Adjusted Trial Balance. This is done by combining the unadjusted trial balance and adjustment columns. Total Adjusted Trial Balance columns to verify debits equal credits.

        4. Sort the adjusted trial balance amounts to the appropriate financial statement columns.

        5. Total statement columns, compute net income or loss, and balance the columns by adding net income or loss.

IX.   **Reversing Entries (Appendix 3C)**

    A. **Reversing entries** are optional; they are recorded in response to accrued assets and accrued liabilities that were created by adjusting entries at the end of a reporting period.

    B. Accounting *without* Reversing Entries—the disadvantage of this approach is the slightly more complex entry required when the cash subsequently changes hands (i.e., when cash is received for the asset that was originally accrued or when cash is paid for the liability that was originally accrued).

    C. Accounting *with* Reversing Entries

        1. A reversing entry is the exact opposite of an adjusting entry.

        2. Reversing entries are prepared after closing entries and dated the first day of the new period.

        5. Procedure is to transfer accrued asset and liability account balances to related revenue and expense accounts creating abnormal balances in these accounts.

        6. The full subsequent cash receipts (and payments) are recorded as increases in revenue (and expense) accounts creating a net balance equal to the amount earned or incurred in that period.

ACCRUAL BASIS ACCOUNTING

(Follows GAAP)

requires that the

Income Statement (for a period)

reports

GAAP Revenue Recognition

ALL REVENUES EARNED in period (Collected or Not)

Minus ALL EXPENSES INCURRED in period (Paid or Not)

Equals Net Income or Net Loss for the period

GAAP Matching

ACCOUNTS MUST BE ADJUSTED TO FOLLOW PRINCIPLES

DEFERRALS

The converse of statements in Visual #3-1 also applies.

Revenue not earned or expense not incurred results in <u>Deferrals</u>*

| UNEARNED = LIABILITY |*

A REVENUE <u>not</u> earned <u>cannot</u> be shown, even if collected.

An EXPENSE <u>not</u> incurred <u>cannot</u> be shown, even if paid.

| PREPAID = ASSET |*

*We defer or postpone the <u>reporting</u> of the collected revenues (as revenues) and prepaid expenses (as expenses) until the revenue is earned and the expense is incurred.

ADJUSTMENTS

TYPE	GENERALIZED* ENTRY	AMOUNT

1. Prepaid items or supplies
  a) initially recorded as assets
	Dr. _____ Expense
	  Cr. The Asset* acct.
		Amount used, or consumed, or expired

b) initially recorded as expenses (alternate treatment)	Dr. the Asset** acct. Cr. _____ Expense	Amount left, or not consumed, or unexpired
2. Accrued expenses (expenses <u>incurred</u> but not yet recorded)	Dr. _____ Expense Cr. _____ Payable	Amount accrued

3. Accrued revenues (revenues <u>earned</u> but not yet recorded)	Dr. _____ Receivable
	  Cr. The Revenue**
	  acct.
		Amount accrued

4. Long-term assets that are depreciable	Dr. Depreciation Expense
	  Cr. Accumulated
	    Depreciation
		Portion of cost allocated to this period as depreciation

5. Unearned revenues (received in advance)
  a) record initially as liability (unearned account)
	Dr. Unearned _____
	  Cr. The Revenue**
	  acct.
		Amount earned to date

b) initially recorded as a revenue (alternate treatment)	Dr. the Revenue** acct. Cr. Unearned_____	Amount still <u>not</u> earned

* Note: (1) Each adjustment affects a Balance Sheet Account and an Income Statement Account

  (2) <u>CASH</u> <u>NEVER</u> appears in an adjustment.

** Title or account name varies.

THE ACCOUNTING CYCLE

STEPS	PURPOSE	TIMING
1. Analyze transactions	Analyze transactions to prepare for journalizing.	During the period
2. Journalize	Record accounts, including debits and credits, in a journal.	During the period
3. Post	Transfer debits and credits from the journal to the ledger.	During the period
4. Prepare unadjusted trial balance	Summarize unadjusted ledger accounts and amounts.	End of period
5. Adjust	Record adjustments to bring account balances up to date; journalize and post adjusting entries.	End of period
6. Prepared adjusted trial balance	Summarize adjusted ledger accounts and amounts.	End of period
7. Prepare statements	Use adjusted trial balance to prepare financial statements.	End of period
8. Close	Journalize and post entries to close temporary accounts.	End of year
9. Prepare post-closing trial balance	Test clerical accuracy of the closing procedures.	End of year
10. Reverse (Optional)	Reverse certain adjustments in the next period (See Appendix 3C)	Beginning of next year

MUSIC WORLD
BALANCE SHEET
DECEMBER 31, 20XX

Assets

Current Assets

Cash	$30,360	
Short-Term Investments	2,000	
Notes Receivable	8,000	
Accounts Receivable	35,300	
Merchandise Inventory	60,400	
Prepaid Insurance	6,600	
Supplies	1,696	
Total Current Assets		$144,356

Investments

Land Held for Future Use		13,950

Property, Plant, and Equipment

Land		$ 4,500	
Building	$20,650		
Less Accumulated Depreciation	8,640	12,010	
Office Equipment	$ 8,600		
Less Accumulated Depreciation	5,000	3,600	
Total Property, Plant, and Equipment			20,110

Intangible Assets

Trademark		500
Total Assets		$178,916

Liabilities

Current Liabilities

Notes Payable	$15,000	
Accounts Payable	25,683	
Salaries Payable	2,000	
Current Portion of Mortgage Payable	10,200	
Total Current Liabilities		$ 52,883

Long-Term Liabilities

Mortgage Payable		27,600
Total Liabilities		$ 80,483

Equity

Common Stock		40,000
Retained Earnings		58,433
Total Liabilities and Equity		$178,916

Chapter Three – Alternate Demonstration Problem #1

On July 1, 20X8, Howard M. Tenant, Inc., rents office space from John Q. Landlord for two years, starting immediately, at a rate of $100 per month, or $2,400 in total. The full $2,400 was paid on this date.

Required:

Record the original transaction on 7/1 and the appropriate adjusting entries at the end of years in 20X8, 20X9, and 2010 from the point of view of Tenant and Landlord.

(If this alternative demonstration problem is not covered in class, see your instructor for the solution.)

Tenant Prepaid Rent

7/01 Prepaid Rent 2400
        Cash   2400

Adjustment
12/31/2008 Rent expense 600
        Prepaid Rent   600
        (6 months used up)

12/31/2009 Rent expense 1200
        Prepaid Rent   1200
        (12 months used up)

12/31/2010 Rent expense 600
        Prepaid Rent   600

Landlord Prepaid Rent

7/01 Cash 2400
        Unearned rent revenue 2400

12/31/08 Unearned rent revenue 600
        rent revenue   600

12/31/09 Unearned rent revenue 1200
        rent revenue   1200

12/31/09 Unearned rent revenue 600
        rent revenue   600

Problem I

The following statements are either true or false. Place a (T) in the parentheses before each true statement and an (F) before each false statement.

1. (T) The effect of a debit to an unearned revenue account and a corresponding credit to a revenue account is to transfer the earned portion of the fee from the liability account to the revenue account.
2. (F) If the accountant failed to make the end-of-period adjustment to remove from the Unearned Fees account the amount of fees earned, the omission would cause an overstatement of assets *Liabilities*
3. (T) The financial effect of a revenue generally occurs when it is earned, not when cash is received.
4. (F) Under the cash basis of accounting, revenues are recognized when they are earned and expenses are matched with revenues. *Accrual*
5. (T) After all closing entries are posted at the end of an accounting period, the Income Summary account balance is zero. *Inc. Sum → Retained*
6. (F) Throughout the current period, one could refer to the balance of the Income Summary account to determine the amount of net income or loss that was earned in the prior accounting period. *Retained earnings*

Problem II

You are given several words, phrases, or numbers to choose from in completing each of the following statements or in answering the following questions. In each case select the one that best completes the statement or answers the question and place its letter in the answer space provided.

_d_ 1. Time periods covered by statements are called:
  a. seasonal periods.
  b. fiscal years.
  c. operating cycles of a business.
  d. accounting periods.
  e. natural business years.

_d_ 2. X Company has four employees who are each paid $40 per day for a five-day work week. The employees are paid every Friday. If the accounting period ends on Wednesday, X Company should make the following entry to accrue wages:
  a. Salaries Expense 800
      Salaries Payable 800
  b. Salaries Expense 800
      Cash 800
  c. Salaries Expense 480
      Salaries Payable... 480
  d. Salaries Expense 320
      Salaries Payable 320
  e. No entry should be made until the salaries are actually paid.

_____C_____ 3 Lori Teach owns a sole proprietorship. During April of 20X8, Lori's business received $250 cash in advance for future services. The following entry should be made when the money is received:

a. Cash 250
    Accounts Receivable   250

b. Accounts Receivable 250
    Unearned Revenue   250

c. Cash 250
    Unearned Revenue   250

d. Unearned Revenue 250
    Services Revenue   250

e. No entry should be made until services are actually rendered.

_____e_____ 4. On December 1, B & B Security Service collected three months' fees of $6,000 in advance of providing services and credited Unearned Security Service Fees. They provided the monthly service from that date forward. The December 31st adjustment will require that Unearned Security Service Fees be:

a. Credited for $ 2,000.

b. Debited for $ 6,000.

c. Credited for $ 6,000.

d. Debited for $ 4,000.

e. Debited for $ 2,000.

_____d_____ 5. The GreenTree Restaurant prepares monthly financial statements. On January 31 the balance in the Supplies account was $1,600. During February, $2,960 of supplies were purchased and debited to Supplies. Assuming a February 28 inventory showed that $1,300 of supplies were on hand, the company should record the following adjusting entry as of February 28:

a. Supplies Expense 300
    Supplies   300

b. Supplies 300
    Supplies Expense...   300

c. Supplies 3,260
    Cash   3,260

d. Supplies Expense 3,260
    Supplies   3,260

_9_ 6. ABC Company's financial statements show the following:

Net income...$195,000

Total revenues...850,000

Total expenses...655,000

ABC's profit margin is:　　　　　　Income　195,000
　　　　　　　　　　　　　　　　　Sales　　850,000

a. 22.9 %

b. 29.8 %

c. 435.9 %

d. 129.8 %

e. 77.1 %

_d_ 7. Based on the following T-accounts and their end-of-period balances, what will be the balance of the (Retained Earnings) account after the closing entries are posted?

Retained Earnings	Dividends	Income Summary
Dec. 31 7,000	Dec. 31 9,600|	29,700 | 3600
7880		500
		920

Revenue　14,880

Revenue	Rent Expense	Salaries Expense
Dec. 31 29,700|	Dec. 31 3,600|	Dec. 31 7,200|

Insurance Expense	Depr. Expense, Equipment	Income Summary
Dec. 31 920|	Dec. 31 500|	29, 700 | 3600

　　　　　　　　　　　　　　　　　　　　　　　　29, 700 │ 3600
　　　　　　　　　　　　　　　　　　　　　　　　　　　│ 500
a. $12,880 Debit.　　　　　　　　　　　　　　　　　│ 920
b. $12,880 Credit.　　　　　　　　　　　　　　　　│ 9600
c. $24,480 Credit.　　　　　　　　　　　　　　　　│ 7200
d. $14,880 Credit.　　　　　　　　Bal 7,880 │ 21,820
e. $10,480 Debit.

_C_ 8. The following information is available from the financial statements of Harvard Company:

Current assets.. $ 195,000
Total assets 850,000
Current liabilities 113,500
Total liabilities..441,500
Stockholder's Equity 408,500

Harvard's (current ratio) is:　　C. Assets　　195,000
a. 1.9　　　　　　　　　　C. liabilities ═ 113,500
b. 2.1

c. 1.7

d. 1.5

e. 5.8

Problem III

Many of the important ideas and concepts discussed in Chapter 3 are reflected in the following list of key terms. Test your understanding of these terms by matching the appropriate definitions with the terms. Record the number identifying the most appropriate definition in the blank space next to each term.

_____ Accounting cycle	_____ Interim financial statements
_____ Accounting period	_____ Long-term investments
_____ Accrual basis accounting	_____ Long-term liabilities
_____ Accrued expenses	_____ Matching principle
_____ Accrued revenues	_____ Natural business year
_____ Adjusted trial balance	_____ Operating cycle
_____ Adjusting entry	_____ Permanent accounts
_____ Annual financial statements	_____ Plant assets
_____ Book value	_____ Post-closing trial balance
_____ Cash basis accounting	_____ Prepaid expenses
_____ Classified balance sheet	_____ Profit margin
_____ Closing entries	_____ Pro forma financial statements
_____ Closing process	_____ Reversing entries**
_____ Contra account	_____ Straight-line depreciation method
_____ Current assets	_____ Temporary accounts
_____ Current liabilities	_____ Time-period principle
_____ Current ratio	_____ Unadjusted trial balance
_____ Depreciation	_____ Unclassified balance sheet
_____ Fiscal year	_____ Unearned revenues
_____ Income Summary	_____ Working papers
_____ Intangible assets	_____ Work sheet*

* *Key term discussed in Appendix 3B.*
** *Key term discussed in Appendix 3C.*

1. Costs incurred in a period that are both unpaid and unrecorded; adjusting entries for recording accrued expenses involve increasing (debiting) expenses and increasing (crediting) liabilities.

2. Ratio of a company's net income to net sales; the percent of income in each dollar of revenue.

3. Allocates equal amounts of an asset's cost (less any salvage value) to depreciation expense during its useful life.

4. List of accounts and balances prepared after adjustments are recorded and posted.

5. Revenues earned in a period that are both unrecorded and not yet received in cash (or other assets); adjusting entries for recording accrued revenues involve increasing (debiting) assets and increasing (crediting) revenues.

6. List of accounts and balances prepared before adjustments have been recorded and posted.

7. Assumes an organization's activities can be divided into specific time periods such as months, quarters, or years.

8. Consecutive 12-month (or 52 week) period chosen as the organization's annual accounting period.

9. Expense created by allocating the cost of plant and equipment to the periods in which they are used.

10. Cash (or other assets) received in advance of providing products or services; a liability.

11. Journal entry at the end of an accounting period to bring an asset or liability account to its proper amount and update the related revenue or expense account.

12. Requires expenses to be reported in the same period as the revenues that were earned as a result of the expenses.

13. The 12-month period that ends when a company's sales activities are at their lowest point.

14. Balance sheet that broadly groups the assets, liabilities and equity accounts.

15. Accounting system that recognizes revenues when cash is received and records expenses when cash is paid.

16. Accounting system that recognizes revenues when earned and expenses when incurred; the basis for GAAP.

17. Account linked with another account and having the opposite normal balance; reported as a subtraction from the other account's balance.

18. Length of time covered by periodic financial statements; also called *reporting period.*

19. Necessary steps to prepare the accounts for recording the transactions of the next period.

20. Financial statements covering periods of less than one year; usually based on one- or three- or six-month periods.

21. Financial statements covering a one-year period; often based on a calendar year, but any consecutive 12-month (or 52-week) period is acceptable.

22. Items paid for in advance of receiving their benefits; classified as assets.

23. An asset's acquisition costs less its accumulated depreciation.

24. Assets such as notes receivable or investments in stocks and bonds that are held for more than the longer of one year or the operating cycle.

25. List of permanent accounts and their balances from the ledger after the closing entries are journalized and posted.

26. Recurring steps performed each accounting period, starting with analyzing transactions and continuing through the post-closing trial balance (or reversing entries).

27. Balance sheet that presents the assets and liabilities in relevant subgroups.

28. Accounts used to record revenues and expenses; they are closed at the end of the period; also called *nominal accounts.*

29. Analyses and other informal reports prepared by accountants when organizing information for formal reports and financial statements.

30. Accounts used to report activities related to one or more future periods; balance sheet accounts whose balances are not closed; also called *real accounts.*

31. Temporary account used only in the closing process to which the balances of revenues and expenses are transferred; its balance is transferred to the retained earnings account.

32. Optional entries recorded at the beginning of a new period that prepare the accounts for the usual journal entries as if adjusting entries had not occurred.

33. Entries recorded at the end of each accounting period to transfer end-of-period balances in revenue and expense accounts to retained earnings.

34. Spreadsheet used to draft an unadjusted trial balance, adjusting entries, adjusted trial balance, and financial statements; an optional step in accounting.

35. Statements that show the effects of the proposed transactions as if they occurred.

36. Long-term assets used to produce or sell products or services; they usually lack physical form and their benefits are uncertain.

37. Cash or other assets that are expected to be sold, collected, or used within one year or the company's operating cycle, whichever is longer.

38. Obligations due to be paid or settled within one year or the operating cycle, whichever is longer.

39. Ratio used to evaluate a company's ability to pay its short-term obligations; calculated by dividing current assets by current liabilities.

40. Obligations that are not due to be paid within one year or the operating cycle, whichever is longer.

41. Tangible long-lived assets used to produce or sell products and services; also called *property, plant and equipment* or fixed assets.

42. Normal time between paying cash for merchandise or employee services and receiving cash from customers.

Problem IV

Complete the following by filling in the blanks.

1. Under the cash basis of accounting, revenues are reported as being earned in the accounting period in which _____, expenses are charged to the period in which _____, and net income for the period is the difference between _____ and _____.

2. Under the accrual basis of accounting, revenues are credited to the period in which _____, expenses are _____ with revenues, and no consideration is given as to when cash is received or disbursed.

3. Revenue accounts have credit balances; consequently, to close a revenue account and make it show a zero balance, the revenue account is _____ , and the Income Summary account is _____ for the amount of the balance.

4. Expense accounts have debit balances; therefore, expense accounts are _____, and the Income Summary account is _____ in closing the expense accounts.

5. Only balance sheet accounts should have balances appearing on the post-closing trial balance because the balances of all temporary accounts are reduced to _____ in the closing procedure.

6. Closing entries are necessary because if at the end of an accounting period the revenue and expense accounts are to show only one period's revenues and expenses, they must begin the period with _____ balances, and closing entries cause the revenue and expense accounts to begin a new period with _____ balances.

7. Closing entries accomplish two purposes: (1) they cause all _____ accounts to begin the new accounting period with zero balances, and (2) they transfer the net effect of the past period's _____ and _____ transactions to the Retained Earnings account.

Problem V

On October 1 of the current year, Harold Lloyd incorporated a business to perform services as a public stenographer. During the month he completed the following transactions:

10/01 Invested $3,000 in the business. *cr.* Cash — Common stock *cr.*

10/01 Paid three months' rent in advance on the office space, $1,245. dr Cash cr prepaid rent

10/01 Purchased office equipment for cash, $925.50. dr cash cr off equip

10/02 Purchased on credit office equipment, $700, and office supplies, $75.50. office equip 700 supplies 75.50 A/P 775.50

10/31 Completed stenographic work during the month and collected cash, $1,725. cash 1725 rev earned 1725

10/31 Declared and paid a dividend in the amount of $725. Retained earnings > Dividends payable / Dividends payable > Cash / cash > Dividends payable > cash

After these transactions were journalized and posted, the company's accounts were as follows:

GENERAL LEDGER

Cash — Account No. 101

DATE	EXPLANATION	P.R.	DEBIT		CREDIT		BALANCE	
Oct. 1	Owner Investment	G-1	3 000 00				3 000 00	
1		G-1			1 245 00		1 755 00	
1		G-1			925 50		829 50	
31		G-2	1 725 00				2 554 50	
31		G-2			725 00		1 829 50	

Office Supplies — Account No. 124

DATE	EXPLANATION	P.R.	DEBIT		CREDIT		BALANCE	
Oct. 2		G-1	75 50				75 50	
Oct 31		2			35 50		40	

Prepaid Rent — Account No. 131

DATE	EXPLANATION	P.R.	DEBIT		CREDIT		BALANCE	
Oct. 1		G-1	1 245 00				1 245 00	
Oct 31		2			415		830 –	

Office Equipment — Account No. 163

DATE	EXPLANATION	P.R.	DEBIT		CREDIT		BALANCE	
Oct. 1		G-1	925 50				925 50	
2		G-1	700 00				1 625 50	

Accumulated Depreciation, Office Equipment — Account No. 164

DATE	EXPLANATION	P.R.	DEBIT		CREDIT		BALANCE	
Oct 31		2			35		35	

Accounts Payable

DATE	EXPLANATION	P.R.	DEBIT	CREDIT	BALANCE
Oct. 2 √		G-1		7 7 5 50	7 7 5 50 √

Common Stock

Account No. 301

DATE	EXPLANATION	P.R.	DEBIT	CREDIT	BALANCE
Oct. 1		G-1		3 0 0 0 00	3 0 0 0 00 √

Dividends

Account No. 303

DATE	EXPLANATION	P.R.	DEBIT	CREDIT	BALANCE
Oct. 31 √		G-2	7 2 5 00		7 2 5 00 √

Stenographic Services Revenue

Account No. 403

DATE	EXPLANATION	P.R.	DEBIT	CREDIT	BALANCE
Oct. 31 √		G-2		1 7 2 5 00	1 7 2 5 00 √

Depreciation Expense, Office Equipment

Account No. 612

DATE	EXPLANATION	P.R.	DEBIT	CREDIT	BALANCE
Oct 31		2	35 -		35 √

Rent Expense

Account No. 640

DATE	EXPLANATION	P.R.	DEBIT	CREDIT	BALANCE
Oct 31		2	415		415 √

Office Supplies Expense

Account No. 650

DATE	EXPLANATION	P.R.	DEBIT	CREDIT	BALANCE
Oct 31		2	35 50		35 50 √

On October 31, Harold Lloyd gathered the following information in preparation for adjusting the company's books and preparing its balance sheet and an income statement.

a. One month's rent had expired. – $\frac{1245}{3}$ = $415 month

b. An inventory of office supplies showed $40 of unused office supplies. 75.50 - 40 =

c. The office equipment had depreciated $35 during October.

Required:

1. Prepare and post journal entries to record the adjustments.

2. After posting the adjusting entries, complete the adjusted trial balance.

3. Using the adjusted trial balance, prepare an income statement and statement of retained earnings for the month of October and a classified balance sheet as of the end of October.

GENERAL JOURNAL   Page 2

DATE	ACCOUNT TITLES AND EXPLANATION	P.R.	DEBIT		CREDIT	
Oct.31 (a)	Rent expense	640	415			
	Prepaid rent	131			415	
(b)	Office Supplies expense.	650	35	50		
	Office Supplies	124			35	50
(c)	Depr. expense		35			
	Accum Depre.				35	

HAROLD LLOYD, INC.

Adjusted Trial Balance

October 31, 20—

			Debit		Credit	
Cash			1 829	50		
Office supplies			40			
Prepaid rent			830			
Office equipment			1 625	50		
Accumulated depreciation, office equipment					35	
Accounts payable					775	50
Common stock					3000	
Dividends			725			
Stenographic services revenue					1 725	
Depreciation expense, office equipment			35			
Rent expense			415			
Office supplies expense			35	50		
Totals			5 535	50	5 535	50

HAROLD LLOYD, INC.

Income Statement

For Month Ended October 31, 20—

Revenue							
Steno Services Revenue						1	725	
Expenses							
Rent expense				415			
Office Supplies Expense				35	50		
Depre. expense office equip				35		(485	50)
Total expenses						1 239	50

HAROLD LLOYD, INC.

Statement of Retained Earnings

For Month Ended October 31, 20—

Retained Earning Dec. 31, 2007							
Net Income				1239	50	1239	50
less Dividend				(725)			
Retained Earning Dec 31, 2008						514	50

HAROLD LLOYD, INC.

Balance Sheet

October 31, 20—

Assets							
Cash			1 829	50			
Office Supplies			40				
Prepaid Rent			830				
Office equipment			1 625	50			
Accum depre. office equip						35	
Total Assets			4 290				
Liabilities						775	50
A/P							
Owners Equity							
Common Stock						3 000	
Retained earnings						514	50
Total Liabilities and Stockholders Equity						4290	

Problem VI

Blade Company has one employee who earns $72.50 per day. The company operates with monthly accounting periods, and the employee is paid each Friday night for a workweek that begins on Monday. Assume the calendar for October appears as shown below:

OCTOBER						
S	M	T	W	T	F	S
	1	2	3	4	⑤	6
7	8	9	10	11	⑫	13
14	15	16	17	18	⑲	20
21	22	23	24	25	㉖	27
28	㉙	㉚	㉛			

$362.50 \left(\frac{3}{5}\right)$

$72.50 \times 2 = \$145$

Required:

1. Enter the four $362.50 weekly wage payments directly in the T-accounts below. Then enter the adjustment for the wages earned but unpaid on October 31 directly in the T-accounts.

Cash		Wages Payable		Wages Expense	
Oct 5 362.50			Oct 31 217.50	Oct 5 362.50	
Oct 12 362.50				Oct 12 362.50	
Oct 19 362.50				Oct 19 362.50	
Oct 26 362.50				Oct 26 362.50	
				Oct 31 217.50	

2. Blade Company's October income statement should show $___1,667.50___ of wages expense, and its October 31 balance sheet should show a $___217.50___ liability for wages payable. The wages earned by its employee but unpaid on October 31 are an example of an ___accrued___ expense.

3. Prepare the journal entry to record payment of a full week's wages to the Blade Company employee on November 2.

	GENERAL JOURNAL						Page 1	
DATE	ACCOUNT TITLES AND EXPLANATION	P.R.	DEBIT			CREDIT		
Nov 2	Wages Expense (2 days)		145					
	Wage Payable		217	50				
	Cash					362	50	

Problem VII

Riverview Properties operates an apartment building. On December 31, at the end of an annual accounting period, its Rent Earned account had a $335,500 credit balance, and the Unearned Rent account had a $3,600 credit balance. The following information was available for the year-end adjustments: (a) the credit balance in the Unearned Rent account resulted from a tenant paying his rent for six months in advance beginning on November 1; (b) also, a tenant in temporary financial difficulties had not paid his rent for the month of December. The amount due was $475.

Required:

1. Enter the necessary adjustments directly in the T-accounts below.

Rent Receivable	Unearned Rent	Rent Earned
Dec 31 475	Dec 31 1200	Nov. 1 3,600	Bal. 335,500
			Dec 31 1200
			Dec. 31 475

2. After the adjustments described above are entered in the accounts, the company's Rent Earned account has a balance of $ 337,175 which will appear on its income statement as revenue earned during the year. Its Unearned Rent account has a balance of $ 2400 , which will appear on the company's balance sheet as a liability . Likewise, the company's Rent Receivable account has a $ 475 balance, and this should appear on its balance sheet as a(n) asset .

Problem VIII

The adjusted trial balance of Homer's Home Shop, Inc. appears below:

HOMER'S HOME SHOP, INC.
Adjusted Trial Balance
December 31, 20---

Cash	$ 2,875	....
Accounts receivable	2,000	....
Shop supplies	725	....
Shop equipment	5,125	....
Accumulated depreciation, shop equipment	....	$ 1,200
Accounts payable	....	575
Wages payable	....	388
Common stock	....	5,500
Retained earnings	30,000	....
Repair services revenue	....	55,785
Wages expense	18,638	....
Rent expense	2,500	....
Shop supplies expense	1,037	....
Depreciation expense, shop equipment	475	....
Miscellaneous expense	73	....
Totals	$63,448	$63,448

Required:

1. Prepare the entries required to close the company's accounts.
2. Prepare a post-closing trial balance.

(handwritten, top right)
Income Summary
	55,785
22,723	
	BAL 33,062
30,000	
	3,062

GENERAL JOURNAL

DATE	ACCOUNT TITLES AND EXPLANATION	P.R.	DEBIT			CREDIT		
	Rent Revenue		55	785				
	Income Summary					55	785	
	Income Summary		22	723				
	Wages expense					18	638	
	rent expense					2	500	
	Supplies expense					1	037	
	Deprc. expense						475	
	Misc. expense						73	
	Income Summary							
	Dividends							

HOMER'S HOME SHOP, INC.

Post-Closing Trial Balance

December 31, 20—

			DEBIT			CREDIT		
	Cash		2	875				
	A/R		2	000				
	Shop Supplies			725				
	Shop Equipment		5	125				
	Accum Deprc., Shop equip					1	200	
	Accounts Payable						575	
	Common Stock						388	
	Retained Earnings					5	500	
						3	062	
			10	725		10	725	

Solutions for Chapter 3

Problem I

1. T
2. F
3. T
4. F
5. T
6. F

Problem II

1. D
2. C
3. C
4. E
5. D
6. A
7. D
8. C

Problem III

26	Accounting cycle	20	Interim financial statements
18	Accounting period	24	Long-term investments
16	Accrual basis accounting	40	Long-term liabilities
1	Accrued expenses	12	Matching principle
5	Accrued revenues	13	Natural business year
4	Adjusted trial balance	42	Operating cycle
11	Adjusting entry	30	Permanent accounts
21	Annual financial statements	41	Plant assets
23	Book value	25	Post-closing trial balance
15	Cash basis accounting	22	Prepaid expenses
27	Classified balance sheet	2	Profit margin
33	Closing entries	35	Pro forma financial statements
19	Closing process	32	Reversing entries**
17	Contra account	3	Straight-line depreciation method
37	Current assets	28	Temporary accounts
38	Current liabilities	7	Time-period principle
39	Current ratio	6	Unadjusted trial balance
9	Depreciation	14	Unclassified balance sheet
8	Fiscal year	10	Unearned revenues
31	Income Summary	29	Working papers
36	Intangible assets	34	Work sheet*

Problem IV

1. they are received in cash; they are paid; revenue receipts; expense disbursements

2. earned; matched

3. debited; credited

4. credited; debited

5. zero

6. zero; zero

7. temporary; revenue; expense

Problem V

1.

Oct. 31	Rent Expense	415.00	
	Prepaid Rent		415.00
31	Office Supplies Expense	35.50	
	Office Supplies		35.50
31	Depreciation Expense, Office Equipment	35.00	
	Accumulated Depreciation, Office Equipment		35.00

Cash

Date	Debit	Credit	Balance
Oct 1	3,000.00		3,000.00
1		1,245.00	1,755.00
1		925.50	829.50
31	1,725.00		2,554.50
31		725.00	1,829.50

Office Supplies

Oct. 2	75.50		75.50
31		35.50	40.00

Prepaid Rent

Oct. 1	1,245.00		1,245.00
31		415.00	830.00

Office Equipment

Oct. 1	925.50		925.50
2	700.00		1,625.50

Accumulated Depr., Office Equipment

Oct. 31		35.00	35.00

Accounts Payable

Date	Debit	Credit	Balance
Oct. 2		775.50	775.50

Common Stock

Oct. 1		3,000.00	3,000.00

Dividends

Oct. 31	725.00		725.00

Stenographic Services Revenue

Oct. 31		1,725.00	1,725.00

Depr. Expense, Office Equipment

Oct. 31	35.00		35.00

Rent Expense

Oct. 31	415.00		415.00

Office Supplies Expense

Oct. 31	35.50		35.50

2.

HAROLD LLOYD, INC.

Adjusted Trial Balance

October 31, 20---

Cash..	$1,829.50	
Office supplies	40.00	
Prepaid rent..	830.00	
Office equipment..	1,625.50	
Accumulated depreciation, office equipment		$ 35.00
Accounts payable		775.50
Common stock		3,000.00
Retained earnings..	725.00	
Stenographic services revenue		1,725.00
Depreciation expense, office equipment..................................	35.00	
Rent expense	415.00	
Office supplies expense	35.50	
Totals..	$5,535.50	$5,535.50

3.

HAROLD LLOYD, INC.

Income Statement

For Month Ended October 31, 20---

Revenue:		
Stenographic services revenue		$1,725.00
Operating expenses:		
Depreciation expense, office equipment.............................	$ 35.00	
Rent expense	415.00	
Office supplies expense...	35.50	
Total operating expenses..		485.50
Net income		$1,239.50

HAROLD LLOYD, INC.

Statement of Retained Earnings

For Month Ended October 31, 20---

Retained earnings, October 1, 20---		$ 0.00
October net income...	$1,239.50	
Less dividends...	725.00	
Excess of income over dividends...		514.50
Retained earnings, October 31, 20---		$514.50

HAROLD LLOYD, INC.
Balance Sheet
October 31, 20---
Assets

Current assets

Cash		$1,829.50
Office supplies		40.00
Prepaid rent..		830.00
Total current assets		2,699.50

Plant assets

Office equipment	$1,625.50	
Less accumulated depreciation	35.00	
Total plant assets		1,590.50
Total assets		$4,290.00 ✓

Liabilities

Current liabilities

Accounts payable..		$ 775.50 ✓

Equity

Common stock...		3,000.00 ✓
Retained earnings		514.50
Total liabilities and equity...		$4,290.00

Problem VI

1.

Cash				Wages Expense		
	Oct. 5	362.50		Oct. 5	362.50	
	12	362.50		12	362.50	
	19	362.50		19	362.50	
	26	362.50		26	362.50	
				31	217.50	

Wages Payable		
	Oct. 31	217.50

2. $1,667.50; $217.50; accrued

3. Nov. 2

Wages Expense..	145.00	
Wages Payable...	217.50	
Cash...		362.50

Problem VII

1.

Rent Receivable					Unearned Rent			
Dec. 31	475				Dec. 31	1,200	Nov. 1	3,600

	Rent Earned	
	Bal.	335,500
	Dec. 31	1,200
	31	475

2. Rent Earned; $337,175; Unearned Rent; $2,400, liability; Rent Receivable; $475, asset.

Problem VIII

1.

Dec. 31	Repair Services Revenue	55,785	
	Income Summary		55,785

Dec. 31	Income Summary	22,723	
	Wages Expense		18,638
	Rent Expense		2,500
	Shop Supplies Expense		1,037
	Depreciation Expense, Shop Equipment		475
	Miscellaneous Expense		73

Dec. 31	Income Summary	33,062	
	Retained Earnings		33,062

2.

HOMER'S HOME SHOP, INC.
Post-Closing Trial Balance
December 31, 20---

Cash	$ 2,875	....
Accounts receivable	2,000	....
Shop supplies	725	....
Shop equipment	5,125	....
Accumulated depreciation, shop equipment	....	$ 1,200
Accounts payable	....	575
Wages payable	....	388
Common stock	....	5,500
Retained earnings (33,062 – 30,000)	....	3,062
Totals	$10,725	$10,725

CHAPTER 4
REPORTING AND ANALYZING
MERCHANDISING OPERATIONS

Learning Objective C1:

Describe merchandising activities and identify income components for a merchandising company.

Merchandisers buy products and resell them. Examples of merchandisers include Wal-Mart, Home Depot, The Limited, and Barnes & Noble. A merchandiser's costs on the income statement include an amount for cost of goods sold. Gross profit, or gross margin, equals sales minus cost of goods sold.

Learning Objective C2:

Identify and explain the inventory asset of a merchandising company.

The current asset section of a merchandising company's balance sheet includes *merchandise inventory,* which refers to the products a merchandiser sells and are available for sale at the balance sheet date.

Learning Objective C3:

Describe both perpetual and periodic inventory systems.

A perpetual inventory system continuously tracks the cost of goods available for sale and the cost of goods sold. A periodic system accumulates the cost of goods purchased during the period and does not compute the amount of inventory or the cost of goods sold until the end of a period.

Learning Objective C4:

Analyze and interpret cost flows and operating activities of a merchandising company.

Cost of merchandise purchases flows into Merchandise Inventory and from there to Cost of Goods Sold on the income statement. Any remaining inventory is reported as a current asset on the balance sheet.

Learning Objective A1:

Compute the acid-test ratio and explain its use to assess liquidity.

The acid-test ratio is computed as quick assets (cash, short-term investments, and current receivables) divided by current liabilities. It indicates a company's ability to pay its current liabilities with its existing quick assets. An acid-test ratio equal to or greater than 1.0 is often adequate.

Learning Objective A2:

Compute the gross margin ratio and explain its use to assess profitability.

The gross margin ratio is computed as gross margin (net sales minus cost of goods sold) divided by net sales. It indicates a company's profitability before considering other expenses.

Learning Objective P1:

Analyze and record transactions for merchandise purchases using a perpetual system.

For a perpetual inventory system, purchases of inventory (net of trade discounts) are added to the Merchandise Inventory account. Purchase discounts and purchase returns and allowances are subtracted from Merchandise Inventory, and transportation-in costs are added to Merchandise Inventory.

Learning Objective P2:

Analyze and record transactions for merchandise sales using a perpetual system.

A merchandiser records sales at list price less any trade discounts. The cost of items sold is transferred from Merchandise Inventory to Cost of Goods Sold. Refunds or credits given to customers for unsatisfactory merchandise are recorded in Sales Returns and Allowances, a contra account to Sales. If merchandise is returned and restored to inventory, the cost of this merchandise is removed from Cost of Goods Sold and transferred back to Merchandise Inventory. When cash discounts from the sales price are offered and customers pay within the discount period, the seller records Sales Discounts, a contra account to Sales.

Learning Objective P3:

Prepare adjustments and close accounts for a merchandising company.

With a perpetual system, it is often necessary to make an adjustment for inventory shrinkage. This is computed by comparing a physical count of inventory with the Merchandise Inventory balance. Shrinkage is normally charged to Cost of Goods Sold. Temporary accounts closed to Income Summary for a merchandiser include Sales, Sales Discounts, Sales Returns and Allowances, and Cost of Goods Sold.

Learning Objective P4:

Define and prepare multiple-step and single-step income statements.

Multiple-step income statements include greater detail for sales and expenses than do single-step income statements. They also show details of net sales and report expenses in categories reflecting different activities.

Learning Objective P5 (Appendix 4A):

Record and compare merchandising transactions using both periodic and perpetual inventory systems.

Transactions involving the sale and purchase of merchandise are recorded and analyzed under both the periodic and perpetual inventory systems. Adjusting and closing entries for both inventory systems are illustrated and explained.

I.   **Merchandising Activities**

Products that a company acquires to resell to customers are referred to as **merchandise** (also called *goods*). A **merchandiser** earns net income by buying and selling merchandise. A **wholesaler** is an *intermediary* that buys products from manufacturers or other wholesalers and sells them to retailers or other wholesalers.

A. Reporting Income for a Merchandiser

Revenue (*net sales*) from selling merchandise minus the **cost of goods sold** (the expense of buying and preparing the merchandise) to customers is called **gross profit** (also called *gross margin*). This amount minus expenses (generally called *operating expenses*) determines the net income or loss for the period.

B. Reporting Inventory for a Merchandiser

1. A merchandiser's balance sheet is the same as a service business with the exception of one additional current asset, **merchandise inventory**, or simply *inventory*.

2. The cost of this asset includes the cost incurred to buy the goods, ship them to the store, and make them ready for sale.

C. Operating Cycle for a Merchandiser

A merchandising company's operating cycle begins by purchasing merchandise and ends by collecting cash from selling the merchandise. Companies try to keep their operating cycles short because assets tied up in inventory and receivables are not productive.

D. Inventory Systems

1. Merchandise available for sale consists of beginning inventory and what it purchases (net cost of purchases). The merchandise available is either sold (cost of goods sold) or kept for future sales (ending inventory).

2. Two alternative inventory systems are used to collect information about cost of goods sold and the cost of inventory:

a. **Perpetual inventory system**—continually updates accounting records for merchandise transactions, specifically, for those records of inventory available for sale and inventory sold.

b. **Periodic inventory system**—updates the accounting records for merchandise transactions only at the *end* of a period.

The following sections of this outline use the perpetual inventory system. Appendix 4A uses the period system (with perpetual results on the side). An instructor can choose to cover either one or both inventory systems.

II.   Accounting for Merchandise Purchases

The invoice serves as a *source document* for this event.

A. Trade Discounts

1. In catalogs, each item has a **list price** or catalog price. An item's intended selling price equals list price minus a given percent called a **trade discount**.

2. A buyer records the net amount of list price minus trade discount.

B. Purchases Discounts

Credit terms for a purchase include the amounts and timing of payments from a buyer to a seller. The amount of time before full payment is due is called the **credit** period.

1. Sellers can grant a **cash discount** to encourage the buyer to pay earlier. A seller views a cash discount as a **sales discount** and a buyer views a cash discount as a **purchase discount.** This reduced payment applies only for the **discount period**.

2. Example: *credit terms*, 2/10 n/30, offers a 2 % discount if the invoice is paid within 10 days of invoice date.

3. Entry for buyer for purchase of merchandise on credit: debit Merchandise Inventory, credit Accounts Payable.

4. Entry for buyer to record payment within discount period: debit Accounts Payable (full invoice amount), credit Cash (amount paid = invoice – discount), credit Merchandise Inventory (amount of discount).

C. Purchase Returns and Allowances

1. *Purchase returns* refer to merchandise a buyer acquires but then returns to the seller.

2. A *purchase allowance* is a reduction in the cost of defective or unacceptable merchandise that a buyer acquires.

3. The buyer issues a **debit memorandum** to inform the seller of a debit made to the supplier's account.

4. Entry for buyer to record purchase return or allowance: debit Accounts Payable or Cash (if refund given) and credit Merchandise Inventory.

5. When goods are returned, a buyer can take a purchase discount on only the remaining balance of the invoice.

D. Transportation Costs and Ownership Transfer

The buyer and seller must agree on who is responsible for paying any freight costs and who bears the risk of loss during transit for merchandising transactions. The point of transfer is called the **FOB** (*free on board*) point.

1. FOB shipping point—buyer accepts ownership when goods depart sellers' place of business; buyer pays shipping costs.

    a. Shipping costs increase the cost of merchandise acquired (cost principle).

    b. Entry for buyer to record shipping costs: Debit Merchandise Inventory, credit Cash or Accounts Payable (if to be paid with merchandise later).

2. FOB destination—ownership of goods transfers to buyer when goods arrive at buyer's place of business; seller pays shipping costs.

    a. Shipping costs are an operating (selling) expense for seller

    b. Entry for seller to record shipping costs: Debit Delivery Expense (or Transportation-Out or Freight-Out), credit Cash.

III. **Accounting for Merchandise Sales**

A. Sales of Merchandise

Each sales transaction involves two parts:

1. Recognize revenue—entry for seller to record: debit Accounts Receivable (or cash), credit Sales (for the invoice amount).

2. Recognize cost— entry for seller to record: debit Cost of Goods Sold, credit Merchandise Inventory (for the cost of the merchandise sold).

B. Sales Discounts

Sales discounts are usually not recorded until a customer actually pays with the discount period.

1. Entry for seller to record collection after discount period— Debit Cash, Credit Accounts Receivable (full invoice amount).

2. Entry for seller to record collection within discount period— debit Cash (invoice amount less discount), debit Sales Discounts (discount amount), credit Accounts Receivable (invoice amount).

3. Sales Discounts is a contra-revenue account; it is subtracted from Sales when computing a company's net sales.

4. Sales discounts are monitored to assess the effectiveness and cost of its discount policy.

C. Sales Returns and Allowances

1. *Sales returns*—merchandise that a customer returns to the seller after a sale.

2. *Sales allowances*—reductions in the selling price of merchandise sold to customers (usually for damaged or defective merchandise that a customer is willing to keep at a reduced price).

3. Entry for seller to record sales returns or allowances: debit Sales Returns and Allowances and credit Accounts Receivable; additional entry if returned merchandise is salable: debit Merchandise Inventory, credit Cost of Goods Sold.

4. Seller prepares a **credit memorandum** to inform buyer of the seller's credit to the buyer's Accounts Receivable (on the seller's books).

IV. **Completing the Accounting Cycle**

A. Adjusting Entries for Merchandisers

Generally same as discussed in chapter 3 for a service business.

1. Additional adjustment needed to update inventory to reflect any loss of merchandise, including theft and deterioration, is referred to as **shrinkage**.

2. Shrinkage is determined by comparing a physical count of the inventory with recorded quantities.

3. Entry to record shrinkage: debit Cost of Goods Sold, credit Merchandise Inventory.

B. Preparing Financial Statements

The financial statement for a merchandiser is similar to those for a service company described in chapters 2 and 3.

1. The income statement mainly differs by the inclusion of *cost of goods sold* and *gross profit*. Net sales is affected by discounts, returns, and allowances, and some additional expenses are possible such as delivery expense and loss from defective merchandise.

2. The balance sheet mainly differs by the inclusion of *merchandise inventory* as part of current assets.

C. Closing Entries

Closing entries are similar to a service business except that some new temporary accounts that arise from merchandising activities must be closed (e.g., Sales Discount, Sales Returns and Allowances, and Cost of Goods Sold). These debit balance accounts are closed with the expense accounts to Income Summary.

V. **Financial Statement Formats**—No specific format is required in practice. Two common income statement formats:

A. Multiple-Step Income Statement

   1. A **multiple-step income statement** has three main parts:

     a. *Gross profit*—net sales minus cost of goods sold),

     b. *Income from operations*—gross profit less operating expenses, and

     c. *Net income*—income from operations adjusted for nonoperating items.

   2. Operating expenses are classified into two sections:

     a. **Selling expenses**—the expenses of promoting sales, making sales, and delivering goods to customers, and

     b. **General and administrative expenses**—expenses related to accounting, human resource management, and financial management.

   3. *Nonoperating activities*—consist of other expenses, revenues, losses, and gains that are unrelated to a company's operations; reported in two sections:

     a. *Other revenues and gains*—interest revenue, dividend revenue, rent revenue, and gains from asset disposals.

     b. *Other expenses and losses*—interest expense, losses from asset disposals, and casualty losses.

B. Single-Step Income Statement

A **single-step income statement** includes cost of goods sold as an operating expense and shows only one subtotal for total expenses, one subtraction to arrive at net income.

C. Classified Balance Sheet

The merchandiser's classified balance sheet reports merchandise inventory as a current asset, usually after accounts receivable.

VI. **Decision Analysis—Acid-Test and Gross Margin Ratios**

A. Acid-Test Ratio

   1. The **acid-test ratio** is used to assess the company's liquidity or ability to pay its current debts; it differs from the current ratio by excluding less liquid current assets.

   2. It is calculated by dividing *quick assets* by current liabilities; quick assets are cash, short-term investments, and current receivables.

   3. Rule of thumb is that the acid-test ratio should have a value of at least 1.0 to conclude that a company is unlikely to face near-term liquidity problems.

    B. Gross Margin Ratio

        1. The **gross margin ratio** is used to assess a company's profitability before considering operating expenses.

        2. It is calculated by dividing *gross margin* (net sales – cost of goods sold) by net sales.

VII.   **Periodic (and Perpetual) Inventory System (Appendix 4A)**

    A. Records merchandise acquisitions, discounts and returns in temporary accounts (Purchases, Purchase Returns, Purchases Discounts) rather than the merchandise inventory account.

    B. Records only the revenue aspect of sales-related events; updates inventory and determines cost of goods sold only at the end or the accounting period.

    C. The Merchandise Inventory account can be updated as part of the adjusting or closing process.

    D. Requires closing additional temporary accounts.

VIII.   **Work Sheet—Perpetual System (Appendix 4B)**

Differs slightly from the work sheet layout for a service company in Chapter 3; includes additional accounts used by a merchandiser: Merchandise Inventory, Sales, Sales Returns and Allowances, Sales Discounts, and Cost of Goods Sold.

COMPONENTS OF NET INCOME (FROM OPERATIONS)

	Steps:
(a) Net Sales	X
(b) – Cost of Goods Sold*	– X
(c) Gross Profit on Sales	X
(d) – Operating Expenses	– X
(e) Net Income (Loss) from Operations	X

COMPONENTS OF COST OF GOODS SOLD

	Steps:
(a) Merchandise Inventory, Beginning of Period	X
(b) + Total Cost of Merchandise Purchases	+ X
(c) Available for Sale	X
(d) – Merchandise Inventory, End of Period	– X
(e) Cost of Goods Sold	X

COMPONENTS COST OF GOODS PURCHASED

		Steps:
(a) Purchases		X
(b) – Purchase Returns & Allowances	X	
and Purchases Discounts	+ X	– X
(c) Net Purchases		X
(d) + Transportation-In		+ X
(e) Total Cost of Merchandise Purchases		X

* Perpetual inventory systems have a cost of goods sold account that continuously accumulates costs as items are sold. In a periodic inventory system this amount is calculated at the end of period.

Financial Accounting, 4e

VISUAL #4-2

THE OUTDOOR STORE
Income Statement
For the Year Ended December 31, 20xx

Sales revenues			
Sales			$700,000
Less: Sales returns and allowances		$ 5,000	
Sales discounts		3,000	8,000
Net sales			$692,000
Cost of goods sold			
Merchandise inventory, January 1			40,300
Purchases		462,000	
Less: Purchase discounts	$12,000		
Purchase returns and Allowances	6,400	18,400	
Net purchases		443,600	
Add: Freight-in		3,600	
Total cost of merchandise purchased			447,200
Goods available for sale			487,500
Merchandise inventory, December 31			70,000
Cost of goods sold			417,500
Gross profit			274,500
Operating expenses			
Selling expenses			
Sales salaries expense		76,000	
Sales commission expense		14,500	
Depreciation expense - Display equip.		13,300	
Utilities expense		6,600	
Insurance expense		4,320	
Total selling expenses			114,720
General and administrative expenses			
Office salaries expense		32,000	
Depreciation expense – building		10,400	
Property tax expense		4,800	
Utilities expense		4,400	
Insurance expense		2,880	
Total administrative expenses			54,480
Total operating expenses			169,200
Income from operations			105,300
Other revenues and gains			
Interest revenue			4,000
Other expenses and losses			
Interest expense			11,000	7,000
Net income			$ 98,300

©The McGraw-Hill Companies, Inc., 2008

Study Guide, Chapter 4

91

The following data was taken from ledger account balances and supplementary data for the Whisk Company for the year ended December 31, 20XX:

Merchandise inventory, 1/1/20XX	$ 20,000
Merchandise inventory, 12/31/20XX	23,000
Purchases	215,000
Purchases discounts	6,000
Purchases returns and allowances	3,000
Sales	400,000
Sales discounts	3,200
Sales returns and allowances	1,800
Transportation-in	10,000

Required:

1. Compute the total cost of merchandise purchases. $206,000

2. Compute the cost of goods sold.

   BI + Purchase + trans − EI =

3. Prepare a multiple-step income statement (only through the gross profit line) for the year ended December 31, 20XX.

(If this alternative demonstration problem is not covered in class, see your instructor for the solution.)

Sales $400,000
Less: Sales Discount $3200
      Sales Rtn & Allow   1800
Total Sales   (5000)
                                                     395,000
COGS   (203,000)
Gross Profit $192,000

Note: Problems I through VI assume the use of a perpetual inventory system. Problem VII (appendix 4A) assumes a periodic inventory system.

Problem I

The following statements are either true or false. Place a (T) in the parentheses before each true statement and an (F) before each false statement.

1. (F) Sales returns and allowances or discounts are not included in the calculation of net sales.
2. (T) On a multiple-step income statement, ending inventory is subtracted from the cost of goods available for sale to determine cost of goods sold.
3. (T) Net sales minus cost of goods sold is gross profit on sales.
4. (T) The balance sheet for a merchandising business is generally the same as for a service business with the exception of the addition of one account.
5. (F) Quick assets include cash, short-term investments, receivables, and merchandise inventory. *NOMI or Prepaid*
6. ( ) A perpetual inventory system may require updating the inventory at the end of every fiscal period.
7. (F) Cash discounts on merchandise purchased are debited to the inventory account. *CR*
8. (T) Transportation costs on merchandise purchased are debited to the inventory account.
9. (F) A debit or credit memorandum may originate with either party to a transaction, but the memorandum gets its name from the action of the selling party exclusively.
10. (T) Recording the purchase of merchandise on account requires a debit to the inventory account and a credit to accounts payable.

Problem II

You are given several words, phrases, or numbers to choose from in completing each of the following statements or in answering the following questions. In each case select the one that best completes the statement or answers the question and place its letter in the answer space provided.

_b_ 1. A method of accounting for inventories in which cost of goods sold is recorded each time a sale is made and an up-to-date record of goods available is maintained is called a:

    a. product inventory system.
    b. perpetual inventory system.
    c. periodic inventory system.
    d. parallel inventory system.
    e. principal inventory system.

_c_ 2. What is the effect on the income statement at the end of an accounting period in which the ending inventory of the prior period was understated and carried forward incorrectly?

    a. Cost of goods sold is overstated and net income is understated.
    b. Cost of goods sold is understated and net income is understated.
    c. Cost of goods sold is understated and net income is overstated.
    d. Cost of goods sold is overstated and net income is overstated.
    e. The errors of the prior period and the current period offset each other, so there is no effect on the income statement.

_D_ 3. Based on the following information, calculate the missing amounts.

Sales.....................................	$28,800	Cost of goods sold.........	_18000_ _?_
Beginning inventory	_? 12,600_	Gross profit....................	$10,800
Purchases	18,000	Expenses........................	_? 7200_
Ending inventory	12,600	Net income	3,600

a. Beginning inventory, $16,200; Cost of goods sold, $12,600; Expenses, $1,800.
b. Beginning inventory, $23,400; Cost of goods sold, $10,800; Expenses, $7,200.
c. Beginning inventory, $9,000; Cost of goods sold, $14,400; Expenses, $3,600.
d. Beginning inventory, $12,600; Cost of goods sold, $18,000; Expenses, $7,200.
e. Beginning inventory, $19,800; Cost of goods sold, $25,200; Expenses, $14,400.

_16 900_ 4. The following information is taken from a single proprietorship's income statement. Calculate ending inventory for the business.

Sales.....................................	$165,250	Purchase returns	$ 390
Sales returns........................	980	Purchase discounts	1,630
Sales discounts....................	1,960	Transportation-in...........	700
Beginning inventory	16,880	Gross profit....................	58,210
Purchases	108,380	Net income	17,360

a. $19,840.
b. 22,080.
c. $21,160.
d. 44,250.
e. Some other amount.

_B_ 5. On July 18, Aught Company sold $1,800 of merchandise on credit, terms 2/10, n/30. On July 21, Aught issued a $180 credit memorandum to the customer who returned a portion of the merchandise purchased. In addition to the journal entry that debits inventory and credits cost of goods sold, what other journal entry is necessary to record the July 21 transaction?

a.	Accounts Receivable	180.00	
	Sales..		180.00
b.	Sales Returns and Allowances...............................	180.00	
	Accounts Receivable...		180.00
c.	Accounts Receivable	900.00	
	Sales Returns and Allowances...............................	180.00	
	Sales..		1,080.00
d.	Sales..	180.00	
	Accounts Receivable...		180.00
e.	Sales Returns and Allowances...............................	180.00	
	Sales..		180.00

___B___ 6. The following information is available from the balance sheet of Foster Company:

Cash	$22,300
Short-term investments	10,500
Accounts receivable	47,360
Merchandise inventory	52,100
Accounts payable	66,800
J. Foster, capital	57,300

Foster's acid-test ratio is:

a. 0.5
b. 1.2
c. 2.0
d. 1.4
e. 2.3

Problem III

Many of the important ideas and concepts discussed in Chapter 4 are reflected in the following list of key terms. Test your understanding of these terms by matching the appropriate definitions with the terms. Record the number identifying the most appropriate definition in the blank space next to each term.

12	Acid-test ratio		Merchandise
18	Cash discount	6	Merchandise inventory
	Cost of goods sold		Merchandiser
	Credit memorandum		Multiple-step income statement
	Credit period		Periodic inventory system
	Credit terms	2.	Perpetual inventory system
5	Debit memorandum		Purchases discount
	Discount period	9.	Retailer
7	EOM		Sales discount
	FOB		Selling expenses
	General and administrative expenses		Shrinkage
1.	Gross margin		Single-step income statement
	Gross margin ratio		Supplementary records
	Gross profit	3.	Trade discount
	Inventory		Wholesaler
8	List price		

1. Net sales minus cost of goods sold; also called *gross profit*. Gross Margin

2. Method that maintains continuous records of the cost of inventory available and the cost of goods sold. Perpetual

3. Reduction from a list or catalog price that can vary for wholesalers, retailers, and consumers. Trade Discount

4. Term used by a seller to describe a cash discount granted to customers for paying within the discount period. Sales Discount

5. Notification that the sender has debited the recipient's account kept by the sender. Debit memo

6. Merchandise a company owns and expects to sell in its normal operations.

7. Abbreviation for *end of month;* used to describe credit terms for some transactions.

8. Catalog price of an item before any trade discount is deducted.

9. Products that a company owns and expects to sell to customers; also called *merchandise inventory*.

10. Description of the amounts and timing of payments that a buyer agrees to make in the future.

11. Time period that can pass before a customer's payment is due.

12. Ratio used to assess a company's ability to settle its current debts with its most liquid assets; defined as quick assets (cash, short-term investments, and current receivables) over current liabilities. Acid test Ratio

13. Term used by a purchaser to describe a cash discount granted to the purchaser for paying within the discount period.

14. Notification that the sender has credited the recipient's account kept by the sender.

15. Method that records the cost of inventory purchased but does not track the quantity available or sold to customers; records are updated at the end of each period to reflect the physical count of goods available.

16. Time period in which a cash discount is available and the buyer can make a reduced payment.

17. Income statement format that includes cost of goods sold as an expense and shows only one subtotal for total expenses.

18. Reduction in the price of merchandise granted by a seller to a buyer when payment is made within the discount period. Cash Discount

19. Expenses of promoting sales, such as displaying and advertising merchandise, making sales, and delivering goods to customers.

20. Products that a company owns and expects to sell to their customers; also called *merchandise*.

21. Expenses that support the operating activities of a business.

22. Abbreviation for *free on board;* the point at which ownership of goods passes to the buyer; *FOB shipping point* (or *factory*) means the buyer pays shipping costs and accepts ownership of the goods at the seller's place of business; *FOB destination* means the seller pays shipping costs and buyer accepts ownership of the goods at the buyer's place of business;

23. Income statement format that shows subtotals between sales and net income and details of net sales and expenses.

24. Inventory losses that occur as a result of theft or deterioration.

25. Cost of inventory sold to customers during a period.

26. Gross margin (net sales minus cost of goods sold) divided by net sales; also called *gross profit ratio*.

27. Entity that earns net income by buying and selling merchandise.

28. Intermediary that buys products from manufacturers or other wholesalers and sells them to retailers or other wholesalers.

29. Information outside the usual accounting records.

30. Intermediary that buys products from manufacturers or wholesalers and sells them to customers.

31. Net sales minus cost of goods sold; also called *gross margin*.

Problem IV

The following amounts appeared on the adjusted trial balance of Valentine Variety Store, Inc. as of December 31, 20X9, the end of its fiscal year:

	Debit	Credit
Cash	$ 4,000	
Merchandise inventory	15,000	
Other assets	8,000	
Liabilities		$ 4,000
Common stock		5,000
Retained earnings		7,300
Sales		80,000
Sales returns and allowances	600	
Cost of goods sold	47,700	
General and administrative expenses	8,000	
Selling expenses	13,000	
Totals	$96,300	$96,300

On December 31, 20X8, the company's merchandise inventory amounted to $13,000. *Supplementary records of merchandising activities during the 20X9 year disclosed the following:*

BI   x = 10,400

Invoice cost of merchandise purchases	$48,500	Purch	52,300
Purchase discounts received	900		62,700
Purchase returns and allowances received	400	GA	(15000)
Cost of transportation-in	2,500	-EI	47,700
Cost of Merchandise Purchased	52,300	COGS	

Required:

Using the data above, complete the Income Statement for Valentine Variety Store, Inc. for December 31, 20x9. Use the form provided below.

VALENTINE VARIETY STORE, INC.

Income Statement

For the Year Ended December 31, 20X9

Sales							80,000	—
less: Sales Rtn. and allowances							(600)	
Net Sales							79	400
COGS							(47	700)
Gross Profit on Sales							31	700
Operating Expenses								
Selling expenses		13	000					
General and Admin. expenses		8	000					
Total Operating expenses							(21	000)
Total Income from Operations							10	700
Other gains and losses (Revenues and expenses)								
Net Income							10	700

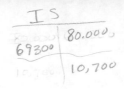

Problem V

Refer to the adjusted trial balance for Valentine Variety Store, Inc. that is presented above in Problem IV.

Required:

Prepare the closing entries for Valentine Variety Store, Inc. Explanations are not necessary.

GENERAL JOURNAL   Page 1

DATE	ACCOUNT TITLES AND EXPLANATION	P.R.	DEBIT			CREDIT		
	Sales		80	000				
	Income Summary					80	000	
	Income Summary		69	300				
	Gen. & Admin expenses					8	000	
	Selling expenses					13	000	
	Sales Rtn & Allowances						600	
	COGS					47	700	
	Income Summary		10	700				
	Retained Earnings					10	700	

Problem VI

1. If a company determines cost of goods sold by counting the inventory at the end of the period and subtracting the inventory from the cost of goods available for sale, the system of accounting for inventories is called a(n) _____Periodic_____.

2. Trade discounts __are not__ (are, are not) credited to the Inventory account.

3. A reduction in a payable that is granted if it is paid within the discount period is a _____Cash_____ discount.

4. A store received a credit memorandum from a wholesaler for unsatisfactory merchandise that the store sent back for credit. The store should record the memorandum with a __Credit__ A/P (debit, credit) to its Inventory account and a __debit__ (debit, credit) to its Accounts Payable account.

MI
A/P

MI

5. The two common systems of accounting for merchandise inventories are the _____ inventory system and the _____ inventory system. Before the availability of computers, the _____ inventory system was most likely used in stores that sold a large volume of relatively low-priced items.

Problem VII (Appendix 4A)

The trial balance that follows was taken from the ledger of Sporthaus Lindner, Inc. at the end of its annual accounting period. Fritz Lindner, the owner of Sporthaus Lindner, Inc. did not make additional investments in the business during 20X8.

SPORTHAUS LINDNER, INC.
Unadjusted Trial Balance
December 31, 20X8

Cash	$ 1,840	
Accounts receivable	2,530	
Merchandise inventory	3,680	
Store supplies	2,070	
Accounts payable		$ 4,370
Salaries payable	---	---
Common stock		2,000
Retained earnings		2,600
Sales		14,260
Sales returns and allowances	1,150	
Purchases	5,750	
Purchase discounts		920
Transportation-in	1,150	
Salaries expense	4,370	
Rent expense	1,610	
Store supplies expense	---	---
Totals	$24,150	$24,150

Required:

Prepare adjusting journal entries and closing journal entries for Sporthaus Lindner using the following information:

    a.   Ending store supplies inventory, $1,150.

    b.   Accrued salaries payable, $690.

    c.   Ending merchandise inventory, $4,830.

Record the adjusting journal entries and closing journal entries in the general journal below.

DATE	ACCOUNT TITLES AND EXPLANATION	P.R.	DEBIT	CREDIT

Solutions for Chapter 4

Problem I

1. F
2. T
3. T
4. T
5. F
6. F
7. F
8. T
9. F
10. T

Problem II

1. B
2. C
3. D
4. A
5. B
6. B

Problem III

12	Acid-test ratio	9	Merchandise
18	Cash discount	20	Merchandise inventory
25	Cost of goods sold	27	Merchandiser
14	Credit memorandum	23	Multiple-step income statement
11	Credit period	15	Periodic inventory system
10	Credit terms	2	Perpetual inventory system
5	Debit memorandum	13	Purchases discount
16	Discount period	30	Retailer
7	EOM	4	Sales discount
22	FOB	19	Selling expenses
21	General and administrative expenses	24	Shrinkage
1	Gross margin	17	Single-step income statement
26	Gross margin ratio	29	Supplementary records
31	Gross profit	3	Trade discount
6	Inventory	28	Wholesaler
8	List price		

Problem IV

VALENTINE VARIETY STORE, INC.
Income Statement
For the Year Ended December 31, 20X9

Revenue:			
Sales		$80,000	
Less: Sales returns and allowances		600	
Net sales			$79,400
Cost of goods sold:			
Merchandise inventory, December 31, 20X8		$13,000	
Purchases	$48,500		
Less: Purchases returns and allowances	$400		
Purchase discounts	900	1,300	
Net purchases		47,200	
Add: Transportation-in		2,500	
Cost of goods purchases		49,700	
Goods available for sale		62,700	
Merchandise inventory, December 31, 20X9		15,000	
Cost of goods sold			47,700
Gross profit from sales			31,700
Operating expenses:			
General and administrative expenses		8,000	
Selling expenses		13,000	
Total operating expenses			21,000
Net income			$10,700

Problem V

Dec. 31	Sales	80,000	
	Income Summary		80,000
31	Income Summary	69,300	
	Sales Returns and Allowances		600
	Cost of Goods Sold		47,700
	General and Administrative Expenses		8,000
	Selling Expenses		13,000
31	Income Summary	10,700	
	Retained Earnings		10,700

Problem VI

1. periodic inventory system

2. are not

3. cash

4. credit, debit

5. periodic, perpetual (these first two answers are interchangeable), periodic

Problem VII (Appendix 4A)

Adjusting Entries

Dec. 31	Store Supplies Expense	920	
	Store Supplies		920
31	Salaries Expense	690	
	Salaries Payable		690

Closing Entries

Dec. 31	Sales	14,260	
	Merchandise Inventory	4,830	
	Purchase Discounts	920	
	Income Summary		20,010
31	Income Summary	19,320	
	Sales Returns and Allowances		1,150
	Merchandise Inventory		3,680
	Purchases		5,750
	Transportation-in		1,150
	Salaries Expense		5,060
	Rent Expense		1,610
	Store Supplies Expense		920
31	Income Summary	690	
	Retained Earnings		690

CHAPTER 5
REPORTING AND ANYLYZING INVENTORIES

Learning Objective C1:

Identify the items making up merchandise inventory.

Merchandise inventory refers to goods owned by a company and held for resale. Three special cases merit our attention. Goods in transit are reported in inventory of the company that holds ownership rights. Goods on consignment are reported in the consignor's inventory. Goods damaged or obsolete are reported in inventory at their net realizable value.

Learning Objective C2:

Identify the costs of merchandise inventory.

Costs of merchandise inventory include expenditures necessary to bring an item to a salable condition and location. This includes its invoice cost minus any discount plus any added or incidental costs necessary to put it in a place and condition for sale.

Learning Objective A1:

Analyze the effects of inventory methods for both financial and tax reporting.

When purchase costs are rising or falling, the inventory costing methods are likely to assign different costs to inventory. Specific identification exactly matches costs and revenues. Weighted average smooths out cost changes. FIFO assigns an amount to inventory closely approximating current replacement cost. LIFO assigns the most recent costs incurred to cost of goods sold and likely better matches current costs with revenues.

Learning Objective A2:

Analyze the effects of inventory errors on current and future financial statements.

An error in the amount of ending inventory affects assets (inventory), net income (cost of goods sold), and equity for that period. Since ending inventory is next period's beginning inventory, an error in ending inventory affects next period's cost of goods sold and net income. Inventory errors in one period are offset in the next period.

Learning Objective A3:

Assess inventory management using both inventory turnover and days' sales in inventory.

We prefer a high inventory turnover, provided that goods are not out of stock and customers are not turned away. We use days' sales in inventory to assess the likelihood of goods being out of stock. We prefer a small number of days' sales in inventory if we can serve customer needs and provide a buffer for uncertainties.

Learning Objective P1:

Compute inventory in a perpetual system using the methods of specific identification, FIFO, LIFO, and weighted average.

Costs are assigned to the cost of goods sold account each time a sale occurs in a perpetual system. Specific identification assigns a cost to each item sold by referring to its actual cost (for example, its net invoice cost). Weighted average assigns a cost to items sold by dividing the current balance in the inventory account by the total items available for sale to determine cost per unit. We then multiply the number of units sold by this cost per unit to get the cost of each sale. FIFO assigns cost to items sold assuming that the earliest units purchased are the first units sold. LIFO assigns cost to items sold assuming that the most recent units purchased are the first units sold.

Learning Objective P2:

Compute the lower of cost or market amount of inventory.

Inventory is reported at market cost when market is lower than recorded cost, called the lower of cost or market (LCM) inventory. Market is typically measured as replacement cost. Lower of cost or market can be applied separately to each item, to major categories of items, or to the entire inventory.

Learning Objective P3 (Appendix 5A):

Compute inventory in a periodic system using the methods of specific identification, FIFO, LIFO, and weighted average.

Periodic inventory systems allocate the cost of goods available for sale between cost of goods sold and ending inventory at the end of a period. Specific identification and FIFO give identical results whether the periodic or perpetual system is used. LIFO assigns costs to cost of goods sold assuming the last units purchased for the period are the first units sold. The weighted average cost per unit is computed by dividing the total cost of beginning inventory and net purchases for the period by the total number of units available. Then, it multiplies cost per unit by the number of units sold to give cost of goods sold.

Learning Objective P4 (Appendix 5B):

Apply both the retail inventory and gross profit methods to estimate inventory. The retail inventory method involves three steps: (1) goods available at retail minus net sales at retail equals ending inventory at retail, (2) goods available at cost divided by goods available at retail equals the cost-to-retail ratio, and (3) ending inventory at retail multiplied by the cost-to-retail ratio equals estimated ending inventory at cost. The gross profit method involves two steps: (1) net sales at retail multiplied by 1 minus the gross profit ratio equals estimated cost of goods sold, and (2) goods available at cost minus estimated cost of goods sold equals estimated ending inventory at cost.

Chapter Outline

I. **Inventory Basics**

A. Determining Inventory Items

Merchandise inventory includes all goods that a company owns and holds for sale. The following inventory items require special attention:

1. Goods in Transit

If ownership has passed to the purchaser, the goods are included in the purchaser's inventory. Ownership is determined by reviewing the shipping terms.

2. Goods on Consignment—goods shipped by the owner, called the **consignor**, to another party, the **consignee**.

a. A consignee sells goods for the owner.

b. The consignor continues to own the consigned goods and reports them in its inventory.

3. Goods Damaged or Obsolete

a. Damaged and obsolete (and deteriorated) goods are not counted in inventory if they cannot be sold.

b. If these goods can be sold at a reduced price, they are included in inventory at their **net realizable value**, the sales price minus the cost of making the sale.

B. Determining Inventory Costs

1. The cost of an inventory item includes its invoice cost minus any discount, plus any added or incidental costs (such as import duties, freight, storage, and insurance necessary to put it in place and condition for sale).

2. The *matching principle* states that inventory costs should be recorded against revenue in the period when inventory is sold. Some companies use the *materiality principle (cost-to-benefit constraint)* to avoid assigning incidental costs to inventory.

C. Internal Controls and Taking a Physical Count

1. The Inventory account under a perpetual system is updated for each purchase and sale, but events (such as theft, loss, damage, and errors) can cause the account balance to be different from the actual inventory on hand.

2. Nearly all companies take a *physical count of inventory* at least once a year; the physical count is used to adjust the Inventory account balance to the actual inventory on hand.

3. Internal controls when taking a physical count of inventory include:

a. *Prenumbered inventory tickets*; each ticket must be accounting for.

    b. Those responsible for the inventory do not count the inventory.

    c. Counters confirm the validity of inventory, including its existence, amount, and quality.

    d. A second count should be performed by a different counter.

    e. A manager confirms that all inventory is ticketed once, and only once.

II.   **Inventory Costing under a Perpetual System**

Major goal is to properly match costs with sales. The *matching principle* is used to decide how much of the cost of goods available for sale is deducted from sales (on the income statement) and how much is carried forward as inventory (on the balance sheet). One of the most important issues in accounting for inventory is determining the per unit cost assigned to inventory items.

A. Inventory Cost Flow Assumptions

Four methods are commonly used to assign costs to inventory and cost of goods sold. Each method assumes a particular pattern for how costs flow through inventory. **Physical flow and cost flow need not be the same.**

    1. First-in, first-out (FIFO)—assumes costs flow in the order incurred.

    2. Last-in, first-out (LIFO)—assumes costs flow in the reverse order occurred.

    3. Weighted average—assumes costs flow in an average of the costs available.

    4. Specific identification—each item can be identified with a specific purchase and invoice. Specific identification is usually only practical for companies with expensive, custom-made inventory.

Note: The following sections assume the use of a perpetual system, the assignment of costs to inventory using a periodic system is described in Appendix 5A.

B. Inventory Costing Illustration

1. Specific identification—As sales occur, cost of goods sold is charged with the actual or invoice cost, leaving actual costs of inventory on hand in the inventory account.

2. First-in, first-out (FIFO)—As sales occur, FIFO charges costs of the earliest units acquired to cost of goods sold, leaving costs of the most recent purchases in inventory.

3. Last-in, first-out (LIFO)—As sales occur, LIFO charges costs of the most recent purchase to cost of goods sold, leaving costs of the earliest purchases in inventory.

4. Weighted average—As sales occur, weighted average computes the average cost per unit of inventory at the time of sale and charges this cost per unit sold to cost of goods sold leaving average cost per unit on hand in inventory. Weighted average equals cost of goods available for sale divided by the units available.

C. Financial Statement Effects of Costing Methods

1. When purchase prices do not change, each inventory costing method assigns the same amounts to inventory and to cost of goods sold. When purchase prices are different, the methods assign different cost amounts. When purchase costs *regularly rise:*

   a. FIFO assigns the lowest amount to cost of goods sold resulting in the highest gross profit and the highest net income. Advantage: Inventory on the balance sheet approximates its current replacement cost; it also mimics the actual flow of goods for most businesses.

   b. LIFO assigns the highest amount to cost of goods sold resulting in the lowest gross profit and the lowest net income. Advantage: Better match of current costs with revenues in computing gross margin.

   c. Weighted average method yields results between FIFO and LIFO. Advantage: Smoothing out of price changes.

   d. Specific identification always yields results that depend on which units are sold. Advantage: Exactly matches costs and revenues.

   When costs *regularly decline*, the reverse occurs for FIFO and LIFO.

D. Tax Effects of Costing Methods

Since inventory costs affect net income, they have potential tax effects.

1. Financial reporting often differs from the method used for tax reporting.

2. Exception: LIFO may only be used for tax purposes if it is also used for financial reporting.

E. Consistency in Costing Methods

1. **Consistency principle** requires the use of the same accounting methods period after period so the financial statements are comparable across periods.

2. Method change is acceptable if it will improve financial reporting. *The full-disclosure principle* requires statement notes report type of change, its justification, and its effect on income.

3. Different methods may be consistently applied to different categories of inventory.

III. **Valuating Inventory at LCM and the Effects of Inventory Errors**

A. Lower of Cost or Market

Accounting principles require that inventory be reported on the balance sheet at the **lower of cost or market (LCM)**.

1. Market is the current replacement cost of purchasing the same inventory items in the usual manner.

2. When the recorded cost of inventory is higher than the replacement cost, a loss is recognized; when the recorded cost is lower, no adjustment is made.

3. Lower of cost or market pricing is applied in one of three ways to:

   a. Each individual item separately,

   b. Major categories of items, or

   c. To the entire inventory.

4. Accounting rules require that inventory be adjusted to market when market is less than cost, but inventory usually cannot be written up to market when market exceeds cost. The **conservatism principle** prescribes the use of the less optimistic amount when more than one estimate of the amount to be received or paid exists and these estimates are about equally likely.

B. Financial Statement Effects of Inventory Errors

An inventory error causes misstatements in cost of goods sold, gross profit, net income, current assets, and equity. It also causes misstatements in the next period's financial statements because ending inventory of one period is the beginning inventory of the next.

1. Income statement effects:

    a. If ending inventory is understated, cost of goods sold is overstated and net income is understated.

    b. If beginning inventory is understated, cost of goods sold is understated and net income is overstated.

    c. If ending inventory is overstated, cost of goods sold is understated and net income is overstated.

    d. If beginning inventory is overstated, cost of goods sold is overstated and net income is understated.

2. Balance sheet effects:

    a. If ending inventory is understated, assets and equity are understated.

    b. If ending inventory is overstated, assets and equity are overstated.

    c. Errors in beginning inventory do not yield misstatements in the end-of-period balance sheet, but they do affect current period's income statement (see 1 above).

IV. **Decision Analysis—Inventory Turnover and Days' Sales in Inventory**

A. Inventory Turnover

   1. **Inventory turnover** is used to measure a company's ability to pay short-term obligations can depend on how quickly inventory is sold.

   2. It is calculated by dividing cost of goods sold by average inventory.

   3. It measures the number of *times* a company's average inventory was sold during an accounting period.

B. Days' Sales in Inventory

   1. **Day's sales in inventory** measure how much inventory is available in terms of the number of days' sales.

   2. It is calculated by dividing ending inventory by cost of goods sold, and then multiplying the result by 365.

   3. It estimates how many days it will take to convert inventory at the end of a period into accounts receivable or cash.

C. Analysis of Inventory Management

Inventory management is a major emphasis for most merchandisers; they must both plan and control inventory purchases and sales. We prefer a high inventory turnover.

V.   Inventory Costing under a Periodic System (Appendix 5A)

Results of periodic vs. perpetual by method:

A. Specific identification—same results as perpetual.

B. First-in, first-out (FIFO)—same results as perpetual.

C. Last-in, first-out (LIFO)—results differ from perpetual because timing of cost assignment changes what is identified as the last cost.

D. Weighted average—results differ from perpetual because timing of cost assignment changes what costs are averaged.

VI.   Inventory Estimation Methods (Appendix 5B)

Inventory sometimes requires estimation for two reasons. First, companies often require interim financial statements, but only take an annual physical count of inventory. Second, companies may require an inventory estimate if some casualty makes taking a physical count impossible. Estimates are usually only required for companies that use the periodic system.

A. Retail Inventory Method

The **retail inventory method** estimates the cost of ending inventory for interim statements in a periodic inventory when a physical count is taken only annually. Steps include:

1. Subtract sales (general ledger amount) from goods available measured at retail price (retail data in supplementary records) to get ending inventory at retail.

2. Find cost ratio by dividing total of goods available at cost by total of goods available at retail.

3. Apply cost ratio to ending inventory at retail to convert to ending inventory at cost.

Note: The cost ratio is also used to convert a physical inventory taken using retail price to cost. Shrinkage can be measured by comparing converted to estimated inventory.

C. Gross Profit Method

The **gross profit method** estimates the cost of ending inventory by applying the gross profit ratio to net sales (at retail). This type of estimate is often used for insurance claims when inventory is destroyed, lost or stolen. Steps include:

1. Determine the normal gross profit percentage from recent years.

2. Find the cost of goods percentage (100% less gross profit percentage).

3. Multiply actual sales by the cost of goods sold percentage to get estimated cost of goods sold.

4. Subtract estimated cost of goods sold from the actual amount of cost of goods available for sale to get estimated ending inventory at cost.

Schedule of Cost of Goods Available

	Units		Cost		Total
Jan. 1 Beginning Inventory	60	@	$10	=	$ 600
Mar. 27 Purchase	90	@	11	=	990
Aug. 15 Purchase	100	@	13	=	1,300
Nov. 6 Purchase	50	@	16	=	800
	300				$3,690

Cost of goods available for sale $3,690

Methods of Assigning Cost to Units in Ending Inventory

(1) **Specific Identification** - requires that each item in an inventory be assigned its <u>actual</u> invoice cost.

(2) **Weighted Average** - a weighted average cost per unit is determined based on total cost and units of goods available for sale. This cost is assigned to units in the ending inventory.

(3) **First-in, First-out (FIFO)** - assumes the first units acquired (beginning inventory) are the first to be sold and that additional sales flow is in the order purchased. Therefore, the costs of the last items received are assigned to the ending inventory.

(4) **Last-in, First-out (LIFO)** - assumes the last units acquired (most recent purchase) are the first units sold. Therefore, the cost of the first items acquired (starting with beginning inventory) are assigned to the ending inventory.

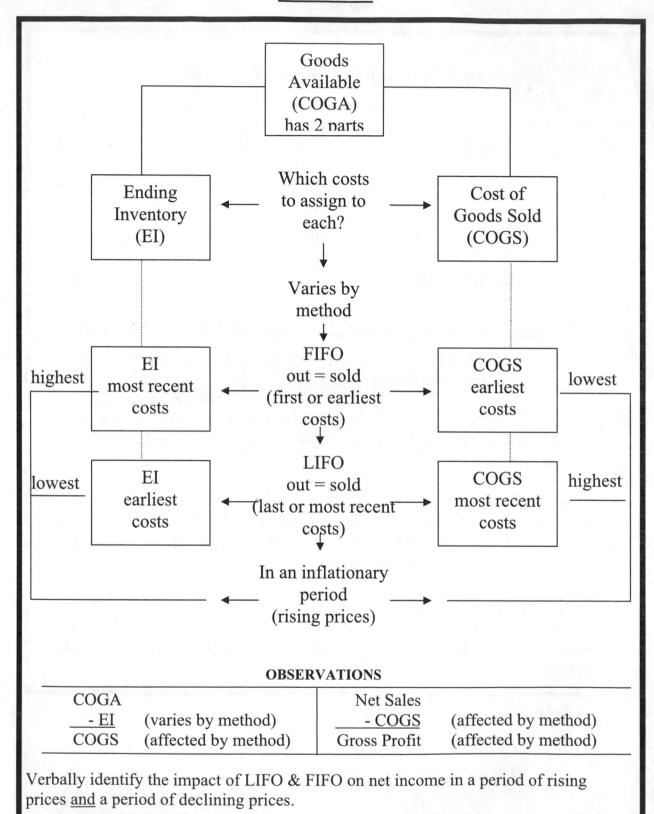

Goods
Available
(COGA)
has 2 parts

Which costs
to assign to
each?

Ending
Inventory
(EI)

Cost of
Goods Sold
(COGS)

Varies by
method

FIFO
out = sold
(first or earliest
costs)

EI
most recent
costs

COGS
earliest
costs

highest

lowest

LIFO
out = sold
(last or most recent
costs)

EI
earliest
costs

COGS
most recent
costs

lowest

highest

In an inflationary
period
(rising prices)

OBSERVATIONS

COGA		Net Sales	
- EI	(varies by method)	- COGS	(affected by method)
COGS	(affected by method)	Gross Profit	(affected by method)

Verbally identify the impact of LIFO & FIFO on net income in a period of rising prices **and** a period of declining prices.

Financial Accounting, 4e

The ABC Company had the following inventory record for the month of January:

Date	Description	# of Items	Unit Price	Item
1/1	Beginning inventory	5	$20	Z1 - Z5
1/5	Sale	2		Z2, Z5
1/11	Purchase	9	12	Z6 - Z14
1/28	Sale	7		Z1, Z3, Z6, Z7, Z8, Z9, Z14

Required:

Assuming a perpetual system is in use, determine the cost of goods sold and the ending inventory using each of the following methods:

1. FIFO

2. LIFO

3. Weighted average

4. Specific identification

(If this alternative demonstration problem is not covered in class, see your instructor for the solution.)

Problem I

The following statements are either true or false. Place a (T) in the parentheses before each true statement and an (F) before each false statement.

1. (F) The merchandise inventory of a business includes goods sold FOB destination if they are not yet delivered.

2. (F) When a perpetual inventory system is used, the dollar amount of ending inventory is determined by counting the units of product on hand, multiplying the count for each product by each product's cost, and adding the costs for all products.

3. ( ) If prices of goods purchased remain unchanged, then all four methods of assigning costs to goods in the ending inventory would yield the same cost figures.

4. ( ) When first-in, first-out inventory pricing is used in a perpetual inventory system, as sales occur the costs of the first items purchased are assigned to cost of goods sold.

5. ( ) If prices are rising, then using the LIFO method of pricing inventory will result in the highest net income.

6. ( ) The conservatism principle supports the lower of cost or market rule.

7. ( ) A misstatement of ending inventory will carry forward and cause misstatements in the succeeding period's cost of goods sold, gross profit, and net income.

8. ( ) The perpetual inventory system uses a Purchases account to record items purchased.

9. ( ) Using FIFO, the perpetual and periodic inventory systems do not result in the same amounts of sales, cost of goods sold, and end-of-period merchandise inventory.

10. ( ) Lower of cost or market may be applied separately to each product, to major categories of products, or to the merchandise inventory as a whole.

Problem II

You are given several words, phrases, or numbers to choose from in completing each of the following statements or in answering the following questions. In each case select the one that best completes the statement or answers the question and place its letter in the answer space provided.

_____ 1. Cisco Company's ending inventory consists of the following:

Product	Units on Hand	Unit Cost	Replacement Cost per Unit
X	100	$10	$ 8
Y	90	15	14
Z	75	8	10

Replacement cost is determined to be the best measure of market. Lower of cost or market for the inventory applied separately to each product is:

a. $2,950

b. $2,810

c. $2,660

d. $3,100

e. Cannot be determined from the information given.

The following information is to be used for questions 2 to 5:

Serese Co. made purchases of a particular product in the current year (20X8) as follows:

Jan.	1	Beginning inventory...	120 units	@	$5.00	=	$ 600
Mar.	7	Purchased..................	250 units	@	$5.60	=	1,400
July	28	Purchased..................	500 units	@	$5.80	=	2,900
Oct.	3	Purchased.................	450 units	@	$6.00	=	2,700
Dec.	19	Purchased..................	100 units	@	$6.20	=	620
		Total	1,420 units				$8,220

Serese Co. made sales on the following dates at $15 a unit:

Jan.	10	70 units
Mar.	15	125 units
Oct.	5	600 units
Total		795 units

The business uses a perpetual inventory system, and the ending inventory consists of 625 units, 500 from the July 28 purchase and 125 from the Oct. 3 purchase.

_____ 2. Using the specific identification cost assignment method, the amounts to be assigned to cost of goods sold and ending inventory respectively are:

    a. $4,465, $3,755

    b. $4,537.50, $3,682.50

    c. $4,570, $3,650

    d. $4,620, $3,600

    e. None of the above.

_____ 3. Using the LIFO cost assignment method, the amounts to be assigned to cost of goods sold and ending inventory respectively are:

    a. $4,465, $3,755

    b. $4,537.50, $3,682.50

    c. $4,570, $3,650

    d. $4,620, $3,600

    e. None of the above.

_____ 4. Using the FIFO cost assignment method, the amounts to be assigned to cost of goods sold and ending inventory respectively are:

    a. $4,465, $3,755

    b. $4,537.50, $3,682.50

    c. $4,570, $3,650

    d. $4,620, $3,600

    e. None of the above.

_____ 5. Using the weighted average cost assignment method, the amounts to be assigned to cost of goods sold and ending inventory respectively are:

   a. $4,465, $3,755
   b. $4,537.50, $3,682.50
   c. $4,570, $3,650
   d. $4,620, $3,600
   e. None of the above.

_____ 6. Atlantis Company uses a periodic inventory system and made an error at the end of year 1 that caused its year 1 ending inventory to be understated by $5,000. What effect does this error have on the company's financial statements?

   a. Net income is understated; assets are understated.
   b. Net income is understated; assets are overstated.
   c. Net income is overstated; assets are understated.
   d. Net income is overstated; assets are overstated.
   e. Net income is overstated; assets are correctly stated.

_____ 7. Trador Company's ending inventory at December 31, 20X8 and 20X7, was $210,000 and $146,000, respectively. Cost of goods sold for 20X8 was $832,000 and $780,000 for 20X7. Calculate Trador's merchandise turnover for 20X8.

   a. 4.7 times.
   b. 4.5 times.
   c. 4.0 times.
   d. 3.8 times.
   e. Cannot be determined from the information given.

_____ 8. Refer to the information presented in question 7. Calculate Trador's days' stock on hand for 20X8.

   a. 78.1 days.
   b. 80.6 days.
   c. 66.1 days.
   d. 92.1 days.
   e. 68.3 days.

Note: Questions 9 – 12 relate to Appendix 5A.

_____ 9. Magnum Company began a year and purchased merchandise as follows:

Jan.	1	Beginning inventory	40 units	@ $17.00
Feb.	4	Purchased	80 units	@ $16.00
May	12	Purchased	80 units	@ $16.50
Aug.	9	Purchased	60 units	@ $17.50
Nov.	23	Purchased	100 units	@ $18.00

The company uses a periodic inventory system and the ending inventory consists of 60 units, 20 from each of the last three purchases. Determine ending inventory assuming costs are assigned on the basis of FIFO.

a. $1,040
b. $1,000
c. $1,069
d. $1,080
e. $1,022

_____ 10. Linder Company began a year and purchased merchandise as follows:

Jan.	1	Beginning inventory	40 units	@ $17.00
Feb.	4	Purchased	80 units	@ $16.00
May	12	Purchased	80 units	@ $16.50
Aug.	9	Purchased	60 units	@ $17.50
Nov.	23	Purchased	100 units	@ $18.00

The company uses a periodic inventory system and the ending inventory consists of 60 units, 20 from each of the last three purchases. Determine ending inventory assuming costs are assigned on the basis of LIFO.

a. $1,040
b. $1,000
c. $1,022
d. $980
e. $1,080.

_____ 11. Box Company began a year and purchased merchandise as follows:

Jan.	1	Beginning inventory	40 units	@ $17.00
Feb.	4	Purchased	80 units	@ $16.00
May	12	Purchased	80 units	@ $16.50
Aug.	9	Purchased	60 units	@ $17.50
Nov.	23	Purchased	100 units	@ $18.00

The company uses a periodic inventory system and the ending inventory consists of 60 units, 20 from each of the last three purchases. Determine ending inventory assuming costs are assigned on the basis of specific invoice prices.

a. $1,000
b. $1,022
c. $1,040
d. $1,080
e. $990

12. Crow Company began a year and purchased merchandise as follows:

Jan.	1	Beginning inventory	40 units	@ $17.00
Feb.	4	Purchased	80 units	@ $16.00
May	12	Purchased	80 units	@ $16.50
Aug.	9	Purchased	60 units	@ $17.50
Nov.	23	Purchased	100 units	@ $18.00

The company uses a periodic inventory system and the ending inventory consists of 60 units, 20 from each of the last three purchases. Determine ending inventory assuming costs are assigned on a weighted average basis.

a. $1,022.00

b. $1,040.00

c. $1,080.00

d. $1,000.00

e. $1,042.50

13. (Appendix 5B) Sanders Company wants to prepare interim financial statements for the first quarter of 20X8. The company uses a periodic inventory system and has an average gross profit rate of 30%. Based on the following information, use the gross profit method to prepare an estimate of the March 31 inventory.

January 1, beginning inventory	$ 97,000
Purchases	214,000
Purchases returns	2,000
Transportation-in	4,000
Sales	404,000
Sales returns	5,000

a. $ 33,700.

b. $193,300.

c. $119,700.

d. $179,900.

e. $ 26,700.

Problem III

Many of the important ideas and concepts discussed in Chapter 5 are reflected in the following list of key terms. Test your understanding of these terms by matching the appropriate definitions with the terms. Record the number identifying the most appropriate definition in the blank space next to each term.

_____ Average cost	_____ Interim statements
_____ Conservatism principle	_____ Inventory turnover
_____ Consignee	_____ Last-in, first-out (LIFO)
_____ Consignor	_____ Lower of cost or market (LCM)
_____ Consistency principle	_____ Net realizable value
_____ Days' sales in inventory	_____ Retail inventory method*
_____ First-in, first-out (FIFO)	_____ Specific identification
_____ Gross profit method*	_____ Weighted average

* *Key term discussed in Appendix 5B*

1. Required method to report inventory at market when market replacement cost is lower than recorded cost.

2. Method to assign cost to inventory that assumes items are sold in the order acquired; earliest items purchased are the first sold.

3. Method to assign cost to inventory where the cost of goods available for sale is divided by number of units available to get per unit cost that is multiplied by the units in inventory.

4. Number of times a company's average inventory is sold during a period; computed by dividing cost of goods sold by the average inventory; also called *merchandise turnover*.

5. Principle encouraging the use of the same accounting methods over time so that the financial statements are comparable across periods

6. Estimate of days needed to convert inventory into receivables or cash; equals the ending inventory divided by cost of goods sold and multiplying by 365; also called *days' stock on hand*.

7. Expected selling price of an item minus the cost of making the sale.

8. Owner of goods who ships them to another party who will sell them for the owner.

9. Procedure to estimate inventory when the past gross profit rate is used to estimate cost of goods sold, which is then subtracted from the cost of goods available for sale.

10. Method to assign cost to inventory when the purchase cost of each item in inventory is identified and used to compute the cost of inventory.

11. Another name for weighted average cost.

12. Method to assign cost to inventory that assumes costs for the most recent items purchased are sold first and charged to cost of goods sold.

13. Principle that seeks to select the less optimistic estimate when two estimates are about equally likely.

14. Financial statements prepared for periods of less than one year.

15. Method to estimate ending inventory based on the ratio of the amount of goods for sale at cost to the amount of goods for sale at retail.

16. One who receives and holds goods owned by another for purposes of selling the goods for the owner.

Problem IV

Complete the following by filling in the blanks.

1. Consistency in the use of an inventory costing method is particularly important if there is to be

    _____.

2. If a running record is maintained for each inventory item of the number of units received as units are received, the number of units sold as units are sold, and the number of units remaining after each   receipt   or   sale,   the   inventory   system   is   called

    _____.

3. When a company changes its accounting procedures, the _____ principle requires that the nature of the change, justification for the change, and the effect of the change on _____ be disclosed in the notes accompanying the financial statements.

4. With a periodic inventory system, an error in taking an end-of-period inventory will cause a misstatement of periodic net income for _____ (one, two) accounting periods because

    _____.

©*The McGraw-Hill Companies, Inc., 2008*

5. When identical items are purchased during an accounting period at different costs, a problem arises as to which costs apply to the ending inventory and which apply to the goods sold. There are at least four commonly used ways of assigning costs to inventory and to goods sold. They are:

   a. _____ ;

   b. _____ ;

   c. _____ ;

   d. _____ ;

6. A major objective of accounting for inventories is the proper determination of periodic net income through the process of matching _____ and _____. The matching process consists of determining how much of the cost of the goods that were for sale during an accounting period should be deducted from the period's _____ and how much should be carried forward as _____ , to be matched against a future period's revenues.

7. Although changing back and forth from one inventory costing method to another might allow management to report the incomes it would prefer, the accounting principle of _____ requires a company to use the same pricing method period after period unless it can justify the change.

8. In separating cost of goods available for sale into cost of goods sold and cost of goods unsold, the procedures for assigning a cost to the ending inventory are also the means of determining _____ because whatever portion of the cost of goods available for sale is assigned to ending inventory, the remainder goes to _____

9. Use of the lower-of-cost-or-market rule places an inventory on the balance sheet at a _____ figure. The argument in favor of this rule provides that any loss should be _____ in the year the loss occurs.

10. When recording a sale of merchandise using a _____ (perpetual, periodic) inventory system, two journal entries must be made. One entry records the revenue received for the sale and the second entry debits the _____ account.

11. (Appendix 5B) In the gross profit method of estimating an ending inventory, an average _____ _____ rate is used to determine estimated cost of goods sold, and the ending inventory is then estimated by subtracting estimated _____ from the cost of goods available for sale.

Problem V

A company uses a perpetual inventory system and during a year had the following beginning inventory, purchases, and sales of Product Z:

Jan.	1	Inventory..	200 units	@	$0.50 =	$100
Mar.	15	Purchased..	400 units	@	0.50 =	200
Apr.	1	Sold...	300 units	@		
June	3	Purchased..	300 units	@	0.60 =	180
July	1	Sold...	200 units	@		
Oct.	8	Purchased..	600 units	@	0.70 =	420
Nov.	1	Sold...	500 units	@		
Dec.	15	Purchased..	500 units	@	0.80 =	400

In the spaces below show the cost that should be assigned to the ending inventory and to the goods sold under the following assumptions:

	Portions Assigned to—	
	Ending Inventory	Cost of Goods Sold
1. A first-in, first-out basis was used to price the ending inventory	$	$
2. A last-in, first-out basis was used to price the ending inventory	$	$

Problem VI (Appendix 5B)

The following end-of-period information about a store's beginning inventory, purchases, and sales is available.

	At Cost	At Retail
Beginning inventory	$ 9,600	$13,000
Net purchases	54,400	69,100
Transportation-in	1,680	
Net sales		69,000

1. Use the above information to estimate the store's ending inventory by the retail method by completing the table below.

   a. The store had goods available for sale during the year calculated as follows:

	At Cost	At Retail
Beginning inventory	$	$
Net purchases		
Transportation-in		
Goods available for sale	$	$

   b. The store's cost ratio was: ....
       $_____ / $_____ x 100 = _____

   c. Of the goods the store had available for sale at retail prices during the year, the following is gone because of sales at retail ....
       Which left the store an estimated ending inventory at retail .... $ _____

   d. And when the store's cost ratio is applied to this estimated ending inventory at retail, the estimated ending inventory at cost is .... $ _____

2. The store took a physical inventory and counted only $12,850 of merchandise on hand (at retail). Calculate the inventory shortage at cost.

Solutions for Chapter 5

Problem I

1. T
2. F
3. T
4. T
5. F
6. T
7. T
8. F
9. F
10. T

Problem II

1. C
2. C
3. D
4. A
5. B
6. A
7. A
8. A
9. D
10. B
11. C
12. A
13. A

Problem III

11	Average cost	14	Interim statements
13	Conservatism principle	4	Inventory turnover
16	Consignee	12	Last-in, first-out (LIFO)
8	Consignor	1	Lower of cost or market (LCM)
5	Consistency principle	7	Net realizable value
6	Days' sales in inventory	15	Retail inventory method*
2	First-in, first-out (FIFO)	10	Specific identification
9	Gross profit method*	3	Weighted average

* *Key term discussed in Appendix 5B*

Problem IV

1.   comparability in the financial statements prepared period after period

2.   a perpetual inventory system

3.   full-disclosure; net income

4.   two; the ending inventory of one period becomes the beginning inventory of the next

5.   (a) specific invoice prices; (b) weighted average cost; (c) first-in, first-out; (d) last-in, first-out

6.   costs; revenues; revenues; merchandise inventory

7.   consistency

8.   cost of goods sold; cost of goods sold

9.   conservative; recognized

10.   perpetual; cost of goods sold

11.   gross profit; cost of goods sold

Problem V

	Portions Assigned to	
	Ending Inventory	Cost of Goods Sold
1.	$750	$550
2.	680	620

Problem VI (Appendix 5B)

1.   Estimate of store's ending inventory using the retail method:

		At Cost	At Retail
a.	Goods for sale		
	Beginning inventory	$ 9,600	$13,000
	Net purchases..	54,400	69,100
	Transportation-in	1,680	
	Goods available for sale..............................	$65,680	82,100
b.	Cost ratio: $65,680/$82,100 x 100 = 80 %...		
c.	Less net sales at retail		69,000
	Ending inventory at retail		$13,100
d.	Ending inventory at cost ($13,100 x 80 %)..	$10,480	

2.   Inventory shortage at cost:

$13,100 - $12,850 = $250
$250 x 80% = $200

CHAPTER 6
REPORTING AND ANALYZING CASH AND INTERNAL CONTROLS

Learning Objective C1:

Define internal control and identify its purpose and principles.

An internal control system consists of the policies and procedures managers use to protect assets, ensure reliable accounting, promote efficient operations, and urge adherence to company policies. It can prevent avoidable losses and help managers both plan operations and monitor company and human performance. Principles of good internal control include establishing responsibilities, maintaining adequate records, insuring assets and bonding employees, separating recordkeeping from custody of assets, dividing responsibilities for related transactions, applying technological controls, and performing regular independent reviews.

Learning Objective C2:

Define cash and cash equivalents and explain how to report them.

Cash includes currency, coins, and amounts on (or acceptable for) deposit in checking and savings accounts. Cash equivalents are short-term, highly liquid investment assets readily convertible to a known cash amount and sufficiently close to their maturity date so that market value is not sensitive to interest rate changes. Cash and cash equivalents are liquid assets because they are readily converted into other assets or can be used to pay for goods, services, or liabilities.

Learning Objective C3:

Identify control features of banking activities.

Banks offer several services that promote the control and safeguarding of cash. A bank account is a record set up by a bank permitting a customer to deposit money for safekeeping and to draw checks on it. A bank deposit is money contributed to the account with a deposit ticket as proof. A check is a document signed by the depositor instructing the bank to pay a specified amount of money to a designated recipient.

Learning Objective A1:

Compute the days' sales uncollected ratio and use it to assess liquidity.

Many companies attract customers by selling to them on credit. This means that cash receipts from customers are delayed until accounts receivable are collected. Users want to know how quickly a company can convert its accounts receivable into cash. The days' sales uncollected ratio, one measure reflecting company liquidity, is computed by dividing the ending balance of receivables by annual net sales, and then multiplying by 365.

$$\frac{A/R}{Sales} \times 365$$

Learning Objective P1:

Apply internal control to cash receipts and disbursements.

Internal control of cash receipts ensures that all cash received is properly recorded and deposited. Attention focuses on two important types of cash receipts: over-the-counter and by mail. Good internal control for over-the-counter cash receipts includes use of a cash register, customer review, use of receipts, a permanent transaction record, and separation of the custody of cash from its recordkeeping. Good internal control for cash receipts by mail includes at least two people assigned to open mail and a listing of each sender's name, amount, and explanation.

Learning Objective P2:

Explain and record petty cash fund transactions.

Petty cash disbursements are payments of small amounts for items such as postage, courier fees, minor repairs, and supplies. A company usually sets up one or more petty cash funds. A petty fund cashier is responsible for safekeeping the cash, making payments from this fund, and keeping receipts and records. A Petty Cash account is debited only when the fund is established or increased in amount. When the fund is replenished, petty cash disbursements are recorded with debits to expense (or asset) accounts and a credit to cash.

Learning Objective P3:

Prepare a bank reconciliation.

A bank reconciliation proves the accuracy of the depositor's and the bank's records. The bank statement balance is adjusted for items such as outstanding checks and unrecorded deposits made on or before the bank statement date but not reflected on the statement. The book balance is adjusted for items such as service charges, bank collections for the depositor, and interest earned on the account.

Learning Objective P4 (Appendix 6A):

Describe the voucher system to control cash disbursements.

A voucher system is a set of procedures and approvals designed to control cash disbursements and acceptance of obligations. The voucher system of control relies on several important documents, including the voucher and its supporting files. A key factor in this system is that only approved departments and individuals are authorized to incur certain obligations.

Learning Objective P5 (Appendix 6B):

Apply the net method to control purchase discounts.

The net method aids management in monitoring and controlling purchase discounts. When invoices are recorded at gross amounts, the amount of discounts taken is deducted from the balance of the Inventory account. This means that the amount of any discounts lost is not reported in any account and is unlikely to come to the attention of management. When purchases are recorded at net amounts, a Discounts Lost account is brought to management's attention as an operating expense. Management can then seek to identify the reason for discounts lost, such as oversight, carelessness, or unfavorable terms.

I. **Internal Control**

   A. Purpose of Internal Control

   A properly designed internal control system is a key part of system design, analysis, and performance. Internal controls do not provide guarantees, but they lower the company's risk of loss. An **internal control system** consists all policies and procedures managers use to:

   1. Protect assets.
   2. Ensure reliable accounting.
   3. Promote efficient operations.
   4. Urge adherence to company policies.

   B. Principles of Internal Control

   Certain fundamental internal control principles apply to all companies. Internal control procedures increase the reliability and accuracy of accounting records. The **principles of internal control** are to:

   1. Establish responsibilities.
   2. Maintain adequate records.
   3. Insure assets and bond key employees.
   4. Separate recordkeeping from custody of assets.
   5. Divide responsibility for related transactions.
   6. Apply technological controls.
   7. Perform regular and independent reviews.

   C. Technology and Internal Control

   Technology provides rapid access to large quantities of data. Examples of technological impacts on internal control:

   1. Reduced processing errors.
   2   More extensive testing of records.
   3. Limited evidence of processing.
   4. Crucial separation of duties.
   5. Increased E-commerce

   D. Limitations of Internal Control

   1. Internal control policies and procedures are applied by people; the human element creates several potential limitations:

      a. Human error—resulting from negligence, fatigue, misjudgment, or confusion.

      b. Human fraud—involves intent by people to defeat internal controls, such as *management override*, for personal gain.

   2. Cost-benefit principle—the costs of internal controls must not exceed their benefits.

II. Control of Cash

Basic guidelines for control of cash include: handling of cash must be separate from recordkeeping of cash, cash receipts are promptly deposited in a bank, and disbursements of cash are made by check.

A. Cash, Cash Equivalents, and Liquidity

1. **Liquidity** refers to a company's ability to pay for its near-term obligations. Cash and similar assets are called **liquid assets** because they can be readily used to settle such obligations.

2. **Cash** includes currency and coins, deposits in bank and checking accounts, many savings accounts, and items that are acceptable for deposit in those accounts.

2. **Cash equivalents** are short-term, highly liquid investment assets meeting two criteria. (Note: only investments purchased within three months of their maturity dates usually satisfy these criteria.)

   a. Readily convertible to a known cash amount.

   b. Sufficiently close to their maturity date so that their market value is not sensitive to interest rate changes.

B. Control of Cash Receipts

Internal control of cash receipts ensures that cash is properly recorded and deposited.

1. Over-the-counter cash receipts:

   a. Record on a cash register at time of sale.

   b. Separate custody from recordkeeping.

2. Cash Over and Short

   Sometimes errors in making change are discovered from differences between the cash in a cash register and the record of the amount of cash receipts.

   a. Record any petty cash shortages/overages in the **Cash Over and Short** account.

   b. Entry to record cash sales with an overage: debit Cash, credit Cash Over and Short, credit Sales.

   c. Entry to record cash sales with a shortage: debit Cash, debit Cash Over and Short, credit Sales.

   d. Report balance of cash over and short account, an income statement account; as part of *miscellaneous expenses* if it has a debit balance or as part of *miscellaneous revenues* if it has a credit balance.

3. Cash receipts by mail:

    a. Preferably, two people should open the mail and prepare a list of cash received; copies should be sent to cashier, recordkeeper in accounting area, and clerks who open mail.

    b. The cashier deposits the money in a bank.

    c. The recordkeeper records the amounts received in the accounting records.

    d. Bank account should be reconciled by another person (see below).

C. Control of Cash Disbursements

To safeguard against theft—require all expenditures be made by check (except for small payments made from petty cash fund) and deny access to the accounting records to anyone, other than the owner, who has authority to sign checks.

1. A **voucher system** is a set of procedures and approvals designed to control cash disbursements and the acceptance of obligations. The voucher system includes procedures for:

    a. Verifying, approving, and recording obligations for eventual cash disbursements.

    b. Issuing checks for payment of verified, approved, and recorded obligations.

    c. Key factors in a voucher system:

        i. Only approved departments and individuals are authorized to incur such obligations.

        ii. Several business documents (purchase requisition, purchase order, invoice, receiving report, and check) are accumulated in a **voucher**, which is an internal document (or file) used to accumulate information to control cash disbursements.

2. Use a **petty cash** system of control as follows:

    a. Write and cash a check to establish petty cash fund. Entry to record establishment: debit Petty Cash, credit Cash.

    b. A petty cash fund is used to pay for small items such as postage, courier fees, minor repairs, and low-cost supplies.

    c. Assign a petty cashier (custodian) to account for the amounts expended and keep receipts.

    d. Entry to record reimbursement: debit the related expense and/or asset accounts for the amounts paid for with petty cash, credit Cash for the amount reimbursed to the petty cash fund.

e. Sometimes, the petty cash payments reported plus the cash remaining will not total to the fund balance.

   i. A shortage is recorded as an expense in the reimbursing entry with a debit to the Cash Over and Short account.

   ii. An overage is recorded with a credit to the Cash Over and Short account in the reimbursing entry.

III. **Banking Activities as Controls**

A. Basic Bank Services

Bank accounts permit depositing money for safeguarding and help control withdrawals.

1. A *bank account* is a record set up by a bank for a customer. To limit access, all persons authorized to write **checks,** documents instructing the bank to pay a specified amount of money to a designated recipient, sign a **signature card**. Each bank deposit is supported by a **deposit ticket**.

2. Electronic Funds Transfer (EFT) is the electronic communication transfer of cash from one party to another.

B. Bank Statement

Once a month, the bank sends each depositor a **bank statement** showing activities in the bank account.

C. Bank Reconciliation

1. A **bank reconciliation** is a report explaining any differences between the checking account balance according to the depositor's records and the balance reported on the bank statement.

2. The balance reported on the bank statement rarely equals the balance in the depositor's accounting records; this is usually due to information that one party has that the other does not. Factors causing the bank statement balance to differ from the depositor's book balance are:

   a. Outstanding checks.

   b. Deposits in transit.

   c. Deductions for uncollectible items and for services

   d. Additions for collections and for interest.

   e. Errors.

3. Steps in preparing the bank reconciliation:

   a. Identify the bank statement balance of the cash account (*balance per bank*).

   b. Identify and list any unrecorded deposits and any bank errors understating the bank balance. Add them to the bank balance.

      c. Identify and list any outstanding checks and any bank errors overstating the bank balance. Deduct them from the bank balance.

      d. Compute the *adjusted bank balance*, also called corrected or reconciled balance.

      e. Identify the company's balance of the cash account (*balance per book*).

      f. Identify and list any unrecorded credit memoranda from the bank, interest earned, and errors understating the book balance. Add them to the book balance.

      g. Identify and list any unrecorded debit memoranda from the bank, service charges, and errors overstating the book balance. Deduct them from the book balance.

      h. Compute the *adjusted book balance*, also called corrected or reconciled balance.

      i. Verify the two adjusted balances from steps d and h are equal. If so, they are reconciled. If not, check for mathematical accuracy and missing data to achieve reconciliation.

    4. A bank reconciliation often identifies unrecorded items that need recording. Only the items reconciling the book balance require adjustment.

      a. All reconciling additions to book balance are debits to cash. Credit depends on reason for addition.

      b. All reconciling subtractions from book balance are credits to cash. Debit depends on reason for subtraction.

IV.   Decision Analysis—Days' Sales Uncollected

    A. One measure of the receivables' nearness to cash is the **days' sales uncollected** ratio (also called *days' sales in receivables*).

    B. It is calculated by dividing accounts receivable by net sales and multiplying the result by 365.

    C. It is used to estimate how much time is likely to pass before the current amount of accounts receivable is received in cash.

V.   Documents in a Voucher System (Appendix 6A)

    A. Purchase Requisition

    B. Purchase Order

    C. Invoice

    D. Receiving Report

    E. Invoice Approval

    F. Voucher

VI. **Controls of Purchases Discounts (Appendix 6B)**

It is very important for a company to take advantage of purchases discounts.

a. Recording inventory purchases using net method provides more control than the gross method, which was described in Chapter 4.

b. The **gross method** of recording purchases initially records the invoice at its *gross* amount ignoring any cash discount.

c. The **net method** records the invoice at its *net* amount of any cash discount. The net method gives management an advantage in controlling and monitoring cash payments involving purchase discounts. Any discounts not taken advantage of are recorded in a **Discounts Lost** expense account. Entries to record the:

1. Purchase of inventory on credit: debit Merchandise Inventory, credit Accounts Payable (for the amount of the invoice net of the discount).

2. Payment of the invoice within the discount period: debit Accounts Payable, credit Cash (for the amount of the invoice net of the discount).

3. Payment of the invoice after the discount period has expired:

   a. As of the date corresponding to the end of the discount period: debit Discounts Lost, credit Accounts Payable (for the amount of the discount).

   b. As of the date of payment: debit Accounts Payable, credit Cash (for the amount of the payment, which is the gross amount of the invoice).

BANK RECONCILIATION

Reasons for differences between bank statement and checkbook balance:	Handle as follows:
Unrecorded deposits	Add to Bank Balance
Outstanding checks	Deduct from Bank Balance
Bank service charges	Deduct from Book Balance
Debit memos	Deduct from Book Balance
Credit memos	Add to Book Balance
NSF checks	Deduct from Book Balance
Interest	Add to Book Balance
Errors	Must analyze individually (bank errors affect bank balance and book errors affect book balance)

The Betsy Dough Company wants to prepare a bank reconciliation for the month of June. When the bank statement for the month of June arrives from the bank, the following steps are performed:

1. The deposits to the bank account, as recorded on the bank statement, are compared to the deposit slips retained by the company. It is noted that the last deposit, of $400, occurred after banking hours on the day of the bank statement and therefore has not been recorded by the bank on this bank statement.

2. Checks returned with the bank statement are compared to the checks written and listed in checkbook. This comparison shows that there are checks outstanding amounting to $1,456.

3. The ending balances on the statement and in the company's books are determined. The ending bank statement balance is exactly $10,129 whereas the books show $9,000.

4. Other information contained on the bank statement, not previously known to the company, is determined. This includes the following: (a) a note from a customer for $200 has been collected by the bank and credited to our account; (b) a check from Frank Ony for $120 previously deposited has been returned for lack of sufficient funds; (c) the bank charged $25 for its services (this includes a $10 fee for the NSF check).

5. A bank reconciliation is prepared; it does not balance! The difference is $18, so a transposition error is looked for (whenever the difference is a multiple of 9, there is a very good chance that there has been an inadvertent exchange of two digits (for example, writing 29 when it should have been 92). An error is found. Check number 141 was written for $235 and cleared the bank for $235, but was recorded in the company records as $253.

Required:

Prepare a bank reconciliation for the Betsy Dough Company at June 30, 20X8.

(If this alternative demonstration problem is not covered in class, see your instructor for the solution.)

Problem I

The following statements are either true or false. Place a (T) in the parentheses before each true statement and an (F) before each false statement.

1. ( ) One of the fundamental principles of internal control states that the person who has access to or is responsible for an asset should not maintain the accounting record for that asset.

2. ( ) Procedures for controlling cash disbursements are as important as those for cash receipts.

3. ( ) When a voucher system is used, duplication of procedures among several departments is instrumental in maintaining control over cash disbursements.

4. ( ) In order to approve an invoice for payment for the purchase of assets, the accounting department of a large company should require copies of the purchase requisition, purchase order, invoice, and receiving report.

5. ( ) After the petty cash fund is established, the Petty Cash account is not debited or credited again unless the size of the fund is changed.

6. ( ) The Cash Over and Short account is usually shown on the income statement as part of miscellaneous revenues if it has a credit balance at the end of the period.

7. ( ) If 20 canceled checks are listed on the current month's bank statement, then no less than 20 checks could have been issued during the current month.

8. ( ) When the net method of recording invoices is used, cash discounts lost are reported as an expense in the income statement; when the gross method is used, cash discounts taken are deducted from purchases in the income statement.

Problem II

You are given several words, phrases, or numbers to choose from in completing each of the following statements or in answering the following questions. In each case select the one that best completes the statement or answers the question and place its letter in the answer space provided.

_____ 1. A voucher system:

a. Permits only authorized individuals to incur obligations that will result in cash disbursements.

b. Establishes procedures for incurring such obligations and for their verification, approval, and recording.

c. Permits checks to be issued only in payment of properly verified, approved, and recorded obligations.

d. Requires that every obligation be recorded at the time it is incurred and every purchase be treated as an independent transaction, complete in itself.

e. Does all of the above.

_____2. Liquidity is:

a. The portion of a corporation's equity that represents investments in the corporation by its stockholders.

b. Cash or other assets that are reasonably expected to be realized in cash or be sold or consumed within one year or one operating cycle of the business.

c. A characteristic of an asset indicating how easily the asset can be converted into cash or used to buy services or satisfy obligations.

d. Obligations that are due to be paid or liquidated within one year or one operating cycle of the business.

e. Economic benefits or resources without physical substance, the value of which stems from the privileges or rights that accrue to their owner.

_____3. A voucher is:

a. An internal business paper (or folder) used to accumulate other papers and information needed to control cash disbursements and to ensure that the transaction is properly recorded.

b. A business form used within a business to ask the purchasing department of the business to buy needed Hems.

c. A document, prepared by a vendor, on which are listed the items sold, the sales prices, the customer's name, and the terms of sale.

d. A form used within a business to notify the proper persons of the receipt of goods ordered and of the quantities and condition of the goods.

e. A document on which the accounting department notes that it has performed each step in the process of checking an invoice and approving it for recording and payment.

_____4. Each of the following items would cause Brand X Sales Company's book balance of cash to differ from its bank statement balance.

A. A service charge made by the bank.

B. A check listed as outstanding on the previous month's reconciliation and that is still outstanding.

C. A customer's check returned by the bank marked "NSF."

D. A deposit which was mailed to the bank on the last day of November and is unrecorded on the November bank statement.

E A check paid by the bank at its correct $422 amount but recorded in error in the General Journal at $442.

F. An unrecorded credit memorandum indicating the bank had collected a note receivable for Brand X Sales Company and deposited the proceeds in the company's account.

G. A check written during November and not yet paid and returned by the bank.

Which of the above items require entries on the books of Brand X Sales Company?

a. A., B., C., and E.

b. A., C., E., and F.

c. A., B., D., and F.

d. A., B., D., E., and G.

e. C., D., E., and F.

_____ 5. A company reported net sales for 20X8 and 20X9 of $560,000 and $490,000 respectively. The year-end balances of accounts receivable were $34,000 and $31,000. Days' sales uncollected for 20X9 is:

   a. 6 days
   b. 20.2 days
   c. 15.8 days
   d. 23.1 days
   e. 24.2 days

Problem III

Many of the important ideas and concepts discussed in Chapter 6 are reflected in the following list of key terms. Test your understanding of these terms by matching the appropriate definitions with the terms. Record the number identifying the most appropriate definition in the blank space next to each term.

_____ Bank reconciliation	_____ Invoice approval*
_____ Bank statement	_____ Liquid assets
_____ Canceled checks	_____ Liquidity
_____ Cash	_____ Net method**
_____ Cash equivalents	_____ Outstanding checks
_____ Cash Over and Short	_____ Petty cash
_____ Check	_____ Principles of internal control
_____ Days' sales uncollected	_____ Purchase order*
_____ Deposit ticket	_____ Purchase requisition*
_____ Deposits in transit	_____ Receiving report*
_____ Discounts Lost**	_____ Signature card
_____ Electronic funds transfer (EFT)	_____ Vendee
_____ Gross method**	_____ Vendor*
_____ Internal control system	_____ Voucher
_____ Invoice	_____ Voucher system

  * Key term discussed in Appendix 6A
 ** Key term discussed in Appendix 6B

1. Form used to report that ordered goods are received and to describe their quantity and condition.

2. Company's ability to pay for its short-term obligations.

3. Expense resulting from failing to take advantage of cash discounts on purchases.

4. Checks written and recorded by the depositor but not yet paid by the bank at the bank statement date.

5. Seller of goods or services.

6. Itemized record of goods prepared by the vendor that lists the customer's name, the items sold, the sales prices, and the terms of sale.

7. Internal file used to store documents and information to control cash disbursements and to ensure that a transaction is properly recorded.

8. Method of recording purchases at the full invoice price without deducting any cash discounts.

9. Resources such as cash that are easily converted into other assets or used to pay for goods, services, or liabilities.

10. Checks that the bank has paid and deducted from the depositor's account.

11. Document containing a checklist of steps necessary for approving an invoice for recording and payment; also called *check authorization*.

12. Document listing merchandise needed by a department and requesting it be purchased.

13. Income statement account used to record cash overages and cash shortages arising from missing petty cash receipts or simple errors.

14. All policies and procedures used to protect assets, ensure reliable accounting, promote efficient operations, and urge adherence to company policies.

15. Procedures and approvals designed to control cash disbursements and acceptance of obligations.

16. Document used by the purchasing department to place an order with a seller (vendor).

17. Report that explains the difference between the book balance of cash and the balance reported on the bank statement.

18. Measure of the liquidity of receivables computed by dividing the current balance of receivables and dividing by the annual (or net) sales, and then multiplying by 365; also called *days' sales in receivables*.

19. Method of recording purchases at the full invoice price less any cash discounts.

20. Buyer or purchaser of goods or services.

21. Short-term, investment assets that are readily convertible into a known cash amount and sufficiently close to their maturity date so that market value is not sensitive to interest rate changes.

22. Includes the signatures of each person authorized to sign checks on the account.

23. Principles requiring management to establish responsibility, maintain records, insure assets, separate recordkeeping from custody of assets, divide responsibility for related transactions, apply technological controls, and perform reviews.

24. Use of electronic communication to transfer cash from one party to another.

25. Lists items such as currency, coins, and checks deposited and their corresponding dollar amounts.

26. Document signed by the depositor instructing the bank to pay a specified amount to a designated recipient.

27. Includes currency, coins, and amounts on deposit in bank checking or savings accounts.

28. Deposits recorded by the company but not yet by its bank.

29. Bank report on the depositor's beginning and ending cash balances, and a listing of its changes for a period.

30. Small amount of cash in a fund to pay minor expenses; accounted for using an imprest system.

Problem IV

Complete the following by filling in the blanks.

1. A (n) _____ form is used by the accounting department in checking and approving an invoice for recording and payment.

2. If the size of the petty cash fund remains unchanged, the Petty Cash account _____ (is, is not) debited in the entry to replenish the petty cash fund.

3. Control of a small business is commonly gained through the direct supervision and active participation of the _____ in the affairs and activities of the business. However, as a business grows, it becomes necessary for the manager to delegate responsibilities and rely on _____ rather than personal contact in controlling the affairs and activities of the business.

4. A properly designed internal control system encourages adherence to prescribed managerial policies;   and   it   also   (a)
   _____ ,   (b)
   _____ , and
   (c) _____ .

5. A good system of internal control for cash requires a _____ of duties so that the people responsible for handling cash and for its custody are not the same people who _____ . It also requires that all cash receipts be deposited in the bank _____ and that all payments, except petty cash payments, be made by _____ .

6. A bank reconciliation is prepared to account for the difference between the _____ and the _____ .

7. An accounting system used to control the incurrence and payment of obligations requiring the disbursement of cash is a _____ .

8. A _____ is commonly used by a selling department to notify the purchasing department of items that the selling department wishes the purchasing department to purchase.

9. The business form commonly used by the purchasing department of a large company to order merchandise is called a(n) _____ .

10. Good internal control follows certain broad principles, including:
    (a) Responsibilities should be clearly established, and, in every situation, _____ should be made responsible for each task.
    (b) Adequate records should be maintained since they provide an important means of protecting _____ .
    (c) Assets should be _____ and employees _____ .
    (d) Recordkeeping for assets and _____ of assets should be separated.
    (e) Responsibility for related transactions should be _____ so that the work of one department or individual may act as a check on the work of others.
    (f) Mechanical devices _____ where practicable.
    (g) Regular and independent _____ of internal control procedures should be conducted.

©The McGraw-Hill Companies, Inc., 2008

11. After preparing a bank reconciliation, journal entries _____ (should, should not) be made to record those items listed as outstanding checks.

12. Days' sales uncollected is used in evaluating the _____ of a company.

Problem V

On November 5 of the current year Cullen Company drew Check No. 23 for $50 to establish a petty cash fund.

Required:

1. Prepare the journal entry to record the establishment of the fund. Do not provide an explanation.

DATE	ACCOUNT TITLES AND EXPLANATION	P.R.	DEBIT	CREDIT

After making a payment from petty cash on November 25, the petty cashier noted that there was only $2.50 cash remaining in the fund. The cashier prepared the following list of expenditures from the fund and requested that the fund be replenished.

Nov. 9	Express freight on merchandise purchased	$ 9.75
12	Miscellaneous expense to clean office	10.00
15	Office supplies	3.50
18	Delivery of merchandise to customer	8.00
23	Miscellaneous expense for collect telegram	3.25
25	Express freight on merchandise purchased	13.00

Check No. 97 in the amount of $47.50 was drawn to replenish the fund.

2. Prepare the journal entry to record the check replenishing the petty cash fund. Do not provide an explanation.

DATE	ACCOUNT TITLES AND EXPLANATION	P.R.	DEBIT	CREDIT

Problem VI

Information about the following eight items is available to prepare Verde Company's December 31 bank reconciliation.

Two checks (1) No. 453 and (2) No. 457 were outstanding on November 30. Check No. 457 was returned with the December bank statement but Check No. 453 was not. (3) Check No. 478, written on December 26, was not returned with the canceled checks; and (4) Check No. 480 for $96 was incorrectly entered in the Cash Disbursements Journal and posted as though it were for $69. (5) A deposit placed in the bank's night depository after banking hours on November 30 appeared on the December bank statement, but (6) one placed there after hours on December 31 did not. (7) Enclosed with the December bank statement was a debit memorandum for a bank service charge and (8) a check received from a customer and deposited on December 27 but returned by the bank marked "Not Sufficient Funds."

Required:

1. If an item in the above list should not appear on the December 31 bank reconciliation, ignore it. However, if an item should appear, enter its number below in the appropriate set of parentheses to show where it should be added or subtracted in preparing the reconciliation.

VERDE COMPANY
Bank Reconciliation
December 31, 20--

Book balance of cash...............	$X,XXX	Bank statement balance..................	$X,XXX
Add:		Add:	
( )		( )	
( )		( )	
( )		( )	
Deduct:		Deduct:	
( )		( )	
( )		( )	
( )		( )	
Reconciled balance..................	$X,XXX	Reconciled balance.........................	$X,XXX

2. Certain of the above items require entries on Verde Company's books. Place the numbers of these items within the following parentheses:

( ), ( ), ( ), ( ), ( ), ( )

Problem VII

The bank statement dated September 30, 20X8, for the Smith Company showed a balance of $2,876.35 which differs from the $1,879.50 book balance of cash on that date. In attempting to reconcile the difference, the accountant noted the following facts:

1. The bank recorded a service fee of $15 that was not recorded on the books of Smith Company.
2. A deposit of $500 was made on the last day of the month but was not recorded by the bank.
3. A check for $176 had been recorded on the Smith Company books as $167. The bank paid the correct amount.
4. A check was written during September but has not been processed by the bank. The amount was $422.85.
5. A check for $1,000 is still outstanding from August.
6. A check for $100 deposited by Smith Company was returned marked "Not Sufficient Funds."
7. A credit memorandum stated that the bank collected a note receivable of $200 for Smith Company and charged Smith a $2 collection fee. Smith Company had not previously recorded the collection.

Required:

Prepare, in good form, a bank reconciliation which shows the correct cash balance on September 30, 20X8.

Problem VIII (Appendix 6B)

The records of ABC Company, which records all purchases at gross amounts, included the following transactions.

June 1   Received shipment of merchandise having \$2,000 invoice price, terms 2/10, n/30.
June 2   Received shipment of merchandise having \$500 invoice price, terms 1/10, n/60.
June 7   Paid for merchandise received on June 1.
July 30   Paid for merchandise received on June 2.

Required:

1. Prepare the journal entries to record the following transactions. Do not provide explanations. Skip a line between entries.

DATE	ACCOUNT TITLES AND EXPLANATION	P.R.	DEBIT	CREDIT

2. Prepare the appropriate journal entries for the ABC Company assuming that the company instead records purchases at net amounts. You may need to use the Discount Lost account. Do not provide explanations. Skip a line between entries.

DATE	ACCOUNT TITLES AND EXPLANATION	P.R.	DEBIT	CREDIT

Solutions for Chapter 6

Problem I

1. T
2. T
3. F
4. T
5. T
6. T
7. F
8. T

Problem II

1. E
2. C
3. A
4. B
5. D

Problem III

17	Bank reconciliation		11	Invoice approval*
29	Bank statement		9	Liquid assets
10	Canceled checks		2	Liquidity
27	Cash		19	Net method**
21	Cash equivalents		4	Outstanding checks
13	Cash Over and Short		30	Petty cash
26	Check		23	Principles of internal control
18	Days' sales uncollected		16	Purchase order*
25	Deposit ticket		12	Purchase requisition*
28	Deposits in transit		1	Receiving report*
3	Discounts Lost**		22	Signature card
24	Electronic funds transfer (EFT)		20	Vendee
8	Gross method**		5	Vendor*
14	Internal control system		7	Voucher
6	Invoice*		15	Voucher system

* *Key term discussed in Appendix 6A*
** *Key term discussed in Appendix 6B*

Problem IV

1. invoice approval
2. is not
3. owner-manager; a system of internal control
4. (a) promotes operational efficiencies; (b) protects the business assets from waste, fraud, and theft; and (c) ensures accurate and reliable accounting data
5. separation; keep the cash records; intact each day, check
6. book balance of cash; bank statement balance
7. voucher system
8. purchase requisition
9. purchase order
10. one person; (b) assets; (c) insured, bonded; (d) custody; (e) divided; (f) should be used; (g) reviews
11. should not
12. liquidity

Problem V

1. Nov. 5	Petty Cash	50.00	
	Cash...		50.00
	Established a petty cash fund.		

2. Nov. 25	Transportation-In (or Inventory if Perpetual system is used)..	22.75	
	Miscellaneous Expenses...	13.25	
	Office Supplies...	3.50	
	Delivery Expense	8.00	
	Cash...		47.50
	Reimbursed the petty cash fund.		

Problem VI

1. Book balance of cash .... $X,XXX   Bank statement balance .... $X,XXX
    Add: Add:
        (   )   (6)
    Deduct: Deduct:
        (4)   (1)
        (7)   (3)
        (8)   (   )

2.   (4), (7), (8)

Problem VII

SMITH COMPANY
Bank Reconciliation
September 30, 20X8

Book balance of cash	$1,879.50	Bank statement balance		$2,876.35
Add:		Add:		
Proceeds of note less				
Collection fee	198.00	Deposit on 9/30/X8		500.00
	2,077.50			3,376.35
Deduct:		Deduct:		
NSF check $100.00		Outstanding checks:		
Service fee 15.00		August	$1,000.00	
Recording error 9.00	124.00	September	422.85	1,422.85
Reconciled balance	$1,953.50	Reconciled balance		$1,953.50

Problem VIII (Appendix 6B)

1.

June 1	Merchandise Inventory		2,000.00	
	Accounts Payable			2,000
2	Merchandise Inventory		500.00	
	Accounts Payable			500.00
7	Accounts Payable		2,000.00	
	Merchandise Inventory			40.00
	Cash			1,960.00
July 30	Accounts Payable		500.00	
	Cash			500.00

2.

June 1	Merchandise Inventory ($2,000 x 98%)		1.960.00	
	Accounts Payable			1,960.00
2	Merchandise Inventory ($500 x 99%)		495.00	
	Accounts Payable			495.00
7	Accounts Payable		1,960.00	
	Cash			1,960.00
12	Discounts Lost		5.00	
	Accounts Payable			5.00
July 30	Accounts Payable		500.00	
	Cash			500.00

CHAPTER 7
REPORTING AND ANALYZING RECEIVABLES

Learning Objective C1:

Describe accounts receivable and how they occur and are recorded.

Accounts receivable are amounts due from customers for credit sales. A subsidiary ledger lists amounts owed by each customer. Credit sales arise from at least two sources: (1) sales on credit and (2) credit card sales. *Sales on credit* refers to a company's granting credit directly to customers. Credit card sales involve customers' use of third-party credit cards.

Learning Objective C2:

Describe a note receivable and the computation of its maturity date and interest.

A note receivable is a written promise to pay a specified amount of money at a definite future date. The maturity date is the day the note (principal and interest) must be repaid. Interest rates are normally stated in annual terms. The amount of interest on the note is computed by expressing time as a fraction of one year and multiplying the note's principal by this fraction and the annual interest rate.

Learning Objective C3:

Explain how receivables can be converted to cash before maturity.

Receivables can be converted to cash before maturity in three ways. First, a company can sell accounts receivable to a factor, who charges a factoring fee. Second, a company can borrow money by signing a note payable that is secured by pledging the accounts receivable. Third, notes receivable can be discounted at (sold to) a financial institution.

Learning Objective A1:

Compute accounts receivable turnover and use it to help assess financial condition.

Accounts receivable turnover is a measure of both the quality and liquidity of accounts receivable. The accounts receivable turnover measure indicates how often, on average, receivables are received and collected during the period. Accounts receivable turnover is computed as net sales divided by average accounts receivable.

Learning Objective P1:

Apply the direct write-off and allowance methods to account for accounts receivable.

The direct write-off method charges Bad Debts Expense when accounts are written off as uncollectible. This method is acceptable only when the amount of bad debts expense is immaterial. Under the allowance method, bad debts expense is recorded with an adjustment at the end of each accounting period that debits the Bad Debts Expense account and credits the Allowance for Doubtful Accounts. The uncollectible accounts are later written off with a debit to the Allowance for Doubtful Accounts.

Learning Objective P2:

Estimate uncollectibles using methods based on sales and accounts receivable.

Uncollectibles are estimated by focusing on either (1) the income statement relation between bad debts expense and credit sales or (2) the balance sheet relation between accounts receivable and the allowance for doubtful accounts. The first approach emphasizes the matching principle using the income statement. The second approach emphasizes realizable value of accounts receivable using the balance sheet.

Learning Objective P3:

Record the receipt of a note receivable.

A note received is recorded at its principal amount by debiting the Notes Receivable account. The credit amount is to the asset, product, or service provided in return for the note.

Learning Objective P4:

Record the honoring and dishonoring of a note and adjustments for interest.

When a note is honored, the payee debits the money received and credits both Notes Receivable and Interest Revenue. Dishonored notes are credited to Notes Receivable and debited to Accounts Receivable (to the account of the maker in an attempt to collect), and Interest Revenue is recorded for interest earned for the time the note is held.

I.   Accounts Receivable

A *receivable* is an amount due from another party. **Accounts Receivable** are amounts due from customers for credit sales.

A. Recognizing Accounts Receivable

Accounts Receivable occur from credit sales to customers.

1. Sales on Credit

Credit sales are recorded by increasing (debiting) Accounts Receivable.

a. The General Ledger continues to keep a single Accounts Receivable account.

b. A supplementary record, called the *accounts receivable ledger*, is created to maintain a separate account for each customer that tracks the balance of each customer.

c. The sum of the individual accounts in the accounts receivable ledger equals the debit balance of the Accounts Receivable account in the general ledger.

d. Entry to record credit sale: debit Accounts Receivable— Customer Name, credit Sales. The debit is posted to the Accounts Receivable account in the general ledger and to the customer account in the accounts receivable ledger.

e. Many larger retailers maintain their own credit cards to grant credit to preapproved customers and to earn interest on unpaid balances. The entries are the same as in d. above except for the possibility of added interest revenue; entry to record interest: debit Interest Receivable, credit Interest Revenue.

2. Credit Card Sales (examples: Visa, MasterCard, American Express)

Sellers allow customers to use third-party credit and debit cards for several reasons:

a. The seller does not have to evaluate each customer's credit standing.

b. The seller avoids the risk of extending credit to customers who may not pay.

c. The seller typically receives cash from the credit card company sooner than had it granted credit directly to customers.

d. A variety of credit options for customers offers a potential increase in sales volume.

e. Entry for credit card sales when cash is received upon deposit of sales receipt: debit Cash (for the amount of sale less the credit card charge), debit Credit Card Expense (for the fee), credit Sales (for the full invoice amount).

    f.   Entry if company must remit the credit card sales receipts to the credit card company and wait for the cash payment: debit Accounts Receivable (for full invoice less the fee), debit Credit Card Expense (for the fee), credit Sales. Entry when payment is received: debit Cash, credit Accounts Receivable.

3.   Valuing Accounts Receivable

    Accounts of customers who do not pay what they promised are uncollectible accounts, commonly called **bad debts**. The total amount of uncollectible accounts is an expense of selling on credit. Two methods are used to account for uncollectible accounts: the direct write-off method and the allowance method.

    a.   **Direct Write-off Method**—records the loss from an uncollectible account receivable when it is determined to be uncollectible.

        i.   Entry to write off uncollectible and recognize loss: debit Bad Debt Expense, credit Accounts Receivable.

        ii.   If a written off account is later collected, this results of a reversal of the write off (see i) and a normal collection of account entry.

        iii.   The **matching principle** requires expenses to be reported in the same accounting period as the sales they helped produce; the direct write-off method usually does not best match sales and expenses because the related expense is not recorded until an account becomes uncollectible, which may be in the next accounting period.

        iv.   The **materiality principle** states that an amount can be ignored if its effect on the financial statements is unimportant to users' business decision,; it permits the use of the direct write-off method when bad debts expenses are very small in relation to a company's other financial statement items.

    b.   **Allowance Method**—matches the *estimated loss* from uncollectibles against the sales they helped produce. At the end of each accounting period, bad debts expense is *estimated* and recorded in an adjusting entry.

        i.   Advantages include that it records bad debt expense when the related sales are recorded and it reports accounts receivable on the balance sheet at the estimated amount of cash to be collected.

ii. Entry to record estimate of bad debt expense: debit Bad Debt Expense, credit Allowance for Doubtful Accounts, a contra-asset account. (This contra account is used instead of Accounts Receivable because, at the time of the adjusting entry, the company does not know which customers will not pay.)

iii. **Realizable value** is the expected proceeds from converting an asset into cash; in the balance sheet, the Allowance for Doubtful Accounts is subtracted from Accounts Receivable to show the amount expected to be collected.

iv. Entry to write off a bad debt (that is, a specific account identified as uncollectible): debit Allowance for Doubtful Accounts, credit Accounts Receivable. (Note that the write-off does not affect the realizable value of accounts receivable.)

v. Recovery of a bad debt requires two journal entries. The first entry is a reversal of the write-off (see iv above) and effectively reinstates the customer's account. The second entry records the collection of the reinstated account.

4. Estimating Bad Debts Expense

The allowance method requires an estimate of bad debts expense to prepare an adjusting entry at the end of the accounting period. There are two common methods:

a. The **percent of sales method**—uses income statement relations to estimate bad debts.

i. Based on experience, company estimates what percentage of credit sales will be uncollectible.

ii. Bad debts expense is calculated as the estimated percentage times sales for the period.

iii. The amount calculated is the estimated bad debt expense for the period; this amount is used in the adjusting entry. The allowance account ending balance rarely equals the bad debt expense because the allowance account was not likely to be zero prior to adjustment.

    b. **Accounts receivable methods**—uses balance sheet relationships.

      i. Goal of the bad debts adjusting entry for these methods is to make the Allowance for Doubtful Accounts balance equal to the portion of accounts receivable that is estimated to be uncollectible. The estimated balance for the allowance account is obtained in one of two ways.

      ii. The **percentage of accounts receivables method** assumes that a given percentage of a company's receivables is uncollectible.

    c. The **aging of accounts receivable method** uses both past and current receivables information to estimate the allowance amount. Specifically:

      i. Each receivable is classified by how long it is past its due date,

      ii. Experience is used to estimate the percent of each uncollectible class (the longer an amount is past due, the more likely it is to be uncollectible),

      iii. The percents are applied to each class and then totaled to get the estimated balance in the Allowance for Doubtful Accounts.

    (See Exhibit 7.11 for an example of an aging schedule.)

    d. Using either of the two methods (described in b and c above), the amount in the adjustment is calculated by determining the amount necessary to bring the allowance account to the desired credit balance.

II.   **Notes Receivable**

A **promissory note** is a written promise to pay a specified amount of money *(*the **principal** of the note*)* usually with **interest** (the cost for borrowing money) either on demand or at a definite future date. Promissory notes are notes payable to the **maker** (person promising to pay) and notes receivable to the **payee** (person to be paid). Sellers sometimes ask for a note to replace an accounts receivable when a customer requests an extension to pay their account.

A. Computing Maturity and Interest

   1. The **maturity date** is the day the note must be repaid.

     a. When the time of the note is expressed in days, its maturity date is the specified number of days after the note's date.

     b. When months are used, the note matures and is payable in the month of its maturity on the *same day of the month* as its original date.

2. Interest Computation:

   Principal of note times the annual interest rate times the time expressed in years. Note that a year has 360 days for interest computations (*the banker's rule*).

B. Recognizing Notes Receivable: debit Notes Receivable for principal or face amount of note; credit will vary (depends on reason note is received). Note that interest is not recorded until earned.

C. Valuing and Settling Notes

   The principal and interest of a note are due on its maturity date.

   1. Recording an Honored Note. The maker of the notes usually *honors* the note and pays it in full; entry (by the payee) to record: debit Cash, credit Notes Receivable, credit Interest Revenue. When a note is dishonored, we remove it from Notes Receivable and charge it back to an Account Receivable.

   2. Recording a Dishonored Note. When the maker does not pay at maturity, the note is *dishonored*; entry (by payee) to record: debit Accounts Receivable (for the principal and interest due), credit Note Receivable (for principal), credit Interest Revenue.

   3. Recording End-of-Period Interest Adjustment. When notes receivable are outstanding at the end of a period, any accrued interest earned is computed and recorded. Entry (by payee) to record: debit Interest Receivable, credit Interest Revenue.

   4. Entry to record honoring of a note if interest has been accrued: debit Cash (for full amount received), credit Interest Receivable (amount previously accrued), credit Interest Revenue (amount earned since accrual date), credit Notes Receivable (face amount of note).

III. **Disposing of Receivables**

   Companies can convert receivables to cash before they are due. Reasons for this include the need for cash or a desire to not be involved in collection activities.

   A. Selling Receivables

      A company can sell all or a portion of its receivables to a finance company or a bank.

      1. Buyer, called a *factor*, charges the seller a *factoring fee* and then takes ownership of the receivables and receives cash when come due.

      2. Entry (by seller of receivables): debit Cash, debit Factoring Fee Expense, credit Account Receivable.

B. Pledging Receivables

A company can pledge its receivables as security for a loan.

1. Borrower retains ownership of the receivables.

2. If borrower defaults on the loan, the lender has the right to be paid from the cash receipts of collections on accounts receivable.

3. The borrower's financial statements must disclose the pledging of the receivables.

V. **Decision Analysis—Accounts Receivable Turnover**

A. The **accounts receivable turnover ratio** measures both the quality (refers to the likelihood of collection without loss) and liquidity of accounts receivable; it indicates how often the average accounts receivable balance was converted to cash during the year.

B. It is calculated by dividing net sales by average accounts receivable.

C. A high turnover in comparison with competitors suggests that management should consider using more liberal credit terms to increase sales. A low turnover suggests management should consider stricter credit terms and more aggressive collection efforts.

VISUAL #7-1
METHODS OF ACCOUNTING FOR BAD DEBTS

	DIRECT WRITE-OFF METHOD	ALLOWANCE METHOD
	Bad debts expense is recorded at the time an account is determined to be uncollectible.	Bad debts expense is estimated and recorded at the end of each accounting period.
Year-end	No adjusting entry	Adjusting entry required: **Bad Debt Expense** XXX **Allowance for Uncollectible Accounts** XXX (The amount is an estimate based on a percentage of sales or a percentage of outstanding accounts receivable. If the estimate is based on sales, the full estimate is used in the adjusting entry. If the estimate is based on accounts receivable the allowance account balance is brought to the amount of the estimate.)

When an account is determined to be uncollectible	Write-off entry required:
	Bad Debts Expense XXX
	  Accounts Receivable/Customer XXX
	(The amount is the balance of the uncollectible account.)
		Write-off entry required:
		Allowance for Uncollectible Accounts XXX
		  Accounts Receivable/Customer XXX
		(The amount is the balance of the uncollectible account.)

When an account previously written off is recovered	1. Reinstate account *by reversing write-off:*
	  Accounts Receivable/Customer XXX
	    Bad Debts Expense XXX
	    (Amount is the account balance that was written off.)
	2. Record collection on account normally:
	  Cash XXX
	    Accounts Receivable/Customer XXX
	    (Amount is the amount collected.)
		1. Reinstate account *by reversing write-off:*
		  Accounts Receivable/Customer XXX
		    Allowance for Uncollectible Accounts XXX
		    (Amount is the account balance that was written off.)
		2. Record collection on account normally:
		  Cash XXX
		    Accounts Receivable/Customer XXX
		    (Amount is the amount collected.)

Advantages:	• Does not require adjusting entry. • Does not require year-end estimating of uncollectibles.	• Matches expense against related revenues. • Reports the net realizable accounts receivable on the balance sheet (a more accurate reporting of assets).
Disadvantages:	• Violates matching, therefore only allowed if qualified under materiality principle. (May be used by a business that anticipates an immaterial amount of uncollectibles.)	• Requires adjusting entry. • Requires year-end estimating of uncollectibles.

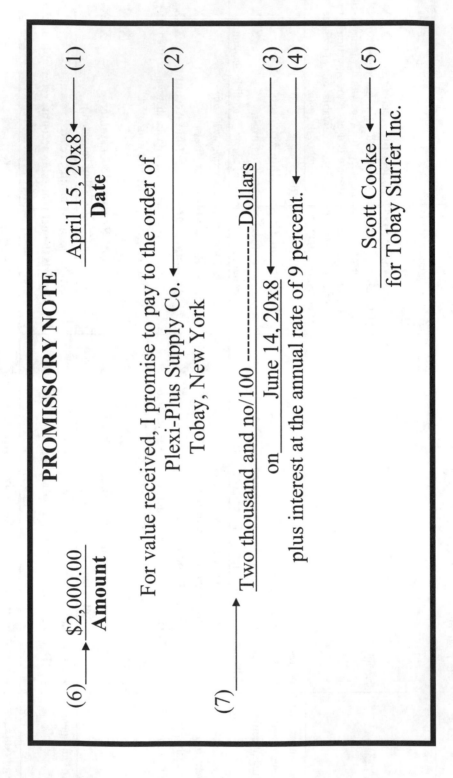

PROMISSORY NOTE

April 15, 20x8 ⟵ (1)
Date

For value received, I promise to pay to the order of ⟵ (2)
Plexi-Plus Supply Co.
Tobay, New York

Two thousand and no/100 ----------------Dollars ⟵ (3)
on___June 14, 20x8 ⟵ (4)
plus interest at the annual rate of 9 percent.

Scott Cooke ⟵ (5)
for Tobay Surfer Inc.

(6) ⟶ $2,000.00
Amount

(7) ⟶

At the end of the year, the M. I. Wright Company showed the following selected account balances:

Sales (all on credit) $300,000

Accounts Receivable 800,000

Allowance for Doubtful Accounts 38,000

Required:

1. Assume the company estimates that 1% of all credit sales will not be collected.

    a. Prepare the proper journal entry to recognize the expense involved.

    b. Present the balances in Accounts Receivable and Allowance for Doubtful Accounts as they would appear on the balance sheet. Also show the net realizable Accounts Receivable.

2. Assume the company estimates that 5% of its accounts receivable will never be collected.

    a. Prepare the proper journal entry to recognize the expense involved.

    b. Present the balances in Accounts Receivable and Allowance for Doubtful Accounts as they would appear on the balance sheet. Also show the net realizable Accounts Receivable.

1. Under each of the two assumptions (described in #1 and #2 above), prepare the proper journal entry for the following event:

    June 3   John Shifty, who owes us $500, informs us that he is broke and cannot pay. We believe him.

(If this alternative demonstration problem is not covered in class, see your instructor for the solution.)

Problem I

The following statements are either true or false. Place a (T) in the parentheses before each true statement and an (F) before each false statement.

1. ( ) If cash from credit card sales is received immediately when the credit card receipts are deposited at the bank, the credit card expense is recorded at the time the sale is recorded.

2. ( ) Businesses with credit customers must maintain a separate account for each customer.

3. ( ) After all entries are posted, the sum of the balances in the Accounts Receivable Ledger should be equal to the balance of the Accounts Receivable account in the General Ledger.

4. ( ) Under the allowance method of accounting for bad debts, accounts receivable are reported on the balance sheet at the amount of cash proceeds expected from their collection.

5. ( ) At the time an adjusting entry to record estimated bad debts expense is made, the credit side of the entry is to Accounts Receivable.

6. ( ) When an account deemed uncollectible is written off against Allowance for Doubtful Accounts, the estimated realizable amount of Accounts Receivable is decreased.

7. ( ) The income statement approach to estimating bad debts is based on the idea that some percentage of credit sales will be uncollectible.

8. ( ) The balance sheet approach to estimating bad debts is based on the idea that some particular percentage of a company's credit sales will become uncollectible.

9. ( ) Aging of accounts receivable requires the review of each account in the accounts receivable ledger.

10. ( ) A 90-day note, dated August 17, matures on November 16.

11. ( ) Although the direct write-off method of accounting for bad debts usually mismatches revenues and expenses, it may be allowed in cases where bad debt losses are immaterial in relation to total net sales and net income.

12. ( ) When a note receivable is discounted without recourse, the bank does not assume the risk of a bad debt loss.

13. ( ) When a note receivable is discounted with recourse, the company that discounts the note has a contingent liability.

14. ( ) A company that pledges its accounts receivable as security for a loan should disclose the fact in the notes to the financial statements.

Problem II

You are given several words, phrases, or numbers to choose from in completing each of the following statements or in answering the following questions. In each case select the one that best completes the statement or answers the question and place its letter in the answer space provided.

_____ 1. Orion Company has decided to write off the account of Jack Irwin against the Allowance for Doubtful Accounts. The $2,100 balance in Irwin's account originated with a credit sale in July of last year. What is the general journal entry to record this write-off?

a.	Allowance for Doubtful Accounts..........................	2,100	
	Accounts Receivable—Jack Irwin.....................		2,100
b.	Accounts Receivable...	2,100	
	Allowance for Doubtful Accounts.....................		2,100
c.	Bad Debts Expense..	2,100	
	Allowance for Doubtful Accounts.....................		2,100
d.	Accounts Receivable...	2,100	
	Accounts Receivable—Jack Irwin.....................		2,100
e.	Bad Debts Expense..	2,100	
	Accounts Receivable...		2,100

_____ 2. Hitech Corporation had credit sales of $3,000,000 in 20X8. Before recording the December 31, 20X8, adjustments, the company's Allowance for Doubtful Accounts had a credit balance of $1,400. A schedule of the December 31,20X8, accounts receivable by age is summarized as follows:

December 31, 20X8 Accounts Receivable	Age of Accounts Receivable	Uncollectible Percent Expected
$285,000	Not due	1.5
87,000	1-45 days past due	8.2
34,000	46-90 days past due	37.0
8,000	over 90 days past due	70.0

Calculate the amount that should appear on the December 31, 20X8, balance sheet as allowance for doubtful accounts.

a. $28,189.

b. $5,600.

c. $25,314.

d. $30,989.

e. $29,589.

_____ 3. Based on the information given in problem 4, what is the general journal entry to record bad debts expense for 20X8?

a. Debit Bad Debts Expense; credit Allowance for Doubtful Accounts.

b. Debit Accounts Receivable; credit Allowance for Doubtful Accounts.

c. Debit Bad Debts Expense; credit Accounts Receivable.

d. Debit Allowance for Doubtful Accounts; credit Bad Debts Expense.

e. Debit Accounts Receivable; credit Bad Debts Expense.

_____4. MBC Company discounts a $25,000 note receivable, with recourse, and receives proceeds of $25,250. MBC's entry to record the transaction would include the following:

a. $25,000 debit to Cash.

b. $250 debit to Interest Expense.

c. $250 credit to Interest Revenue.

d. $25,250 credit to Notes Receivable.

e. None of the above.

_____5. Westing Company had net sales of $500,000 and $400,000 for 20X9 and 20X8, respectively. Accounts receivable at December 31, 20X9 and 20X8, were $45,000 and $55,000. What is Westing's accounts receivable turnover for 20X9?

a. 11.1 times.

b. 10.0 times.

c. 20.0 times.

d. 9.0 times.

e. None of the above.

Problem III

Many of the important ideas and concepts discussed in Chapter 7 are reflected in the following list of key terms. Test your understanding of these terms by matching the appropriate definitions with the terms. Record the number identifying the most appropriate definition in the blank space next to each term.

_____	Accounts receivable	_____	Maker of a note
_____	Accounts receivable turnover	_____	Matching principle
_____	Aging of accounts receivable	_____	Materiality principle
_____	Allowance for Doubtful Accounts	_____	Maturity date of a note
_____	Allowance method	_____	Payee of a note
_____	Bad debts	_____	Principal of a note
_____	Direct write-off method	_____	Promissory note (or note)
_____	Interest	_____	Realizable value

1. Measure of both the quality and liquidness of accounts receivable; indicates how often receivables are received and collected during the period; computed by dividing net sales by average accounts receivable.

2. Entity who signs a note and promises to pay it at maturity.

3. Procedure that (1) estimates and matches bad debts expense with its sales for the period and (2) reports accounts receivable at estimated realizable value.

4. Entity to whom a note is made payable.

5. Method that records the loss from an uncollectible accounts receivable at the time it is determined to be uncollectible; no attempt is made to estimate bad debts.

6. Implies an amount can be ignored if its effect on financial statements is unimportant to users.

7. Accounts of customers who do not pay what they have promised to pay; an expense of selling on credit; also called _uncollectible accounts_.

8. Requires expenses to be reported in the same period as the sales they helped produce.

9. Expected proceeds from converting an asset into cash.

10. Contra asset account with a balance approximating uncollectible accounts receivable; also called *Allowance for Uncollectible Accounts*.

11. Date when principal and interest of a note are due.

12. Process of classifying accounts receivable by how long they are past due for purposes of estimating uncollectible accounts.

13. Amounts due from customers for credit sales.

14. Written promise to pay a specified amount either on demand or at a definite future date.

15. Charge for using money (or assets) until repaid at a future date.

16. Amount that the signer of a note agrees to pay back when it matures, not including interest.

Problem IV

On December 12, Lark Company received from Guy Hall, a customer, $300 in cash and a $1,500, 12%, 60-day note dated December 11 in granting a time extension on Hall's past-due account. On December 31, Lark Company recorded the accrued interest on the note, and Guy Hall paid the note and its interest on the following February 9. Prepare the journal entries to record these transactions.

DATE	ACCOUNT TITLES AND EXPLANATION	P.R.	DEBIT			CREDIT		
Dec. 12								
	Received cash and a note in granting a time extension							
	on a past-due account.							
31								
	To record accrued interest on a note receivable.							
Feb 9								
	Received payment of a note and interest.							

Problem V

On March 1, Lark Company accepted a $1,200, 12%, 60-day note dated that day from a customer, Mary Dale, in granting a time extension on the customer's past-due account. When Lark Company presented the note for payment on April 30, it was dishonored, and on December 20 Lark Company wrote off the debt as uncollectible. Prepare the journal entries to record the dishonor and the write-off against the company's Allowance for Doubtful Accounts.

DATE	ACCOUNT TITLES AND EXPLANATION	P.R.	DEBIT		CREDIT	
Apr 30						
	To charge the account of Mary Dale for her					
	dishonored $1,200, 12%, 60-day note.					
Dec. 20						
	To write off the uncollectible note of Mary Dale.					

Problem VI

Marin Company uses the allowance method in accounting for bad debt losses, and over the past several years it has experienced an average loss equal to one-fourth of 1% of its credit sales. During 20X8 the company sold $928,000 of merchandise on credit, including a $98 credit sale to Gus Bell on March 5, 20X8. The $98 had not been paid by the year's end.

1. If at the end of 20X8 Marin Company, in providing for estimated bad debt losses, assumes history will repeat, it will provide an allowance for 20X8 estimated bad debts equal to _____ % of its $928,000 of 20X8 charge sales; and the adjusting entry to record the allowance will appear as follows:

DATE	ACCOUNT TITLES AND EXPLANATION	P.R.	DEBIT		CREDIT	
20X1						
Dec. 31						
	To record estimated bad debts					

2. The debit of the foregoing entry is to the expense account, _____, which is closed to the _____ account at the end of the accounting period, just as any other expense account is closed.

3. The effect of the foregoing adjusting entry on the 20X8 income statement of Marin Company is to cause an estimated amount of bad debts expense to be deducted from the $928,000 of revenue from 20X8 charge sales. This complies with the accounting principle of _____.

4. The credit of the foregoing adjusting entry is to the contra account _____. On the December 31, 20X8, balance sheet, the balance of this contra account is subtracted from the balance of the _____ account to show the amount that is expected to be realized from the accounts receivable.

5. On March 31, 20X9, the Accounts Receivable controlling account and the Allowance for Doubtful Accounts account of Marin Company had the following balances:

Accounts Receivable		Allowance for Doubtful Accounts	
Mar. 31 65,625			Mar. 31 4,475

A balance sheet which was prepared on March 31, 20X9, would show that Marin Company expects to collect $ _____ of its accounts receivable.

6. On April 1, 20X9, Marin Company decided the $98 account of Gus Bell (sale made on March 5 of the previous year) was uncollectible and wrote it off as a bad debt. Prepare the journal entry and post to the above T-accounts the portions affecting the accounts.

DATE	ACCOUNT TITLES AND EXPLANATION	P.R.	DEBIT		CREDIT	
20X2						
Apr. 1						
	To write off the account of Gus Bell					

7. If a balance sheet was prepared immediately after the journal entry writing off the uncollectible account of Gus Bell was posted, it would show that Marin Company expected to collect $ _____ of its accounts receivable. Consequently, the write-off _____ (did, did not) affect the net balance sheet amount of accounts receivable. Likewise, the journal entry writing off the account did not record an expense because the expense was anticipated and recorded in the _____ entry made on December 31, 20X8 (which corresponds to the year of the sale).

Problem VII

Pell Company sells almost exclusively for cash, but it does make a few small charge sales, and it also occasionally has a small bad debt loss, which it accounts for by the direct write-off method.

1. Give below the entry made by Pell Company on February 5 to write off the $55 uncollectible account of Joan Bond (the goods were sold during the previous period.)

DATE	ACCOUNT TITLES AND EXPLANATION	P.R.	DEBIT			CREDIT		
Feb. 5								

2. Writing off the foregoing bad debt directly to the Bad Debts Expense account violates the accounting principle of _____. However, due to the accounting principle _____, the direct write-off is permissible in this case because the company's bad debt losses are very small in relation to its sales.

Problem VIII

A company that ages its accounts receivable and increases its allowance for doubtful accounts to an amount sufficient to provide for estimated bad debts had a $75 debit balance in its Allowance for Doubtful Accounts account on December 31. If on that date it estimated that $1,800 of its accounts receivable were uncollectible, it should record a year-end adjusting entry crediting $ _____ to its Allowance for Doubtful Accounts account.

Problem IX

Pierce Company allows its customers to use two credit cards: the University National Bank credit card and the Community Credit Card. Using the information given below, prepare the journal entries for Pierce Company to record the following credit card transactions:

a) University National Bank charges a 3% service fee for sales on its credit card. As a commercial customer of the bank, Pierce Company receives immediate credit when it makes its daily deposit of sales receipts.

    May 2   Sold merchandise for $525 to customers who used the University National Bank credit card.

DATE	ACCOUNT TITLES AND EXPLANATION	P.R.	DEBIT	CREDIT

b) Community Credit Card Company charges 4% of sales for use of its card. Pierce Company submits accumulated sales receipts to Community Company and is paid within 30 days.

    May 3   Sold merchandise for $675 to customers using the Community Credit Card. Submitted receipts to Community Company for payment

       30   Received amount due from Community Credit Card Company.

DATE	ACCOUNT TITLES AND EXPLANATION	P.R.	DEBIT	CREDIT

Solutions for Chapter 7

Problem I

1. T
2. T
3. T
4. T
5. F
6. F
7. T
8. F
9. T
10. F
11. T
12. F
13. T
14. T

Problem II

1. A
2. E
3. A
4. C
5. B

Problem III

13	Accounts receivable		2	Maker of a note
1	Accounts receivable turnover		8	Matching principle
12	Aging of accounts receivable		6	Materiality principle
10	Allowance for Doubtful Accounts		11	Maturity date of a note
3	Allowance method		4	Payee of a note
7	Bad debts		16	Principal of a note
5	Direct write-off method		14	Promissory note (or note)
15	Interest		9	Realizable value

Problem IV

Dec. 12	Cash	300	
	Notes Receivable	1,500	
	Accounts Receivable--Guy Hall		1,800
31	Interest Receivable ($1,500 x .12 x 20/360)	10	
	Interest Revenue		10
Feb. 9	Cash	1,530	
	Interest Receivable		10
	Interest Revenue		20
	Notes Receivable		1,500

Problem V

Apr. 30	Accounts Receivable--Mary Dale	1,224	
	Interest Revenue		24
	Notes Receivable		1,200
Dec. 20	Allowance for Doubtful Accounts	1,224	
	Accounts Receivable--Mary Dale		1,224

Problem VI

1. One fourth of 1%, or .25%

Dec. 31	Bad Debts Expense	2,320	
	Allowance for Doubtful Accounts		2,320

2. Bad Debts Expense, Income Summary

3. matching revenues and expenses

4. Allowance for Doubtful Accounts, Accounts Receivable

5. $61,150

6.
Apr. 1	Allowance for Doubtful Accounts	98	
	Accounts Receivable—Gus Bell....................................		98

Accounts Receivable			Allowance for Doubtful Accounts		
Mar. 31	65,625			Mar. 31	4,475
		Apr. 1 98	Apr. 1 98		

7. $61,150; did not; adjusting.

Problem VII

1. Feb. 5 Bad Debts Expense.. 55
      Accounts Receivable--Joan Bond   55

2. Matching revenues and expenses; materiality

Problem VIII

$1,875

Problem IX

a) May 2 Cash.. 509.25
     Credit Card Expense ($525 x 0.03)...................................... 15.75
      Sales   525

b) May 3 Accounts Receivable--Community Company......................... 648.00
     Credit Card Expense ($675 x 0.04)....................................... 27.00
      Sales 675.00

    30 Cash.. 648.00
      Accounts Receivable--Community Company................   648.00

CHAPTER 8
REPORTING AND ANALYZING LONG-TERM ASSETS

Learning Objective C1:

Describe plant assets and issues in accounting for them.

Plant assets are tangible assets used in the operations of a company and have a useful life of more than one accounting period. Plant assets are set apart from other tangible assets by two important features: use in operations and useful lives longer than one period. The four main accounting issues with plant assets are (1) computing their costs, (2) allocating their costs to the periods they benefit, (3) accounting for subsequent expenditures, and (4) recording their disposal.

Learning Objective C2:

Explain depreciation and the factors affecting its computation.

Depreciation is the process of allocating to expense the cost of a plant asset over the accounting periods that benefit from its use. Depreciation does not measure the decline in a plant asset's market value or its physical deterioration. Three factors determine depreciation: cost, salvage value, and useful life. Salvage value is an estimate of the asset's value at the end of its benefit period. Useful (service) life is the length of time an asset is productively used.

Learning Objective C3:

Explain depreciation for partial years and changes in estimates.

Partial-year depreciation is often required because assets are bought and sold throughout the year. Depreciation is revised when changes in estimates such as salvage value and useful life occur. If the useful life of a plant asset changes, for instance, the remaining cost to be depreciated is spread over the remaining (revised) useful life of the asset.

Learning Objective A1:

Compare and analyze alternative depreciation methods.

The amount of depreciation expense per period is usually different for different methods, yet total depreciation expense over an asset's life is the same for all methods. Each method starts with the same total cost and ends with the same salvage value. The difference is in the pattern of depreciation expense over the asset's life. Common methods are straight-line, double-declining-balance, and units-of-production.

Learning Objective A2:

Compute total asset turnover and apply it to analyze a company's use of assets.

Total asset turnover measures a company's ability to use its assets to generate sales. It is defined as net sales divided by average total assets. While all companies desire a high total asset turnover, it must be interpreted in comparison with that for prior years and its competitors.

Learning Objective P1:

Apply the cost principle to compute the cost of plant assets.

Plant assets are recorded at cost when purchased. Cost includes all normal and reasonable expenditures necessary to get the asset in place and ready for its intended use. The cost of a lump-sum purchase is allocated among its individual assets.

Learning Objective P2:

Compute and record depreciation using the straight-line, units-of-production, and declining-balance methods.

The straight-line method divides cost less salvage value by the asset's useful life to determine depreciation expense per period. The units-of-production method divides cost less salvage value by the estimated number of units the asset will produce over its life to determine depreciation per unit. The declining-balance method multiplies the asset's beginning-of-period book value by a factor that is often double the straight-line rate.

Learning Objective P3:

Distinguish between revenue and capital expenditures, and account for them.

Revenue expenditures expire in the current period and are debited to expense accounts and matched with current revenues. Ordinary repairs are an example of revenue expenditures. Capital expenditures benefit future periods and are debited to asset accounts. Examples of capital expenditures are extraordinary repairs and betterments.

Learning Objective P4:

Account for asset disposal through discarding or selling an asset.

When a plant asset is discarded, sold, or exchanged, its cost and accumulated depreciation are removed from the accounts. Any cash proceeds from discarding or selling an asset are recorded and compared to the asset's book value to determine gain or loss.

Learning Objective P5:

Account for natural resource assets and their depletion.

The cost of a natural resource is recorded in a noncurrent asset account. Depletion of a natural resource is recorded by allocating its cost to depletion expense using the units-of-production method. Depletion is credited to an Accumulated Depletion account.

Learning Objective P6:

Account for intangible assets.

An intangible asset is recorded at the cost incurred to purchase it. The cost of an intangible asset with a definite useful life is allocated to expense using the straight-line method, which is called *amortization*. Goodwill and intangible assets with an indefinite useful life are not amortized—they are annually tested for impairment. Intangible assets include patents, copyrights, leaseholds, goodwill, and trademarks.

Learning Objective P7 (Appendix 8A):

Account for asset exchanges.

For an asset exchange with commercial substance, a gain or loss is recorded based on the difference between the book value of the asset given up and the market value of the asset received. For an asset exchange without commercial substance, no gain or loss is recorded, and the asset received is recorded based on book value of the asset given up.

Chapter Outline

Section 1—Plant Assets

I.   **Cost Determination**

Plant assets are tangible assets used in a company's operations that have a useful life of more than one accounting period. Consistent with *cost principle*, plant assets are recorded at cost when acquired. Cost includes all normal and reasonable expenditures necessary to get the asset in place and ready for its intended use.

A. **Land**—has an unlimited life and is not usually used up over time. Cost includes:

1. The total amount paid for the land.

2. Real estate commissions, title insurance fees, legal fees, and any accrued property taxes paid by the purchaser.

3. Payments for surveying, clearing, grading, and draining, and government assessments for public roadways, sewers, and sidewalks are included in the cost of land.

4. Removal of any existing structures (less proceeds from sale of salvaged material). These costs are charged to the land account. Land is not depreciated.

B. **Land Improvements**—costs that increase the usefulness of the land. Land improvements have limited useful lives and are used up.

1. Examples include parking lot surfaces, driveways, fences, and lighting systems.

2. Costs are charged to a separate Land Improvement account so that their costs can be allocated to the periods they benefit.

C. **Buildings**

1. When purchased, costs usually includes its purchase price, brokerage fees, taxes, title fees, attorney costs, and all expenditures to make it ready for its intended use including any necessary repairs or renovations such as wiring, lighting, flooring and wall coverings.

2. If constructed for own use, cost includes materials and labor plus a reasonable amount of indirect overhead costs, such as heat, lighting, power, and depreciation on machinery used to construct the asset. Cost also includes design fees, building permits, and insurance during construction (but not after it is placed in use; insurance then becomes an operating expense).

D. **Machinery and Equipment**

Costs include all normal and necessary expenditures to purchase and prepare them for intended use, including purchase price, taxes, transportation charges, insurance while in transit, and the installing, assembling and testing of the machinery and equipment.

E. **Lump-Sum Purchase**

1. A lump-sum purchase is the purchase of plant assets as a group in a single transaction for a lump-sum price.

2. Individual asset cost is determined by allocating the cost of the purchase among the different types of assets acquired based on their *relative market values*.

II. **Depreciation**—The process of allocating the cost of a plant asset to expense in the accounting periods benefiting from its use.

A. Factors in Computing Depreciation

1. **Cost**—consists of all necessary and reasonable expenditures to acquire the plant asset and to prepare it for its intended use.

2. **Salvage value**—an estimate of the asset's value at the end of its benefit period (also called *residual value* or *scrap value*).

3. **Useful life**—length of time the asset is expected to be productively used in a company's operations (also called *service life*). Factors affecting useful life include:

   a. Wear and tear from use in operations.

   b. **Inadequacy**—the insufficient capacity of plant assets to meet the company's growing productive demands.

   c. **Obsolescence**—refers to a plant asset that is no longer useful in producing goods or services with a competitive advantage because of new inventions and improvements.

B. Depreciation Methods

Depreciation methods are used to allocate a plant asset's cost over the accounting periods in its useful life.

1. Straight-line method—charges the same amount to expense for each period of the asset's useful life; most frequently used method. *Computation:*

   a. Cost minus salvage value (equals the *depreciable cost)* divided by the useful life equals annual depreciation expense.

   b. Can be expressed as a rate by dividing 100% by the number of periods in the assets' useful life.

2. Units-of-production method—charges a varying amount to expense for each period of an asset's useful life depending on its usage. *Computation:*

   a. Cost minus salvage value divided by the total number of units expected to be produced during its useful life equals the depreciation per unit.

   b. Depreciation cost per unit times number of units produced in the period equals the period's depreciation expense.

3. Declining-balance method—an **accelerated depreciation method** that yields larger depreciation expense during the early years of an asset's life and less depreciation in the later years. *Computation:*

    a. Multiply the asset's beginning-of-period book value by a multiple of the straight-line rate. (Do not consider salvage value.) **Book value** is computed as the asset's cost less its accumulated depreciation.

    b. A common depreciation rate for the declining-balance method is double the straight-line rate; called the *double-declining-balance method.*

4. Comparing depreciation methods—while the amount of depreciation expense per period differs for different methods, total depreciation expense is the same over a given asset's useful life.

5. Depreciation for tax reporting—differences between financial and tax accounting systems are normal and expected.

    a. Many companies use accelerated depreciation in computing taxable income because it postpones tax payments by charging higher depreciation expense in the early years and lower amounts in the later years.

    b. Federal income tax law rules for depreciating assets are called the **Modified Accelerated Cost Recovery System (MACRS)**.

    c. MACRS is not acceptable for financial reporting because it often allocates costs over an arbitrary period that is less than the asset's useful life.

C. Partial-Year Depreciation

When an asset is purchased (or disposed of) at a time other than the beginning or end of an accounting period, depreciation is recorded for the part of the year the asset was in use.

D. Change in Estimates for Depreciation

Depreciation is based on estimates of salvage value and useful life; later, new information may indicate these estimates are inaccurate.

1. Use the new estimate to compute depreciation for current and future periods by revising the deprecation expense computation by spreading the cost yet to be depreciated over the remaining useful life.

2. The revision is referred to as a **change in an accounting estimate** and is reflected in future financial statements; not in prior statements.

E. Reporting Depreciation

1. Both the cost and accumulated depreciation of plant assets are reported on the balance sheet or in its notes.

2. To satisfy the full-disclosure principle, the depreciation method(s) used must be disclosed in notes.

3. Plant assets are reported on the balance sheet at book value; not at market value; emphasis on cost rather than market value is based on the *going concern principle*.

4. Accumulated Depreciation is a contra asset account with a normal credit balance. It does *not* represent funds accumulated to buy new assets when the currently owned assets are replaced.

III. **Additional Expenditures**

In recording additional expenditures for an assets' operation, maintenance, repair, and improvement, the company must decide whether to capitalize (that is, debit an asset account) or expense them.

A. Types of Additional Expenditures

1. **Revenue expenditures** (also called *income statement expenditures*) are additional costs of plant assets that do not materially increase the asset's life or productive capabilities; they are recorded as expenses and reported on the income statement.

2. **Capital expenditures** (also called *balance sheet expenditures*) are additional costs of plant assets that provide benefits extending beyond the current period; they are debited to asset accounts and reported on the balance sheet.

B. Ordinary Repairs

1. **Ordinary repairs** are expenditures to keep an asset in normal, good operating condition.

2. Ordinary repairs are treated as revenue expenditures; their costs are reported as expenses on the income statement.

C. Betterments and Extraordinary Repairs

1. **Betterments** (also called improvements) are expenditures that make a plant asset more efficient or productive.

2. **Extraordinary repairs** are expenditures extending the asset's useful life beyond its original estimate.

3. Since betterments and extraordinary repairs benefit future periods, both are debited to the asset account as capital expenditures.

IV. **Disposals of Plant Assets**—Assets may be discarded, sold, or exchanged.

  A. Discarding Plant Assets

    1. Entry to record disposal of plant assets when *fully depreciated* (when accumulated depreciation is less than the asset's cost): debit Accumulated Depreciation, credit the plant asset account.

    2. Entry to record disposal of plant assets when *not fully depreciated* (when accumulated depreciation is less than the asset's cost): first, record depreciation expense through date discarded, then debit Accumulated Depreciation, debit Loss on Disposal (for the remaining book value), credit the plant asset account.

  B. Selling Plant Assets

  First, record depreciation expense through date sold, then:

    1. Entry to record sale at book value: debit cash, debit Accumulated Depreciation, credit the plant asset account.

    2. Entry to record sale above book value: debit cash, debit Accumulated Depreciation, credit Gain on Disposal, credit the plant asset account.

    3. Entry to record sale below book value: debit cash, debit Loss on Disposal, debit Accumulated Depreciation, credit the plant asset account.

V. **Section 2—Natural Resources**—assets that are physically consumed when used. Examples include timber, mineral deposits, and oil and gas fields. Since they are consumed when used, they are also called *wasting assets*.

  A. Cost Determination and Depletion

    1. Natural resources are recorded at cost, which includes all expenditures necessary to acquire the resource and prepare it for its intended use.

    2. **Depletion** is the process of allocating the cost of a natural resource to the period when it is consumed.

    3. Natural resources are reported on the balance sheet at cost less *accumulated depletion*.

    4. The depletion expense per period is based on the units extracted; entry to record depletion: debit Depletion Expense, credit Accumulated Depletion.

  B. Plant Assets Used in Extracting Resources

  When the usefulness of plant assets used in extracting resources is directly related to the depletion of the natural resource, their costs are depreciated using the units-of-production method in proportion to the depletion of the natural resource.

VI. **Section 3 -- Intangible Assets**—nonphysical assets (used in operations) that confer on their owners long-term rights, privileges, or competitive advantages.

A. Cost Determination and Amortization

1. An intangible asset is recorded at cost when purchased. Its cost is systematically allocated to expense over its estimated useful life through a process called **amortization**. If an intangible asset has an **indefinite useful life**, it should not be amortized.

2. Amortization is similar to depreciation and depletion, except that only the straight-line method is generally used for amortization.

3. The effects of amortization are recorded in a contra account called Accumulated Amortization. The gross acquisition cost and accumulated amortization are disclosed in the balance sheet.

B. Types of Intangibles

1. **Patent**—an exclusive right granted to its owner to manufacture and sell a patented machine or device, or to use a process, for 20 years.

2. **Copyright**—the exclusive right given to its owner to publish and sell a musical, literary, or artistic work during the life of the creator plus 70 years.

3. **Leasehold**—**lessee** is granted the right to use property by the **lessor**, the property's owner.

4. **Leasehold improvements**—alterations or improvements to leased property, such as partitions, painting, and storefronts.

5. **Franchises and Licenses**—rights that a company or government grants an entity to deliver a product or service under specified conditions.

6. **Trademarks and Trade Names**—symbols, names, phrases, or jingles identified with a company, product, or service.

7. **Goodwill**—meaning in accounting: the amount by which the value of a company exceeds the value of its individual assets and liabilities; implies the company as a whole has certain value attributes not measured among its individual assets and liabilities.

VII. **Decision Analysis—Total Asset Turnover**

A. **Total asset turnover** is a measure of a company's ability to use its assets most efficiently and effectively.

B. Calculated by dividing net sales by average total assets.

C. It is safe to say that all companies desire a high total asset turnover. However, interpreting a company's total asset turnover requires an understanding of the company's operations.

1. Some operations are capital intensive, meaning that a relatively large amount is invested in assets to generate sales, which would suggest a lower total asset turnover.

2. Other operations are labor intensive, meaning that they generate sales more by the efforts of people than the use of assets; a higher total asset turnover would be expected.

VIII. **Exchanging Plant Assets (Appendix 8A)** Many plant assets are disposed of by exchanging them for newer assets. In a typical exchange, a *trade-in allowance* is received on the old asset and the balance is paid in cash. Accounting for the exchange depends on whether the transaction has *commercial substance*. An exchange has commercial substance if the company's future cash flows change as a result of the transaction. If an asset exchange has commercial substance, a gain or loss is recorded based on the difference between the book value of the asset given up and the market value of the asset received. If an asset exchange lacks commercial substance, no gain or loss is recorded, and the asset received is recorded based on book value of the asset given up.

A. **Exchange with Commercial Substance: A Loss**

When the book value of the assets given up (cash paid plus book value of the old equipment) is more than the market value of the equipment received, a loss is recorded. Entry: debit the new equipment for market value, debit Loss on Exchange of Assets (difference between the book value of the assets given up and the market value of the new asset), debit Accumulated Depreciation for the old equipment, credit Equipment (old) for cost of the old equipment, credit cash for the cash paid.

B. **Exchange with Commercial Substance: A Gain**

When the market value of the equipment received is more than the book value of the assets given up (cash paid plus book value of the old equipment), a gain is recorded. Entry: debit the new equipment for market value, debit Accumulated Depreciation for the old equipment, credit Equipment (old) for cost of the old equipment, credit cash for the cash paid, and credit Gain on Exchange of Assets for the gain (difference between market value of the new asset and the book value of the assets given up).

C. **Exchange without Commercial Substance**

If the transaction lacks commercial substance, any gain or loss which would have been recorded when the transaction had commercial substance is not recorded. The unrecognized gain is subtracted from the new asset's market value to determine its cost basis. The cost basis of the new asset also can be computed by summing the book values of the assets given up.

FORMULAS FOR DEPRECIATION METHODS

1. STRAIGHT LINE

$$\frac{\text{Cost - Estimated salvage}}{\text{Estimated useful life}} = \frac{\text{Annual}}{\text{Depreciation}}$$

2. UNITS OF PRODUCTION

a) $\dfrac{\text{Cost - Estimated salvage}}{\text{Predicted units of production}} = $ Depreciable Cost per Unit

b) $\begin{array}{c}\text{CPU x units produced}\\ \text{in period}\end{array} = \begin{array}{c}\text{Depreciation}\\ \text{for PERIOD}\end{array}$

(In last year, depreciate to estimated salvage value; never depreciate below this amount.)

3. DOUBLE-DECLINING BALANCE

Book Value (beginning of year) x RATE* = Depreciation (for that year)

*RATE → The rate used is constant and it is twice what the straight line rate would have been for this asset.
(In the last year, depreciate to estimated salvage value; never depreciate below this amount.)

The New Times Company purchased a new machine on January 1, 20X6. The new machine cost $120,000, had an estimated useful life of five years, and an estimated salvage value of $15,000 at the end of its useful life. It was expected that the machine would produce 210,000 widgets during its useful life.

The company used the machine for exactly three years. During these three years, the annual production of widgets was 80,000, 50,000, and 30,000 units, respectively.

On January 1, 20X9, the machine is sold for $45,000.

Required:

1. Calculate the depreciation expense for each of the first three years using:
   a. Straight-line
   b. Units-of-production
   c. Double-declining-balance
2. Prepare the proper journal entry for the sale of the machine under each of the three different depreciation methods.

(If this alternative demonstration problem is not covered in class, see your instructor for the solution.)

Problem I

The following statements are either true or false. Place a (T) in the parentheses before each true statement and an (F) before each false statement.

1. ( ) Cost is the basis for recording the acquisition of a plant asset.

2. ( ) The cost of a plant asset constructed by a business for its own use would include depreciation on the machinery used in constructing the asset.

3. ( ) Depreciation is a process of determining the value of assets.

4. ( ) The cost of extraordinary repairs which extend the service life of an asset should be debited to a Repairs Expense account.

5. ( ) The service life of a plant asset can be affected by inadequacy or obsolescence.

6. ( ) Accelerated depreciation methods increase taxable income in the early years of an asset's life.

7. ( ) Straight-line depreciation charges each year of an asset's life with an equal amount of expense.

8. ( ) Double-declining-balance depreciation applies twice the straight-line rate to the beginning-of-the-year book value of an asset to calculate each year's depreciation expense.

9. ( ) When an asset exchange has commercial substance, a gain or loss is recorded based on the difference between the book value of the asset given up and the market value of the asset received.

10. ( ) Total asset turnover is calculated by dividing average total assets by net sales.

11. ( ) The cost of making an ordinary repair to a machine should be classified as a revenue expenditure.

12. ( ) The credit balance in accumulated depreciation represents funds accumulated to buy new assets when the presently owned assets must be replaced.

13. ( ) If a cost is incurred to modify an existing plant asset for the purpose of making it more efficient or more productive, the cost should be classified as an extraordinary repair.

14. ( ) A betterment is recorded by reducing accumulated depreciation.

15. ( ) Natural resources appear on the balance sheet at cost less accumulated depreciation.

16. ( ) The depletion cost of any mined but unsold natural resources that are held for sale is carried forward on the balance sheet as a current asset.

17. ( ) Trademarks and organization costs are intangible assets and must be amortized over the asset's useful life (not to exceed 40 years).

18. ( ) The amortization entry for the costs of leasehold improvements would debit Rent Expense and credit Leasehold Improvements.

19. ( ) The cost of all intangible assets must be amortized over 40 years.

Problem II

You are given several words, phrases, or numbers to choose from in completing each of the following statements or in answering the following questions. In each case select the one that best completes the statement or answers the question and place its letter in the answer space provided.

_____ 1. Jocelyn Leland, CPA, paid $165,000 to purchase approximately two acres of land and the building on it to be used as an office. The building was appraised at $84,000 and the land was appraised at $126,000. What amount should be debited to the Land account?

    a. $165,000

    b. $211,000

    c. $126,000

    d. $ 66,000

    e. $ 99,000

_____ 2. Flintstone Company depreciated a machine that cost $21,600 on a straight-line basis for three years under the assumption it would have a five-year life and a $3,600 trade-in value. At that point, the manager realized that the machine had three years of remaining useful life, after which it would have an estimated $2,160 trade-in value. Determine the amount of depreciation to be charged against the machine during each of the remaining years in its life.

    a. $3,240

    b. $1,800

    c. $2,640

    d. $2,880

    e. $3,888

_____ 3. Busy Bee Industries installed a machine in its factory at a cost of $84,000 on May 1, 20X8. The machine's useful life is estimated at eight years with a $9,000 salvage value. Determine the machine's 20X8 depreciation using the double-declining-balance method of depreciation.

    a. $14,000

    b. $10,500

    c. $21,000

    d. $12,500

    e. $18,750

_____ 4. Spacely's Sprockets purchased a machine on September 1 for $400,000. The machine's useful life was estimated at six years or 500,000 units of product with a $25,000 trade-in value. During Its second year, the machine produced 87,000 units of product. Assuming units-of-production depreciation, calculate the machine's second-year depreciation.

    a. $69,600

    b. $66,667

    c. $65,250

    d. $62,500

    e. $31,250

_____5. A machine that cost $40,000 and had been depreciated $30,000 was exchanged for a new machine in a transaction which had commercial substance. The new machine had an estimated 10-year life and market value of $50,000. If $33,000 cash was paid, at what amount should the new machine be recorded in the accounts? (Appendix 8A)

a. $10,000
b. $40,000
c. $50,000
d. $43,000
e. $33,000

_____6. The Romeo Company exchanged its used bottle-capping machine for a new bottle capping machine. The old machine cost $14,000, and the new one had a market value of $19,000. Romeo had taken $12,000 depreciation on the old machine and paid $18,500 cash for the new machine. If the transaction had commercial substance, what gain or loss should be recorded on the exchange? (Appendix 8A)

a. No gain or loss
b. $ 500 gain
c. $1,500 loss
d. $1,500 gain
e. $4,500 gain

_____7. Cherokee Company had a bulldozer destroyed by fire. The bulldozer originally cost $16,000, but insurance paid only $14,200. Accumulated depreciation on this bulldozer was $2,000. The gain or loss from the fire is:

a. No gain or loss
b. $ 200 gain
c. $ 200 loss
d. $ 1,800 loss
e. $16,000 loss

_____8. Following is selected year-end financial statement information from the Mega Life Inc.:

	12/31/X8	12/31/X9
Total assets	$18,500	$20,000
Total liabilities	12,750	11,900
Net sales	73,000	88,550
Total expenses	48,200	53,150

What is the total asset turnover for 20X9?

a. 4.4
b. 2.9
c. 0.2
d. 4.6
e. 1.8

_____9. Fleet Lines made a $3,000 modification to one of its trucks that made the truck more efficient. The $3,000 should be debited to which account?

    a. Trucks

    b. Accumulated Depreciation, Trucks

    c. Betterments

    d. Extraordinary Repairs

    e. Capital Expenditures

_____10. The process of allocating the cost of a patent to expense over time:

    a. Is called depletion.

    b. Is sometimes called depreciation.

    c. Is usually done by the declining-balance method over 50 years.

    d. Is seldom limited to less than 40 years.

    e. Should be accomplished in 20 years or less.

Problem III

Many of the important ideas and concepts discussed in Chapter 8 are reflected in the following list of key terms. Test your understanding of these terms by matching the appropriate definitions with the terms. Record the number identifying the most appropriate definition in the blank space next to each term.

_____ Accelerated depreciation method	_____ Leasehold
_____ Amortization	_____ Leasehold improvements
_____ Betterments	_____ Lessee
_____ Book value	_____ Lessor
_____ Capital expenditures	_____ Licenses
_____ Change in an accounting estimate	_____ Modified Accelerated Cost Recovery
_____ Copyright	System (MACRS)
_____ Cost	_____ Natural resources
_____ Declining-balance method	_____ Obsolescence
_____ Depletion	_____ Ordinary repairs
_____ Depreciation	_____ Patent
_____ Extraordinary repairs	_____ Plant assets
_____ Franchises	_____ Revenue expenditures
_____ Impairment	_____ Salvage value
_____ Inadequacy	_____ Straight-line depreciation
_____ Indefinite useful life	_____ Total asset turnover
_____ Intangible assets	_____ Trademark or trade (brand) name
_____ Land improvements	_____ Units-of-production depreciation
_____ Lease	_____ Useful life

1. Depreciation system required by federal income tax law.

2. Estimate of amount to be recovered at the end of an asset's useful life; also called _residual_, or _scrap, value_.

3. Condition in which, because of new inventions and improvements, a plant asset can no longer be used to produce goods or services with a competitive advantage.

4. Method that charges a varying amount to depreciation expense per period of an asset's useful life depending on usage.

5. Assets that increase the benefits of land, have a limited useful life, and are depreciated.

6. Measure of a company's ability to use its assets to generate sales; calculated by dividing net sales by average total assets.

7. Method that determines depreciation charge for the period by multiplying a depreciation rate (up to twice the straight-line rate) by the asset's beginning-period book value.

8. Process of allocating the cost of an intangible asset to expense over its estimated useful life.

9. Method that allocates an equal portion of the total depreciation for a plant asset (cost minus salvage) to each accounting period in its useful life.

10. Total cost of an asset less its accumulated depreciation (or depletion, or amortization).

11. Method that produces larger depreciation charges in the early years of an asset's life and smaller charges in its later years.

12. Length of time an asset will be productively used in the operations of a business; also called *service life*.

13. Condition in which the capacity of plant assets is too small to meet the company's productive demands.

14. Expenditures to make a plant asset more efficient or productive; also called *improvements*.

15. Additional costs of plant assets that provide material benefits extending beyond the current period; also called *balance sheet expenditures*.

16. Change in an accounting estimate that results from new information, subsequent developments, better insight, or improved judgment.

17. Expenditures reported on the current income statement as an expense because they do not provide benefits in future periods.

18. Repairs to keep a plant asset in normal, good operating condition; treated as a revenue expenditure.

19. Major repairs that extend the service life of a plant asset beyond prior expectations; treated as a capital expenditure.

20. Right giving the owner the exclusive privilege to publish and sell musical, literary, or artistic work during the creator's life plus 50 years.

21. All normal and reasonable expenditures necessary to get a plant asset in place and ready for its intended use.

22. Process of allocating the cost of natural resources to periods when they are consumed.

23. Process of allocating the cost of a plant asset to expense in the periods benefiting from its use.

24. Nonphysical assets (used in operations) that confer on their owners long-term rights, privileges, or competitive advantages.

25. Alterations or improvements to leased property such as partitions and storefronts.

26. Contract specifying the rental of property.

27. Exclusive right granted to its owner to manufacture and sell an item or use a process for 20 years.

28. Rights the lessor grants to the lessee under the terms of a lease.

29. Tangible assets used in a company's operations that have a useful life of more than one period.

30. Party to a lease who secures the right to possess and use the property from another party (the lessor).

31. Symbol, name, phrase, or jingle identified with a company, product, or service.

32. Assets physically consumed when used; examples are timber, mineral deposits, and oil and gas fields; also called *wasting assets*.

33. Party to a lease who grants another party (the lessee) the right to possess and use property.

34. Privileges granted by a company or government to sell a product or service under specified conditions.

35. Another term for *franchises*.

36. Diminishment of an asset value.

37. Asset life that is not limited by legal, regulatory, contractual, competitive, economic, or other factors.

Problem IV

Complete the following by filling in the blanks.

1. Land has an unlimited useful life, is not consumed when it is used, and therefore is not subject to _____. Costs that increase the usefulness of the land, such as parking lots or fences, should be classified as _____.

2. There are several factors that affect the useful life of some assets. These factors include:
   a. _____
   b. _____
   c. _____

3. The method of depreciation currently used by most companies for financial accounting purposes is _____. The most commonly used accelerated method of depreciation for financial accounting purposes is_____.

4. While MACRS is required for tax purposes, it is not acceptable for financial accounting because it allocates depreciation over an arbitrary recovery period that is _____
   _____.

5. Two types of revenue expenditures are _____ repairs and purchases of _____. Two types of capital expenditures are: _____ repairs and _____.

6. The tax advantage of accelerated depreciation is that _____ .

7. Trucks held for sale by a dealer and land held for future expansion are not classified as plant assets because _____.

8. Depreciation allocates and charges the cost of an asset's usefulness to _____. Depreciation does not measure the asset's decline in _____ or its physical _____.

9. The book value of a plant asset is its "value" as shown by the books and consists of its _____ minus its _____.

10. Regardless of what leads to a disposal of a plant asset, the journal entry or entries for the disposal should:

   a. Record _____ and _____ up to the date of the disposal.

   b. Remove the _____ and _____ account balances relating to the disposal.

   c. Record any _____ as a result of the disposal.

   d. Record any _____ or _____ that result from comparing the _____ of the asset with any cash received or paid as a result of the disposal.

Problem V

A machine was purchased for $7,000, terms 2/10, n/60, FOB vendor's factory. The invoice was paid within the discount period along with $175 of freight charges. The employees of the company that bought it installed the machine on a special concrete base. The concrete base and special power connections for the machine cost $575, and the wages of the employees during the period in which they installed the machine amounted to $425. The employees accidentally dropped the machine while moving it onto its special base, causing damages to the machine, which cost $125 to repair. As a result of all this, the cost of the machine for accounting purposes should be:

$_____

Problem VI

A machine with a cost of $8,000, an estimated eight-year service life, and an $800 salvage value, was purchased on July 1, 20X8. It was estimated that the machine would produce 144,000 units of product during its life, and it produced 10,000 units during its first year. The depreciation expense for 20X8 was:

   1. $_____ calculated on a straight-line basis.

   2. $_____ calculated using the units-of-production method.

   3. $_____ calculated using the double-declining-balance method.

Problem VII (Appendix 8A)

A machine that cost $45,000 and had been depreciated $20,000 was exchanged for a new machine that had a market value of $55,000. Assuming the balance was paid in cash prepare the general journal entry to record the transaction under each of the following unrelated assumptions:

   1. Cash paid was $28,000, and the transaction had commercial substance.

   2. Cash paid was $35,000 and the transaction had commercial substance.

   3. Cash paid was $28,000, and the transaction did not have commercial substance.

DATE	ACCOUNT TITLES AND EXPLANATION	P.R.	DEBIT	CREDIT

Solutions for Chapter 8

Problem I

1. T
2. T
3. F
4. F
5. T
6. F
7. T
8. T
9. T
10. F
11. T
12. F
13. T
14. F
15. F
16. T
17. T
18. F
19. F

Problem II

1. E
2. D
3. A
4. C
5. C
6. C
7. B
8. D
9. A
10. E

Problem III

11	Accelerated depreciation method	28	Leasehold
8	Amortization	25	Leasehold improvements
14	Betterments	30	Lessee
10	Book value	33	Lessor
15	Capital expenditures	35	Licenses
16	Change in an accounting estimate	1	Modified Accelerated Cost Recovery System (MACRS)
20	Copyright		
21	Cost	32	Natural resources
7	Declining-balance method	3	Obsolescence
22	Depletion	18	Ordinary repairs
23	Depreciation	27	Patent
19	Extraordinary repairs	29	Plant assets
34	Franchises	17	Revenue expenditures
36	Impairment	2	Salvage value
13	Inadequacy	9	Straight-line depreciation
37	Indefinite useful life	6	Total asset turnover
24	Intangible assets	31	Trademark or trade (brand) names
5	Land improvements	4	Units-of-production depreciation
26	Lease	12	Useful life

Problem IV

1. depreciation; land improvements
2. (a) wear and tear
   (b) inadequacy
   (c) obsolescence
3. straight-line; declining-balance
4. usually much shorter than the estimated service life of an asset
5. ordinary; assets with low costs; extraordinary; betterments
6. the payment of income taxes is deferred
7. they are not being used in the production or sale of other assets or services
8. the accounting periods that benefit from the asset's use; market value; deterioration
9. cost; accumulated depreciation
10. (a) depreciation expense; accumulated depreciation
    (b) asset; accumulated depreciation
    (c) cash received or paid
    (d) gain; loss; book value

Problem V

$7,000 - ($7,000 x 2%) + $175 + $575 + $425 = $8,035

Problem VI

1. ($8,000 - $800) ÷ 8 x 6/12 = $450

2. [($8,000 - $800) ÷144,000] x 10,000 = $500

3. (100%/8) x 2 = 25% double-declining-balance rate

   $8,000 x 25% x 6/12 = $1,000

Problem VII

(a)	Machinery..	32,000	
	Accumulated Depreciation Machinery	20,000	
	Cash ($35,000 - $28,000)		7,000
	Machinery..		45,000
(b)	Machinery..	35,000	
	Accumulated Depreciation Machinery	20,000	
	Loss on Exchange of Machinery	4,000	
	Cash ($35,000 - $21,000)		14,000
	Machinery..		45,000
(c)	Machinery..	35,000	
	Accumulated Depreciation Machinery	20,000	
	Gain on Exchange of Machinery		8,000
	Cash ($35,000 - $33,000)		2,000
	Machinery..		45,000

CHAPTER 9
REPORTING AND ANALYZING CURRENT LIABILITIES

Learning Objective C1:

Describe current and long-term liabilities and their characteristics.

Liabilities are probable future payments of assets or services that past transactions or events obligate an entity to make. Current liabilities are due within one year or the operating cycle, whichever is longer. All other liabilities are long term.

Learning Objective C2:

Identify and describe known current liabilities.

Known (determinable) current liabilities are set by agreements or laws and are measurable with little uncertainty. They include accounts payable, sales taxes payable, unearned revenues, notes payable, payroll liabilities, and the current portion of long-term debt.

Learning Objective C3:

Explain how to account for contingent liabilities.

If an uncertain future payment depends on a probable future event and the amount can be reasonably estimated, the payment is recorded as a liability. The uncertain future payment is reported as a contingent liability (in the notes) if (*a*) the future event is reasonably possible but not probable or (*b*) the event is probable but the payment amount cannot be reasonably estimated.

Learning Objective A1:

Compute the times interest earned ratio and use it to analyze liabilities.

Times interest earned is computed by dividing a company's net income before interest expense and income taxes by the amount of interest expense. The times interest earned ratio reflects a company's ability to pay interest obligations.

Learning Objective P1:

Prepare entries to account for short-term notes payable.

Short-term notes payable are current liabilities; most bear interest. When a short-term note's face value equals the amount borrowed, it identifies a rate of interest to be paid at maturity.

Learning Objective P2:

Compute and record *employee* payroll deductions and liabilities.

Employee payroll deductions include FICA taxes, income taxes, and voluntary deductions such as pensions and charities. They make up the difference between gross and net pay.

Learning Objective P3:

Compute and record *employer* payroll expenses and liabilities.

An employer's payroll expenses include employees' gross earnings, any employee benefits, and the payroll taxes levied on the employer. Payroll liabilities include employees' net pay amounts, withholdings from employee wages, any employer-promised benefits, and the employer's payroll taxes.

Learning Objective P4:

Account for estimated liabilities, including warranties and bonuses.

Liabilities for health and pension benefits, warranties, and bonuses are recorded with estimated amounts. These items are recognized as expenses when incurred and matched with revenues generated.

Learning Objective P5 (Appendix 9A):

Identify and describe the details of payroll reports, records and procedures.

Employers report FICA taxes and federal income tax withholdings using Form 941. FUTA taxes are reported on Form 940. Earnings and deductions are reported to each employee and the federal government on Form W-2. An employer's payroll records often include a payroll register for each pay period, payroll checks and statements of earnings, and individual employee earnings reports.

Chapter Outline

I. **Characteristics of Liabilities**

   A. Defining Liabilities

   A liability is a probable future payment of assets or services that a company is presently obligated to make as a result of past transactions or events. Note three crucial factors:

   1. Past transaction or event.

   2. Present obligation.

   3. Future payment of assets or services.

   B. Classifying Liabilities

   1. **Current liabilities** (also called *short-term liabilities*)—Obligations due within one year or the company's operating cycle, whichever is longer.

   2. **Long-term liabilities**—Obligations not expected to be paid within the longer of one year or the company's operating cycle.

   C. Uncertainty in Liabilities—answers to the following questions are often decided when a liability is incurred; however, one or more may be uncertain for some liabilities:

   1. Whom to pay?

   2. When to pay?

   3. How much to pay?

II. **Known (Determinable) Liabilities**—Set by agreements, contracts, or laws and are measurable. Examples of these liabilities in the *current* classification include:

   A. Accounts Payable

   Amounts owed to suppliers for products or services purchased with credit; also known as *trade accounts payable*.

   B. Sales Taxes Payable

   Amounts the seller has collected as sales taxes from customers when sales occur, which have not yet been remitted to the proper governmental agency.

   1. Entry (by seller) to record cash sale subject to sales tax: debit Cash, credit Sales, credit Sales Taxes Payable.

   2. Entry (by seller) when sales taxes are remitted: debit Sales Tax Payable, credit Cash.

C. Unearned Revenues

Amounts received in advance from customers for future products or services; also known as *deferred revenues, collections in advance and prepayments*.

1. Entry to record receipt of amounts in advance for future products or services: debit Cash, credit Unearned Revenue.

2. Entry to record revenue for that portion earned: debit Unearned Revenue, credit Revenue.

D. Short-Term Notes Payable

Written promise to pay a specified amount on a definite future date within one year or the company's operating cycle, whichever is longer. Can arise from many transactions; two common examples:

1. Note given to extend credit period; interest-bearing note is substituted for an overdue account payable.

   a. Entry to record partial payment on account and substitution of note payable for overdue amount: debit Accounts Payable, credit Cash, credit Notes Payable.

   b. Entry to record payment when note becomes due: debit Note Payable, debit Interest Expense, credit Cash.

2. Note given to borrow from bank
   Entries (by borrower) to record:

   a. Receipt of cash when note is signed: debit Cash, credit Note Payable.

   b. Payment of principal and interest: debit Note Payable, debit Interest Expense, credit Cash.

   c. Accrual of interest when notes payable are outstanding at the end of a period: debit Interest Expense, credit Interest Payable.

   d. Payment of note when interest has been accrued: debit Interest Expense (amount incurred since accrual date), debit Interest Payable (amount previously accrued), debit Notes Payable, credit Cash (for full amount paid).

E. Payroll Liabilities

An employer incurs several expenses and liabilities from salaries and wages earned, from employee benefits, and from payroll taxes levied on the employer.

1. **Gross pay**—total compensation an employee earns (includes wages, salaries, commissions, bonuses).

2. **Net pay**—gross pay less all deductions; also called *take-home pay*.

3. **Payroll deductions**—amounts withheld from an employee's gross pay, either required or voluntary; commonly called *withholdings*. The employer withholds payroll deductions from employees' pay and is obligated to remit to the designated organizations.

   a. Employee FICA taxes (*Social Security* and *Medicare taxes*) equal current rate times gross wages *subject to tax*. (For year 2005, Social Security tax is 6.2% of the *first* $90,000 earned by the employee in the calendar year and Medicare tax is 1.45% of *all* amounts earned by the employee).

   b. Employee federal income tax withholding is determined from tables published by the IRS based on employee's annual earnings rate and the number of *withholding allowances* claimed.

   c. Employee voluntary deductions (charitable contributions, medical insurance premiums, pension contributions, and union dues) are withheld and reported as part of the employer's current liabilities until paid.

4. Illustrative entry (by employer) to accrue payroll expenses and liabilities: debit Salaries Expense, credit FICA-Social Securities Taxes Payable, credit FICA-Medicare Taxes Payable, credit Employee Federal Income Taxes Payable, credit Employee Medical Insurance Payable, credit Employee Union Dues Payable, credit Accrued Payroll Payable (for the amount of the net pay).

5. Employer payroll taxes are recorded as expenses and current liabilities. Employer taxes include:

   a. Employer FICA taxes—employers must pay FICA taxes *equal in amount* to the FICA taxes withheld from their employees.

   b. Federal and state unemployment taxes—Employers must pay a federal unemployment tax on wages and salaries paid to their employees. (For year 2005, employers were required to pay FUTA taxes of as much as 6.2% on the first $7,000 earned by each employee; this tax can be reduced by a credit of up to 5.4% for taxes paid to a state program.) All states place a payroll tax for unemployment insurance on employers; the amounts vary.

        c. Illustrative entry (by employer) to record payroll tax expense and related liabilities: debit Payroll Tax Expense, credit FICA-Social Securities Taxes Payable, credit FICA-Medicare Taxes Payable, credit State Unemployment Taxes Payable, credit Federal Unemployment Taxes Payable.

    F. Multi-Period Known Liabilities—often include unearned revenues and notes payable that extend over multiple periods.

III.   **Estimated Liabilities**—Known obligations of uncertain amounts that can be reasonably estimated. Examples are:

    A. Health and Pension Benefits

        1. Employers often pay all or part of medical, dental, life, and disability insurance, and many employers also contribute to pension plans.

        2. Illustrative entry to record these benefits: debit Employee Benefits Expense, credit Employee Medical Insurance Payable, credit Retirement Program Payable.

    B. Vacation Benefits—Estimated and recorded by the employer during the weeks the employees are working and earning the vacation time.

        1. Many employers offer paid vacations.

        2. Entry to record: debit Vacation Benefits Expense, credit Vacation Benefits Payable. When employees take vacation, employer reduces (debits) the Vacation Benefits Payable and credits Cash.

    C. Bonus Plans

        1. Many companies offer bonuses to employees; many bonuses depend on net income.

        2. The related expense and liability are recorded in a year-end adjusting entry.

    D. Warranty Liabilities

        1. A **warranty** is a seller's obligation to replace or correct a product (or service) that fails to perform as expected within a specified period.

        2. To comply with the *full disclosure* and *matching principles*, the seller reports the expected warranty expense in the period when revenue from the sale of the product or service is reported. The warranty obligation is reported as a liability even though the amount, payee, and date are uncertain. The costs are probably and the amount can be estimated based on past experience.

    E. Multi-Period Estimated Liabilities
        Reported as both current and long-term depending on when payment will be made.

IV.   **Contingent Liabilities**—Potential obligation that depends on a future event arising from past transactions.

    A. Accounting for Contingent Liabilities – depends on the likelihood that a future event will occur and the ability to estimate the future amount owed if this event occurs. Three categories of contingent liabilities:

       1. Future event is probable and the amount can be reasonably estimated. Record as a liability.

       2. Future event is remote. Do not record or disclose in notes.

       3. Future event is reasonably possible. Disclose in notes.

    B. Reasonably Possible Contingent Liabilities – Examples:

       1. Potential legal claims—recorded in the accounts only if payment for damages is probable *and* the amount can be reasonably estimated; if can't be reasonably estimated or is less than probable but reasonably possible, disclose in notes.

       2. Debt guarantees (of a debt owed by another company)— require disclosure if potential liabilities are reasonably possible.

       3. Other contingencies (e.g., environmental damages, possible tax assessments, insurance losses, and government investigations)—require disclosure if potential liabilities are reasonably possible.

       4. Uncertainties – not contingent liabilities because they are future events not arising from past transactions.

V.   **Decision Analysis—Times Interest Earned Ratio**

    A. The **times interest earned ratio** is a measure of risk that a business will not earn sufficient income to cover interest.

    B. It is calculated by dividing income before interest expense and income taxes by interest expense.

VI.   **Payroll Reports, Records, and Procedures (Appendix 9A)**

    A. Payroll Reports—employers are required to prepare and submit the following reports:

       1. Employer's Quarterly Federal Tax Return (IRS Form 941) Filed within one month after the end of each calendar quarter to report FICA and income withholding taxes owed and remitted.

       2. Annual Federal Unemployment Tax Return (IRS Form 940) Must be mailed on or before January 31 following the end of each tax year to report an employer's FUTA taxes.

3. Wage and Tax Statement (Form W-2)

Must be given to employees on or before January 31 following the year covered by the report; employers must give each employee an annual report of the employee's wages subject to FICA and federal income taxes and the amounts of these taxes withheld.

B. Payroll Records

1. Payroll Register

A record for a pay period that shows the pay period dates and the hours worked, gross pay, deductions, and net pay of each employee; contains all the data needed to record payroll (for each pay period) in the General Journal.

2. Payroll Check

Generally accompanied with a detachable *statement of earnings* showing gross pay, deductions, and net pay.

3. **Employee's Earnings Report**

A record of an employee's hours worked, gross earnings, deductions, net pay, and certain personal information about the employee; contains the data the employer needs to prepare a Form W-2.

C. Payroll Procedures

1. Computing Federal Income Taxes

Computed using a wage bracket withholding table based on gross pay, number of personal exemptions, the employee's tax status, and pay period.

a. Withholding allowance—a number that is used to reduce the amount of federal income tax withheld from an employee's pay, and which corresponds to the personal exemptions the employee is allowed to subtract from annual earnings in calculating taxable income.

b. Form W-4—withholding allowance certificate form. Filed by employee with employer to identify personal exemptions claimed.

2. Payroll Bank Account

A separate **payroll bank account** is used in a company with many employees.

a. One check for total payroll is drawn on the regular bank account or an *electronic funds transfer* for this amount is executed to provide deposit for the payroll bank account.

b. Individual payroll checks are drawn on payroll account.

c. Helps with internal control and reconciling the regular bank account.

VII. Income Taxes (Appendix 9B)

   A. Income Tax Liabilities

      1. Corporations (but not sole proprietorships or partnerships) are subject to income taxes and must estimate their tax liability when preparing financial statements.

      2. Entry to record estimated income tax liability: debit Income Taxes Expense, credit Income Taxes Payable.

   B. Deferred Income Tax Liabilities

      1. Income tax laws and GAAP are different.

      2. *Temporary differences* arise when the tax return and the income statement report a revenue or expense in different years. When temporary differences exist, corporations compute income taxes expense on the income reported on the income statement; the result is that the income taxes expense is different from the amount payable to the government; this difference is the **deferred income tax liability.**

      3. Entry to record estimated income tax liability when there are temporary differences: debit Income Taxes Expense, credit Income Taxes Payable, credit Deferred Income Tax Liability (for the difference).

      4. Temporary differences can also cause corporations to pay income taxes *before* they are reported on the income statement as an expense. The corporation then reports a *Deferred Income Tax Asset* on its balance sheet.

On November l, 20X8, Orleaon Co. borrowed $200,000 for 90 days at 9% by signing a note.

Required:

1. Assume that the face value of the note equals the principal of the loan. Prepare the general journal entries to record issuing the note, accrual of interest at the end of 20X8 and the payment of the note at maturity.

2. Assume that the face value of the note ($204,500) includes both the principal of the loan and the interest to be paid at maturity. Prepare the general journal entries to record issuing the note, accrual of interest at the end of 20X8 and the payment of the note at maturity.

(If this alternative demonstration problem is not covered in class, see your instructor for the solution.)

Problem I

The following statements are either true or false. Place a (T) in the parentheses before each true statement and an (F) before each false statement.

1. ( ) An example of an estimated liability is a warranty.

2. ( ) Contingent liabilities are generally not recognized on the balance sheet.

3. ( ) A corporation would report a deferred income tax liability when reported income tax expense for the year is greater than the amount of tax actually paid.

4. ( ) Federal unemployment taxes are withheld from employees' wages at the rate of 1.45% on the first $61,200 earned.

5. ( ) Social Security taxes are levied equally on the employee and the employer.

6. ( ) Employee benefit costs represent expenses to the employer in addition to the direct costs of salaries and wages.

7. ( ) Each time a payroll is recorded, a separate journal entry usually is made to record the employer's FICA and state and federal unemployment taxes.

8. ( ) Since federal income taxes withheld from an employee's wages are expenses of the employee, not the employer, they should not be treated as liabilities of the employer.

9. ( ) Since Jon Company has very little employee turnover, the company has received a very favorable merit rating. As a result, Jon Company should expect to pay substantially smaller amounts of FICA taxes than normal.

10. ( ) Select Company's income before interest and taxes is $292,400 and interest expense is $86,000. Select's times interest earned is 3.4 times.

11. ( ) (Appendix 9A) An employer's FICA taxes are reported annually on a Form 940.

12. ( ) (Appendix 9A) If an employer's total FUTA taxes for the year are $100 or less, the amount due may be remitted annually rather than quarterly.

13. ( ) (Appendix 9A) As the number of withholding allowances claimed increases, the amount of income tax to be withheld increases.

14. ( ) (Appendix 9A) A special payroll bank account is used to replenish the regular bank account after all the employees are paid.

Problem II

You are given several words, phrases, or numbers to choose from in completing each of the following statements or in answering the following questions. In each case select the one that best completes the statement or answers the question and place its letter in the answer space provided.

_____ 1. On November 1, 20X8, Profitable Company borrowed $50,000 by giving a 90-day, 12% note payable. The company has an annual, calendar-year accounting period and does not make reversing entries. What amount should be debited to Interest Expense on January 30, 20X9?

a. $6,000

b. $1,500

c. $1,000

d. $ 500

e. $ 0

For the next two questions, use the following information as to earnings and deductions taken from a company's payroll records for the pay period ended November 15:

Employee's Name	Earnings to End of Previous Week	Gross Pay This Week	Federal Income Taxes	Medical Insurance Deducted
Rita Hawn......................................	$25,700	$ 800	$155.00	$ 35.50
Dolores Hopkins..........................	930	800	134.00	35.50
Robert Allen	76,100	1,000	193.00	42.00
Calvin Ingram.............................	18,400	740	128.00	42.00
		$3,340	$610.00	$155.00

_____ 2. Employees' FICA taxes are withheld at an assumed rate of 6.2% on the first $90,000 earned for Social Security and 1.45% of all wages earned for Medicare. The journal entry to accrue the payroll should include a:

a. Debit to Accrued Payroll Payable for $3,340.

b. Debit to FICA Taxes Payable for $255.51.

c. Debit to Payroll Taxes Expense for $765.

d. Credit to FICA Taxes Payable for $255.51.

e. Credit to Accrued Payroll Payable for $2,575.

_____ 3. Assume a state unemployment tax rate of 5.4% on the first $7,000 paid each employee and a federal unemployment tax rate of 0.8% on the first $7,000 paid each employee. The journal entry to record the employer's payroll taxes resulting from the payroll should include a debit to Payroll Taxes Expense for:

a. $305.11

b. $277.91

c. $293.23

d. $349.03

e. The entry does not include a debit to Payroll Taxes Expense.

Problem III

Many of the important ideas and concepts that are discussed in Chapter 9 are reflected in the following list of key terms. Test your understanding of these terms by matching the appropriate definitions with the terms. Record the number identifying the most appropriate definition in the blank space next to each term.

_____	Contingent liability	_____ Gross pay
_____	Current liabilities	_____ Known liabilities
_____	Current portion of long-term debt	_____ Long-term liabilities
_____	Deferred income tax liability**	_____ Merit rating
_____	Employee benefits	_____ Net pay
_____	Employee earnings report*	_____ Payroll bank account*
_____	Estimated liability	_____ Payroll deductions
_____	Federal depository bank*	_____ Payroll register*
_____	FICA taxes	_____ Short-term note payable
_____	Form 940*	_____ SUTA
_____	Form 941*	_____ Times interest earned
_____	Form W-2*	_____ Wage bracket withholding table*
_____	Form W-4*	_____ Warranty
_____	FUTA	

* Key term discussed in Appendix 9A.
** Key term discussed in Appendix 9B.

1. Corporation income taxes that are deferred until future years because of temporary differences between GAAP and tax rules.

2. Obligation of an uncertain amount that can be reasonably estimated.

3. Potential liability that depends on a future event arising from a past transaction.

4. Table of the amounts of income tax withheld from employee's wages.

5. A withholding allowance certificate, filed with the employer, identifying the number of withholding allowances claimed.

6. Obligations due within a year or the company's operating cycle, whichever is longer; paid using current assets or by creating other current liabilities.

7. Portion of long-term debt due within one year or the operating cycle, whichever is longer; reported under current liabilities.

8. Annual report by an employer to each employee showing the employee's wages subject to FICA and federal income taxes along with amounts withheld.

9. Taxes assessed on both employers and employees; for Social Security and Medicare programs.

10. Ratio of income before interest expense (and any income taxes) divided by interest expense; reflects risk of interest commitments when income varies.

11. Agreement that obligates the seller to correct or replace a product or service when if fails to perform properly within a specified period.

12. IRS form used to report an employer's federal unemployment taxes (FUTA) on an annual filing basis.

13. Rating assigned to an employer by a state based on the employer's record of employment.

14. Additional compensation paid to or on behalf of employees, such as premiums for medical, dental, life, disability insurance, and contributions to pension plans.

15. Payroll taxes on employers assessed by the federal government to support its unemployment insurance program.

16. State payroll taxes on employers to support its unemployment programs.

17. Total compensation earned by an employee.

18. Current obligation in the form of a written promissory note.

19. Obligations of a company with little uncertainty; set by agreements, contracts or laws; also called *definitely determinable liabilities*.

20. Amounts withheld from an employee's gross pay; also called *withholdings*.

21. Obligations *not* requiring payment within one year or the operating cycle, whichever is longer.

22. Gross pay less all deductions; also called *take-home pay*.

23. Record of an employee's net pay, gross pay, deductions, and year-to-date information.

24. Bank account used solely for paying employees; each pay period an amount equal to the total employees' net pay is deposited in it and the payroll checks are drawn on it.

25. IRS form filed to report FICA taxes owed and remitted.

26. Record for a pay period that shows the pay period dates, regular and overtime hours worked, gross pay, net pay, and deductions.

27. Bank authorized to accept deposits of amounts payable to the federal government.

Problem IV

Complete the following by filling in the blanks.

1. A debt guarantee is an example of a _____ liability.

2. Good employer merit ratings give employers a reduction in their state unemployment tax rates as a reward for _____.

3. The two components of FICA taxes are _____ and _____.

4. Employers pay FICA taxes _____ to those withheld from employees.

5. (Appendix 9A) According to law, a _____ showing wages earned and taxes withheld must be given by the employer to each employee within one month after the year-end.

6. (Appendix 9A) The amount to be withheld from an employee's wages for federal income taxes is determined   by   (a) _____ and

   (b)_____.

7. (Appendix 9A) According to the Federal Insurance Contributions Act, an employer must file an Employer's Quarterly Federal Tax Return (Form _____ within one month after the end of each _____.

8. (Appendix 9A) The _____ contains all the data needed to prepare the general journal entry to record payroll.

9. (Appendix 9A) An employee's working time, gross earnings, deductions, and net pay for a full year   are   summarized   in   an   _____ _____ .

Problem V

Glitz Company estimates that future costs to satisfy its product warranty obligation amount to 3% of sales. In January, the company sold merchandise for $50,000 cash and paid $1,200 to repair products returned for warranty work. Prepare the journal entries related to the product warranty.

DATE	ACCOUNT TITLES AND EXPLANATION	P.R.	DEBIT		CREDIT	

Problem VI

The following information as to earnings and deductions for the pay period ended November 15 was taken from a company's payroll records:

Employee's Name	Earnings to End of Previous Week	Gross Pay This Week	Federal Income Taxes	Medical Insurance Deducted
Rita Hawn..	$25,700	$ 800	$155.00	$ 35.50
Dolores Hopkins............................	930	800	134.00	35.50
Robert Allen..................................	89,900	1,000	193.00	42.00
Calvin Ingram..............................	18,400	740	128.00	42.00
		$3,340	$610.00	$155.00

Required:

1. Calculate the employees' FICA taxes withheld assuming a rate of 6.2% on the first $90,000 earned for Social Security and 1.45% of all wages earned for Medicare, and prepare the journal entry to accrue the payroll under the assumption that all of the employees work in the office.
2. Prepare the journal entry to record the employer's payroll taxes resulting from the payroll. Assume a state unemployment tax rate of 2% on the first $7,000 paid each employee and a federal unemployment tax rate of 0.8% on the first $7,000 paid each employee.

DATE	ACCOUNT TITLES AND EXPLANATION	P.R.	DEBIT	CREDIT

Problem VII (Appendix 9A)

The Payroll Register of Whiteman Sales for the first week of the year follows. The deductions and net pay of the first three employees have been calculated and entered.

1. Use an assumed 8% FICA tax rate (Medicare and Social Security have been combined for this problem) and complete the payroll information opposite the name of the last employee, Fred Clarke. In addition to FICA taxes, Mr. Clarke should have $111 of federal income taxes, $20 of medical insurance, and no union dues withheld from his wages, which are chargeable to office salaries. The overtime premium rate is 50%.

PAYROLL REGISTER

EMPLOYEE'S NAME	CLOCK CARD NUMBER	DAILY TIME							TOTAL HOURS	O.T. HOURS	REG. PAY RATE		REGULAR PAY		O.T. PREMIUM PAY		GROSS PAY		
		M	T	W	T	F	S	S											
Delbert Landau	12	8	8	8	7	4	0	0	35		11	00	385	00			385	00	1
Maria Garza	9	8	8	8	5	4	0	0	35		12	00	396	00			396	00	2
Ralph Webster	15	8	8	7	8	4	0	0	35		13	00	455	00			455	00	3
Fred Clarke	4	8	8	8	8	8	4	0	44	4	14	00							4
																			5

Week ending January 8, 20--

	DEDUCTIONS									PAYMENT				DISTRIBUTION					
	FICA TAXES		FEDERAL INCOME TAXES		MEDICAL INSURANCE		UNION DUES		TOTAL DEDUC-TIONS		NET PAY		CHECK NUMBER	SALES SALARIES		OFFICE SALARIES		DELIVERY WAGES	
1	30	80	65	00	20	00	10	00	125	80	259	20						385	00
2	31	68	63	00	20	00	10	00	124	68	271	32		396	00				
3	36	40	68	00	20	00	10	00	134	40	320	60		455	00				
4																			
5																			

2. Complete the Payroll Register by totaling its columns, and prepare the journal entry to record its information.

DATE	ACCOUNT TITLES AND EXPLANATION	P.R.	DEBIT	CREDIT

Whiteman Sales uses a special payroll bank account in paying its employees. Each payday, after the general journal entry recording the information of its Payroll Register is posted, a single check for the total of the employees' net pay is drawn and deposited in the payroll bank account. This transfers funds equal to the payroll total from the regular bank account to the payroll bank account. Then special payroll checks are written on the payroll bank account and given to the employees. For the January 8 payroll, four payroll checks beginning with payroll Check No. 102 were drawn and delivered to the employees. Record this information in the Payroll Register.

3. Prepare the journal entry to record the transfer of cash to the payroll bank account for the January 8 payroll.

DATE	ACCOUNT TITLES AND EXPLANATION	P.R.	DEBIT	CREDIT

4. Prepare the journal entry to record the payroll taxes levied on Whiteman Sales as a result of the payroll entered in its January 8 Payroll Register. The company has a merit rating that reduces its state employment tax rate to 1% of the first $7,000 paid each employee. (Assume the federal unemployment tax rate is 0.8%.)

DATE	ACCOUNT TITLES AND EXPLANATION	P.R.	DEBIT	CREDIT

Solutions for Chapter 9

Problem I

1. T
2. T
3. T
4. F
5. T
6. T
7. T
8. F
9. F
10. T
11. F
12. T
13. F
14. F

Problem II

1. D
2. D
3. A

Problem III

3	Contingent liability		17	Gross pay
6	Current liabilities		19	Known liabilities
7	Current portion of long-term debt		21	Long-term liabilities
1	Deferred income tax liability**		13	Merit rating
14	Employee benefits		22	Net pay
23	Employee earnings report*		24	Payroll bank account*
2	Estimated liability		20	Payroll deductions
27	Federal depository bank*		26	Payroll register*
9	FICA taxes		18	Short-term note payable
12	Form 940*		16	SUTA
25	Form 941*		10	Times interest earned
8	Form W-2*		4	Wage bracket withholding table*
5	From W-4*		11	Warranty
15	FUTA			

* *Key term discussed in Appendix 9A.*
** *Key term discussed in Appendix 9B.*

©*The McGraw-Hill Companies, Inc., 2008*

Problem IV

1. contingent
2. providing stable employment for employees
3. Social Security taxes; Medicare taxes
4. Equal
5. Form W-2 (Wage and Tax Statement)
6. (a) the amount of his or her wages; (b) the number of his or her withholding allowances
7. 941; calendar quarter
8. Payroll Register
9. Employee's Individual Earnings Record

Problem V

Jan. --	Warranty Expense ($50,000 x 0.03)	1,500.00	
	Estimated Warranty Liability		1,500.00
--	Estimated Warranty Liability	1,200.00	
	Cash		1,200.00

Problem VI

Nov. 15	Office Salaries Expense	3,340.00	
	FICA Taxes Payable		199.71
	Employees' Federal Income Taxes Payable		610.00
	Employees' Hospital Insurance Payable		155.00
	Accrued Payroll Payable		2,375.29

($800 + $800 + $100 + $740) x .062 = $151.28
$3,340 x .0145 = $48.43
$151.28 + $48.43 = $199.71

15	Payroll Taxes Expense	222.11	
	FICA Taxes Payable		199.71
	State Unemployment Taxes Payable		16.00
	Federal Unemployment Taxes Payable		6.40

$800 x 0.02 = $16
$800 x 0.008 = $6.40

Problem VII (Appendix 9A)

1.

PAYROLL REGISTER

EMPLOYEE'S NAME	CLOCK CARD NUMBER	M	T	W	T	F	S	S	TOTAL HOURS	O.T. HOURS	REG. PAY RATE		REGULAR PAY		O.T. PREMIUM PAY		GROSS PAY		
Delbert Landau	12	8	8	8	7	4	0	0	35		11	00	385	00			385	00	1
Maria Garza	9	8	8	8	5	4	0	0	35		12	00	396	00			396	00	2
Ralph Webster	15	8	8	7	8	4	0	0	35		13	00	455	00			455	00	3
Fred Clarke	4	8	8	8	8	8	4	0	44	4	14	00	560	00	84	00	644	00	4
													1,796	00	84	00	1,880	00	5

Week ending January 8, 20--

	FICA TAXES		FEDERAL INCOME TAXES		HOSPITAL INSURANCE		UNION DUES		TOTAL DEDUC-TIONS		NET PAY		CHECK NUMBER	SALES SALARIES		OFFICE SALARIES		DELIVERY WAGES	
1	30	80	65	00	20	00	10	00	125	80	259	20	102					385	00
2	31	68	63	00	20	00	10	00	124	68	271	32	103	396	00				
3	36	40	68	00	20	00	10	00	134	40	320	60	104	455	00				
4	51	52	111	00	20	00			182	52	461	48	105			644	00		
5	150	40	307	00	80	00	30	00	567	40	1,312	60		851	00	644	00	385	00

2. Jan. 8   Sales Salaries Expense 851.00
            Office Salaries Expense 644.00
            Delivery Wages Expense 385.00
                FICA Taxes Payable.. 150.40
                Employees' Federal Income Taxes Payable 307.00
                Employees' Medical Insurance Payable 80.00
                Employees' Union Dues Payable.. 30.00
                Accrued Payroll Payable 1,312.60

3. Jan. 8   Accrued Payroll Payable 1,312.60
                Cash... 1,312.60

4. Jan. 8   Payroll Taxes Expense 184.24
                FICA Taxes Payable.. 150.40
                State Unemployment Taxes Payable................................... 18.80
                Federal Unemployment Taxes Payable............................... 15.04

©The McGraw-Hill Companies, Inc., 2008

Study Guide, Chapter 9

213

CHAPTER 10
REPORTING AND ANALYZING LONG-TERM LIABILITIES

Learning Objective C1:

Explain the types and payment patterns of notes.

Notes repaid over a period of time are called *installment notes* and usually follow one of two payment patterns: (1) decreasing payments of interest plus equal amounts of principal or (2) equal total payments. Mortgage notes also are common.

Learning Objective C2 (Appendix 10A):

Explain and compute the present value of an amount(s) to be paid at a future date(s).

The basic concept of present value is that an amount of cash to be paid or received in the future is worth less than the same amount of cash to be paid or received today. Another important present value concept is that interest is compounded; meaning interest is added to the balance and used to determine interest for succeeding periods. An annuity is a series of equal payments occurring at equal time intervals. An annuity's present value can be computed using the present value table for an annuity (or a calculator).

Learning Objective C3 (Appendix 10C):

Describe the accrual of bond interest when bond payments do not align with accounting periods.

Issuers and buyers of debt record the interest accrued when issue dates or accounting periods do not coincide with debt payment dates.

Learning Objective C4 (Appendix 10D):

Describe the accounting for leases and pensions.

A lease is a rental agreement between the lessor and the lessee. When the lessor retains the risks and rewards of asset ownership (an *operating lease*), the lessee debits Rent Expense and credits Cash for its lease payments. When the lessor substantially transfers the risks and rewards of asset ownership to the lessee (a *capital lease*), the lessee capitalizes the leased asset and records a lease liability. Pension agreements can result in either pension assets or pension liabilities.

Learning Objective A1:

Compare bond financing with stock financing.

Bond financing is used to fund business activities. Advantages of bond financing versus stock include (1) no effect on owner control, (2) tax savings, and (3) increased earnings due to financial leverage. Disadvantages include (1) interest and principal payments and (2) amplification of poor performance.

Learning Objective A2:

Assess debt features and their implications.

Certain bonds are secured by the issuer's assets; other bonds, called *debentures,* are unsecured. Serial bonds mature at different points in time; term bonds mature at one time. Registered bonds have each bondholder's name recorded by the issuer; bearer bonds are payable to the holder. Convertible bonds are exchangeable for shares of the issuer's stock. Callable bonds can be retired by the issuer at a set price. Debt features alter the risk of loss for creditors.

Learning Objective A3:

Compute the debt-to-equity ratio and explain its use.

Both creditors and equity holders are concerned about the relation between the amount of liabilities and the amount of equity. A company's financing structure is at less risk when the debt-to-equity ratio is lower, as liabilities must be paid and usually with periodic interest.

Learning Objective P1:

Prepare entries to record bond issuance and bond interest expense.

When bonds are issued at par, Cash is debited and Bonds Payable is credited for the bonds' par value. At bond interest payment dates (usually semiannual), Bond Interest Expense is debited and Cash credited; the latter for an amount equal to the bond par value multiplied by the bond contract rate.

Learning Objective P2:

Compute and record amortization of bond discount.

Bonds are issued at a discount when the contract rate is less than the market rate, making the issue (selling) price less than par. When this occurs, the issuer records a credit to Bonds Payable (at par) and debits both Discount on Bonds Payable and Cash. The amount of bond interest expense assigned to each period is computed using either the straight-line or effective interest method.

Learning Objective P3:

Compute and record amortization of bond premium.

Bonds are issued at a premium when the contract rate is higher than the market rate, making the issue (selling) price greater than par. When this occurs, the issuer records a debit to Cash and credits both Premium on Bonds Payable and Bonds Payable (at par). The amount of bond interest expense assigned to each period is computed using either the straight-line or effective interest method. The Premium on Bonds Payable is allocated to reduce bond interest expense over the life of the bonds.

Learning Objective P4:

Record the retirement of bonds.

Bonds are retired at maturity with a debit to Bonds Payable and a credit to Cash at par value. The issuer can retire the bonds early by exercising a call option or purchasing them in the market. Bondholders can also retire bonds early by exercising a conversion feature on convertible bonds. The issuer recognizes a gain or loss for the difference between the amount paid and the bond carrying value.

Learning Objective P5:

Prepare entries to account for notes.

Interest is allocated to each period in a note's life by multiplying its beginning-period carrying value by its market rate at issuance. If a note is repaid with equal payments, the payment amount is computed by dividing the borrowed amount by the present value of an annuity factor (taken from a present value table) using the market rate and the number of payments.

I. Basics of Bonds

Projects that demand large amounts of money often are funded from bond issuances.

A. Bond Financing

 1. A **bond** is its issuer's written promise to pay an amount identified as the par value of the bond with interest.

   a. Most bonds require the issuer to make periodic interest payments.

   b. The **par value of a bond**, also called the *face amount* or *face value*, is paid at a specified future date known as the *maturity date*.

 2. Advantages of bonds

   a. *Bonds do not affect owner control.*

   b. *Interest on bonds is tax deductible.*

   c. *Bonds can increase return on equity.* A company that earns a higher return with borrowed funds than it pays in interest on those funds increases its return on equity. This process is called *financial leverage* or *trading on the equity.*

 3. Disadvantages of bonds

   a. *Bonds can decrease return on equity.* A company that earns a lower return with borrowed funds than it pays in interest on those funds decreases its return on equity.

   b. *Bonds require payment of both periodic interest and par value at maturity.* Equity financing, by contrast, does not require any payments because cash withdrawals (dividends) are paid at the discretion of the owner (board).

B. Bond Trading

 1. Bonds can be traded on exchanges including both the New York Stock Exchange and the American Stock Exchange.

 2. A bond *issue* consists of a large number of bonds (denominations of $1,000 or $5,000, etc.) that are sold to many different lenders.

 3. Market value (price) is expressed as a percentage of par (face) value. Examples: bonds issued at 103 ½ means that they are sold for 103.5% of their par value. Bonds issued at 95 means that they are sold for 95% of their par value.

C. Bond-Issuing Procedures

Governed by state and federal laws. Bond issuers also insure they do not violate any existing contractual agreements.

1. **Bond indenture** is the contract between the bond issuer and the bondholders; it identifies the obligations and rights of each party. A bondholder may also receive a **bond certificate** that includes specifics such as the issuer's name, the par value, the contract interest rate, and the maturity date.

2. Issuing corporation normally sells its bonds to an investment firm (the *underwriter*), which resells the bonds to the public.

3. A *trustee* (usually a bank or trust company) monitors the issuer to ensure it complies with the obligations in the indenture.

II. **Bond Issuances**

A. Issuing Bonds at Par—bonds are sold for face amount.

Entries are:

1. Issue date: debit Cash, credit Bonds Payable (face amount).

2. Interest date: debit Interest Expense, credit Cash (face times bond interest rate times interest period).

3. Maturity date: debit Bonds Payable, credit Cash (face amount).

B. Bond Discount or Premium—bonds are sold for an amount different than the face amount.

1. **Contract rate**—(also called *coupon rate, stated rate*, or *nominal rate*) annual interest rate *paid* by the issuer of bonds (applied to par value).

2. **Market rate**—annual rate borrowers are willing to pay and lenders are willing to accept for a particular bond and its risk level.

3. When contract rate and market rate are equal, bonds sell at par value; when contract rate is above market rate, bonds sell at a *premium* (above par); when the contract rate is below market rate, bonds sell at a *discount* (below par).

C. Issuing Bonds at a Discount—sell bonds for *less* than par value.

1. The **discount on bonds payable** is the difference between the par (face) value of a bond and its lower issuance price.

2. Entry to record issuance at a discount: debit Cash (issue price), debit Discount on Bonds Payable (amount of discount), credit Bonds Payable (par value).

3. Discount on Bonds Payable is a contra liability account; it is *deducted* from par value to yield the **carrying (book) value** of the bonds payable.

4. Amortizing a Bond Discount

    a. Total bond interest expense is the *sum* of the interest payments and bond discount (or can be computed by comparing total amount borrowed to total amount repaid over life).

    b. Discount must be systematically reduced (*amortized*) over the life of the bond to report periodic interest expense incurred.

    c. Requires crediting Discount on Bonds Payable when bond interest expense is recorded (payment and/or accruals) and increasing Interest Expense by the amortized amount.

    d. Amortizing the discount increases book value; at maturity, the unamortized discount equals zero and the carrying value equals par value.

5. Straight-line amortization—allocates an equal portion of the total discount to bond interest expense in each of the six-month interest periods.

D. Issuing Bonds at a Premium—sell bonds for *more* than par value.

1. The **premium on bonds payable** is the difference between the par value of a bond and its higher issuance price.

2. Entry to record issuance at a premium: debit Cash (issue price), credit Premium on Bonds Payable (amount of premium), credit Bonds Payable (par value).

3. Premium on Bonds Payable is an adjunct liability account; it is added to par value to yield the carrying (or book) value of the bonds payable.

4. Amortizing a Bond Premium

    a. Total bond interest expense incurred is the interest payments *less* the bond premium.

    b. Premiums must be systematically reduced (*amortized*) over the life of the bond to report periodic interest expense incurred.

    c. Requires debiting Premium on Bonds Payable when bond interest expense is recorded (payment and/or accruals) and decreasing Interest Expense by the amortized amount.

    d. Amortizing the premium decreases book value; at maturity, book value = face value.

5. Straight-line amortization allocates an equal portion of the total premium to bond interest expense in each of the six-month interest periods.

E. Bond Pricing

The price of a bond is the present value of the bond's future cash flows discounted at the current market rate. Present value tables can be used to compute price, which is the *combination of* the:

1. Present Value of a Discount Bond. Present value of the maturity payment is found by using single payment table, the market rate, and number of periods until maturity.

2. Present Value of a Premium Bond. Present value of the semiannual interest payments is found by using annuity table, the market rate, and number of periods until maturity.

3. Present values found in present value tables in Appendix B at the end of this book.

III. **Bond Retirement**

A. Bond Retirement at Maturity

1. Carrying value at maturity will always equal par value.

2. Entry to record bond retirement at maturity: debit Bonds Payable, credit Cash.

B. Bond Retirement Before Maturity

1. Two common approaches to retire bonds before maturity:

a. Exercise a call option—pay par value plus a call premium.

b. Purchase them on the open market.

2. Difference between the purchase price and the bonds' carrying value is recorded as a gain (or loss) on retirement of bonds.

C. Bond Retirement by Conversion

Convertible bondholders have the right to convert their bonds to stock. If converted, the carrying value of bonds is transferred to equity accounts and no gain or loss is recorded.

IV. **Long-Term Notes Payable**

Notes are issued to obtain assets, such as cash. Notes are typically transacted with a single lender, such as a bank.

A. **Installment Notes**—obligations requiring a series of periodic payments to the lender.

1. Entry to record issuance of an installment note for cash: debit Cash, credit to Notes Payable.

2. Payments include interest expense accruing to the date of the payment plus a portion of the amount borrowed (*principal*).

a. Equal total payments consist of changing amounts of interest and principal.

b. Entry to record installment payment: debit Interest Expense (issue rate times the declining carrying value of note), debit Notes Payable (for difference between the equal payment and the interest expense), credit Cash for the amount of the equal payment.

B. Mortgage Notes and Bonds

A **mortgage** is a legal agreement that helps protect a lender if a borrower fails to make required payments. A *mortgage contract* describes the mortgage terms.

1. Accounting for mortgage notes and bonds—same as accounting for unsecured notes and bonds.

2. Mortgage agreements must be disclosed in financial statements.

V. **Decision Analysis—Debt Features and the Debt-to-Equity Ratio**

Collateral Agreements—reduce the risk of loss for both bonds and notes; unsecured bonds and notes are riskier because the issuer's obligation to pay interest and principal has the same priority as all other unsecured liabilities in the event of bankruptcy.

A. Features of Bonds and Notes

1. Secured or Unsecured

a. **Secured bonds** and notes have specific assets of the issuer pledged (or *mortgaged*) as collateral.

b. Unsecured bonds and notes also called *debentures*, are backed by the issuer's general credit standing. Unsecured debt is riskier than secured debt.

2. Term or Serial

a. **Term bonds** and notes are scheduled for maturity on one specified date.

b. **Serial bonds** and notes mature at more than one date (often in series) and are usually repaid over a number of periods.

3. Registered or Bearer

a. **Registered bonds** are issued in the names and addresses of their holders. Bond payments are sent directly to registered holders.

b. **Bearer bonds**, also called *unregistered* bonds, are made payable to whoever holds them (the bearer). Many bearer bonds are also **coupon bonds**; which are interest coupons that are attached to the bonds.

4. Convertible and/or Callable

a. **Convertible bonds** and notes can be exchanged for a fixed number of shares of the issuing company's common stock.

b. **Callable bonds** and notes have an option exercisable by the issuer to retire them at a stated dollar amount before maturity.

B. Debt-to-Equity Ratio

1. Knowing the level of debt helps in assessing the risk of a company's financing structure.

2. A company financed mainly with debt is riskier than a company financed mainly with equity because liabilities must be repaid.

3. Debt-to-equity ratio measures the risk of a company's financing structure.

4. Debt-to-equity ratio is computed by dividing total liabilities by total equity.

VI.   **Present Values of Bonds and Notes (Appendix 10A)**

   A.   Present Value Concepts

      1.   Cash paid (or received) in the future has less value now than the same amount of cash paid (or received) today.

      2.   An amount borrowed equals the present value of the future payment.

      3.   *Compounded interest* means that interest during a second period is based on the total of the amount borrowed plus the interest accrued from the first period.

      4.   Present Value tables can be used to determine the present value of future cash payments of a single amount or an annuity.

   B.   Present Value Tables (Complete tables in Appendix B)

      1.   Present values can be computed using a formula or a table.

      2.   Present value of $1 table is used to compute present value of a single payment.

      3.   Present value of an annuity of $1 table is used to compute present value of a series of equal payments (annuity).

   C.   Applying a Present Value Table (Complete tables in Appendix B)

      1.   Determine the column with the interest rate.

      2.   Determine the row with the periods hence.

      3.   The column and row will intersect at the factor number.

      4.   To convert the single payment to its present value, multiply this amount by the factor.

   D.   Present Value of an Annuity (Complete tables in Appendix B)

      1.   Determine the column with the interest rate.

      2.   Determine the row with the number of periods.

      3.   The column and row will intersect at the factor number.

      4.   To convert the annuity to its present value, multiply the annuity amount by the factor.

   E.   Compounding Periods Shorter than a Year

      1.   Interest rates are generally stated as annual rates.

      2.   They can be allocated to shorter periods of time.

VII.   **Effective Interest Amortization (Appendix 10B)**

   A   Effective Interest Amortization of a Discount Bond

      1.   The straight-line method yields changes in the bonds' carrying value while the amount for bond interest expense remains constant.

      2.   The **effective interest method** allocates total bond interest expense over the bonds' life in a way that yields a constant rate of interest.

©The McGraw-Hill Companies, Inc., 2008

3. The key difference between the two methods lies in computing bond interest expense. Instead of assigning an equal amount of bond interest expense in each period, the effective interest method assigns a bond interest expense amount that increases over the life of a discount bond.

4. Both methods allocate the same amount of bond interest expense to the bonds' life, but in different patterns.

5. Except for differences in amounts, journal entries recording the expense and updating the Discount on Bonds Payable account balance are the same under both methods.

B   Effective Interest Amortization of a Premium Bond

1. As noted above, the **effective interest method** allocates total bond interest expense over the bonds' life in a way that yields a constant rate of interest.

2. Except for differences in amounts between the two methods (that is, the straight-line and effective interest methods), journal entries recording the expense and updating the Premium on Bonds Payable account are the same under both methods.

VIII. Issuing Bonds Between Interest Dates (Appendix 10C)

A. Procedure used to simplify recordkeeping:

1. Buyers pay the purchase price plus any interest accrued since the prior interest payment date.

2. This accrued interest is repaid to these buyers on the next interest date.

3. Entry to record issuance of bonds between interest dates: debit Cash, credit Interest Payable (for any interest accrued since the prior interest payment date), credit Bonds Payable.

4. Entry to record first semiannual interest payment for bonds issued between interest dates: debit Interest Payable (for amount accrued in entry above), debit Interest Expense (for interest accrued since issuance date), credit Cash.

B. Accruing Bond Interest Expense

1. Necessary when bond's interest period does not coincide with issuer's accounting period.

2. Adjusting entry is necessary to record bond interest expense accrued since the most recent interest payment and requires amortization of the premium or discount for this period.

3. Affects the subsequent interest payment date entry.

VIV. Leases and Pensions (Appendix 10D)

A. Lease Liabilities

A **lease** is a contractual agreement between a *lessor* (asset owner) and a *lessee* (asset renter or tenant) that grants the lessee the right to use the asset for a period of time in return for cash (rent) payments.

1. **Operating leases** are short-term (or cancelable) leases in which the lessor retains the risks and rewards of ownership.

   a. Lessee records lease payments as expenses.

   b. Lessor records lease payments as revenues.

2. **Capital leases** are long-term (or noncancelable) leases in which the lessor transfers substantially all risks and rewards of ownership to the lessee. The lease must meet *any one of the four* following criteria:

   a. Transfer title of leased asset to lessee.

   b. Contain a bargain purchase option.

   c. Have lease term of 75% or more of leased asset's useful life.

   d. Have present value of leased payments of 90% or more of leased asset's market value.

   Failure to meet one of the criteria results in *off-balance-sheet financing* (not recorded on the balance sheet).

   Capital leases are recorded as assets and liabilities. The asset is depreciated. At each lease payment date, the liability is amortized to record interest expense incurred.

B. Pension Liabilities

   A pension plan is a contractual agreement between an employer and its employees for the employer to provided benefits (payments) to employees after they have retired.

   1. Employer records their payment into pension plan as a debit to Pension Expense and a credit to Cash.

   2. Based on contracted benefits, pension plans can be overfunded (resulting in plan assets) or underfunded (resulting in plan liabilities).

Chapter Ten – Alternate Demonstration Problem #1
(Appendix 10B)

ABC Company issued $200,000 face value bonds on January 1, 20X6, with semiannual interest payments to be made on June 30 and December 31 at a contract rate of 10%. The bonds were scheduled to mature five years after they were issued. ABC Company uses the effective interest method of amortization.

On January 1, 20X9, three years after the bonds were issued, the company repurchased 40% of the outstanding bonds for $79,000.

Required:

<u>Part A</u>

1. Assume that the bonds were issued when the market rate of interest was 9%. Prepare a schedule showing the bond interest expense and amounts of amortization for the life of the bonds.

2. Prepare the journal entry to record the bond issuance.

3. Prepare journal entries for the first two interest payments.

4. Prepare the journal entry to recognize the partial repurchase of the bonds.

<u>Part B</u>

Redo Part A under the assumption that the market rate on the bonds when issued was 16%.

(If this alternative demonstration problem is not covered in class, see your instructor for the solution.)

Problem I

The following statements are either true or false. Place a (T) in the parentheses before each true statement and an (F) before each false statement.

1. (　) Interest expense on installment notes is calculated each period as the interest rate multiplied by the beginning-of-period principal balance.

2. (　) Bondholders do not share in either management or earnings of the issuing corporation.

3. (　) Bondholders are creditors of the issuing corporation.

4. (　) If bonds are sold at par value, the entry to record the sale has a debit to Cash and a credit to Bonds Payable.

5. (　) Investors will be willing to pay more than par (buy at a premium) for bonds when the market rate of interest is higher than the contract rate of interest.

6. (　) To determine the price of bonds, the present value of the future cash flows is calculated by discounting the amounts to be received in the future at the contract rate of interest.

7. (　) If the market rate of interest is 12%, it is 4% semiannually.

8. (　) The straight-line method of amortizing bond premium allocates an equal portion of the premium to each interest period.

9. (　) When the straight-line method is used to amortize bond premium or bond discount, interest expense as a percentage of carrying amount is the same each period the bonds are outstanding.

10. (　) Callable bonds are bonds that can be redeemed at the option of the investor.

11. (　) The debt-to-equity ratio is computed by dividing total liabilities by total equity.

12. (　) The carrying amount of a payable decreases each year by the amount of discount amortized that year.

13. (　) The process of allocating the interest on a noninterest-bearing note payable is called amortizing the discount.

14. (　) (Appendix 10A) The concept of present value is based on the idea that the right to receive $1 a year from now is worth more than $1 today.

15. (　) (Appendix 10A) Receiving $500 on June 30 and $500 on December 31 has the same present value as receiving $1,000 on December 31.

16. (　) (Appendix 10A) If a note requires quarterly payments and the borrower could obtain a 12% annual rate of interest in borrowing money, a 3% quarterly interest rate should be used to determine the present value of the note.

17. (　) (Appendix 10B) To calculate the amount of interest expense each period using the effective interest method, the beginning of-period carrying amount of the bonds must be multiplied by the market rate of interest at the time the bonds were issued.

18. (　) (Appendix 10D) In a capital lease the lessor retains substantially all the risks and rewards of ownership.

19. ( ) (Appendix 10D) Based on contracted benefits, an overfunded pension plan will result in plan assets.

20. ( ) (Appendix 10D) Operating leases are generally short-term and cancelable.

Problem II

You are given several words, phrases, or numbers to choose from in completing each of the following statements or in answering the following questions. In each case select the one that best completes the statement or answers the question and place its letter in the answer space provided.

_____1. On December 31, the interest payment date, the carrying value of Taylor Company's issued bonds is $106,000. The bonds have a par value of $100,000. On January 1, Taylor buys and retires the outstanding bonds. The market price on this date is 103.5. The entry to retire the bonds includes a:

    a. $6,000 credit to Premium on Bonds Payable.

    b. $3,500 debit to Loss on Retirement of Bonds.

    c. $3,500 credit to Gain on Retirement of Bonds.

    d. $2,500 credit to Gain on Retirement of Bonds.

    e. $100,000 credit to Cash.

_____2. Commonly used payment patterns on installment notes include:

    a. Installment payments consisting of equal amounts of interest and equal amounts of principal.

    b. Installment payments of accrued interest plus equal amounts of principal.

    c. Installment payments that are equal in total amount and consist of changing amounts of interest and principal.

    d. A and C

    e. B and C

_____3. Unsecured bonds that are supported by only the general credit standing of the issuer are called:

    a. Callable bonds

    b. Sinking fund bonds

    c. Serial bonds

    d. Coupon bonds

    e. Debentures

_____ 4. (Appendix 10A) Indigo, Inc., is offered a contract whereby it will be paid $15,000 every six months for the next five years. The first payment will be received six months from today. What will the company be willing to pay for this contract if it expects a 16% annual return on the investment? [Use the appropriate present value table in the Appendix B.]

    a. $ 10,209.00

    b. $ 6,948.00

    c. $100,651.50

    d. $ 59,890.50

    e. Cannot be determined from information provided.

_____ 5. (Appendix 10A) On June 30,20X1, the DEF Corporation sold bonds with a face value of $100,000. The contract rate of bond interest was 9% with interest payments on December 31 and June 30. The bonds mature in 10 years. When the bonds were sold, the market rate of bond interest was 12%. How much money did the DEF Corporation receive when it sold the bonds? (Use the present value tables in Appendix B and round amounts to the nearest whole dollar.)

    a. $119,252

    b. $110,042

    c. $100,000

    d. $ 82,795

    e. $ 83,052

_____ 6. (Appendix 10B) How is the interest expense for each period calculated when the effective interest method is used to amortize bond discount?

    a. The par value of the bonds is multiplied by the contract rate of bond interest.

    b. The par value of the bonds is multiplied by the market rate of bond interest which applied to the bonds at the time the bonds were issued.

    c. The beginning balance of the bond liability is multiplied by the market rate of bond interest which applied to the bonds at the time the bonds were issued.

    d. The beginning balance of the bond liability is multiplied by the contract rate of bond interest.

    e. The total amount of discount at the time of issue is divided by the number of periods to maturity and added to the cash payment of interest.

_____ 7. (Appendix 10B) On June 30, 20X8, the DEF Corporation sold bonds with a face value of $100,000. The contract rate of bond interest was 9% with interest payments on December 31 and June 30. The bonds mature in 10 years. When the bonds were sold, the market rate of bond interest was 12% and they were issued for $82,795. What is the entry to record the payment of interest on December 31, 20X8? DEF uses the effective interest method of amortizing bond discount or premium.

a. Interest Expense... 4,500.00
   Cash...   4,500.00
b. Interest Expense... 4,968.00
   Cash...   4,500.00
   Discount on Bonds Payable.............................   468.00
c. Interest Expense... 6,000.00
   Cash...   6,000.00
d. Interest Expense... 4,500.00
   Premium on Bonds Payable............................... 1,500.00
   Cash...   6,000.00
e. Interest Expense... 4,500.00
   Cash...   4,230.00
   Discount on Bonds Payable.............................   270.00

Problem III

Many of the important ideas and concepts discussed in Chapter 10 are reflected in the following list of key terms. Test your understanding of these terms by matching the appropriate definitions with the terms. Record the number identifying the most appropriate definition in the blank space next to each term.

_____ Annuity
_____ Bearer bonds
_____ Bond
_____ Bond certificate
_____ Bond indenture
_____ Callable bonds
_____ Capital leases**
_____ Carrying value of bonds
_____ Contract rate
_____ Convertible bonds
_____ Coupon bonds
_____ Debt-to-equity ratio
_____ Discount on bonds payable
_____ Effective interest method*
_____ Installment note

_____ Lease**
_____ Market rate
_____ Mortgage
_____ Off-balance-sheet financing**
_____ Operating leases**
_____ Par value of a bond
_____ Pension plan**
_____ Premium on bonds payable
_____ Registered bonds
_____ Secured bonds
_____ Serial bonds
_____ Sinking fund bonds
_____ Straight-line method
_____ Term bonds
_____ Unsecured bonds

 * Key term discussed in Appendix 10B.
** Key term discussed in Appendix 10D.

1. Contract between the bond issuer and the bondholders; identifies the parties' rights and obligations.

2. Difference between a bond's par value and its lower issue price or carrying value; occurs when the contract rate is less than the market rate.

3. Interest rate borrowers are willing to pay and lenders are willing to accept for a specific debt agreement at its risk level.

4. Allocates interest expense over the bond life to yield a constant rate of interest; interest expense for a period is found by multiplying the balance of the liability at the beginning of the period by the bond market rate at issuance; also called *interest method*.

5. Bonds that bondholders can exchanged for a set number of the issuer's shares.

6. Bonds made payable to whoever holds them (the *bearer*); also called *unregistered bonds*.

7. Net amount at which bonds are reported on the balance sheet; equals the par value of the bonds less any unamortized discount or plus any unamortized premium; also called *carrying amount*.

8. Legal agreement that protects a lender by giving the lender the right to be paid from the cash proceeds from the sale of the borrower's assets identified in the mortgage.

9. Difference between bond's par value and its higher issue price or carrying value; occurs when the contract rate is higher than the market rate.

10. Bonds that require the issuer to make deposits to a separate account; bondholders are repaid at maturity from that account.

11. Bonds consisting of separate amounts that mature at different dates.

12. Bonds with interest coupons attached to their certificates; bondholders detach coupons when they mature and present them to a bank or broker for collection.

13. Bonds that give the issuer an option to retire them at a stated amount prior to maturity.

14. Interest rate specified in a bond indenture; multiplied by the bonds' par value to determine the interest paid each period; also called *coupon rate*, *stated rate*, or *nominal rate*.

15. Amount the bond issuer agrees to pay at maturity and the amount on which interest payments are based; also called *face amount* or *face value*.

16. Series of equal payments at equal intervals.

17. Measures the risk of a company's financing structure.

18. Method allocating an equal amount of interest expense to each period in the life of bonds.

19. Liability requiring a series of periodic payments to the lender.

20. Bonds owned by investors whose names and addresses are recorded by the issuer; interest payments are made to the registered owners.

21. Written promise to pay the bond's par (or face) value and interest at a stated contract rate; often issued in denominations of $1,000.

22. Bonds backed only by the issuer's credit standing; almost always riskier than secured bonds; also called *debentures*.

23. Bonds scheduled for payment (mature) at a single specified date.

24. Bonds that have specific assets of the issuer pledged as collateral.

25. Document containing bond specifics such as the issuer's name, bond par value, contract interest rate, and maturity date.

26. Contractual agreement between *lessor* and *lessee* that grants a lessee the right to use an asset for a period of time in return for cash payments.

27. Short-term (or cancelable) leases in which lessor retains risks and rewards of ownership.

28. Acquisition of assets by agreeing to liabilities not reported on the balance sheet.

29. Contractual agreement between an employer and its employees to provide benefits to employees after they retire.

30. Long-term leases in which the lessor transfers substantially all risk and rewards of ownership to the lessee.

Problem IV

Complete the following by filling in the blanks.

1. Two important rights given to the owner of a bond are:

    a. _____
    _____, and

    b. _____
    _____.

2. Often a corporation cannot obtain debt financing without providing security to the creditors by the issuance of a _____.

3. The rate of interest a corporation agrees to pay on a bond issue is called the _____ rate. This rate is applied to the _____ value of the bonds to determine the amount of interest that must be paid.

4. If a corporation offers to sell a bond issue when the contract rate of interest is below the market rate, the bonds will sell at a _____ and if it offers to sell bonds when the contract rate is above the market rate, the bonds will sell at a _____.

5. A $1,000 bond with a contract rate of bond interest of 9% would provide semiannual interest payments of $_____.

6. Bonds that may be redeemed at the issuing company's option are known as _____ bonds.

7. (Appendix 10C) When a corporation sells bonds between interest dates, it collects accrued interest from the purchasers. On the interest payment date, the accrued interest is _____ to the purchaser.

8. The accounting procedure for allocating a discount to each period in the life of a bond is called
_____.

9. The terms of installment notes payable require one of two payment plans:

    a. _____
    _____, or

    b. _____
    _____.

10. When the issuing company retires bonds, it recognizes a gain or loss for the difference between the
_____ and the retirement price.

11. (Appendix 10D) Capital leases must meet one of the following four criteria:
   a. _____
   b. _____
   c. _____
   d _____

Problem V

(Appendix 10C) On December 15, 20X8, Candida Corporation deposited a bond indenture with the trustee of its bondholders authorizing it to issue $1,000,000 of 10.2%, 20-year bonds dated January 1, 20X9, and upon which interest is payable each June 30 and December 31. The bonds were issued at par plus accrued interest on February 1, 20X9.

1. Prepare the 20X9 journal entries for this bond issue.

DATE	ACCOUNT TITLES AND EXPLANATION	P.R.	DEBIT			CREDIT		
20X9 Feb 1								
	Sold $1,000,000 of 10.2%, 20-year bonds at par plus							
	one month's accrued interest.							
June 30								
	Paid the semiannual interest on the bonds.							
Dec. 31								
	Paid the semiannual interest on the bonds.							

2. Post to the T-account below the portions of the above entries that affect bond interest expense and then complete the statement that follows.

```
               Bond Interest Expense
_____|_____
                               |
                               |
                               |
                               |
                               |
```

Candida Corporation's 20X9 income statement should show $_____ of bond interest expense and its 20X10 income statement should show $_____ of bond interest expense.

Problem VI

On January 1, 20X8, a day on which the market rate of interest for Bullock Company's bonds was 10%, Bullock Company sold bonds having a $100,000 par value, a five-year life, and on which interest was to be paid semiannually at a 9% annual rate. The bonds were issued for $ 96,138.

1. The buyer of these bonds received two rights:
    (a) the right to receive $_____ in interest at the end of each six-month interest period throughout the five-year life of the bond issue, and
    (b) the right to receive $_____ at the end of the bond issue's life.

2. Bullock Corporation's journal entry to record the sale of the bonds would be as follows:

DATE	ACCOUNT TITLES AND EXPLANATION	P.R.	DEBIT	CREDIT
20X8 Jan. 1				
	Sold bonds at a discount			

3. At the end of the first semiannual interest period Bullock Corporation calculated the number of dollars of interest to be paid to bondholders as follows:
    $ _____ x _____ % = $ _____

4. (Appendix 10B) Using the effective interest method, the company then calculated the amount of interest expense to be recorded at the end of the first semiannual interest period as follows:
    $ _____ x _____ % = $ _____

5. (Appendix 10B) Next, the company determined the amount of discount to be amortized with this calculation:
    $ _____ - $ _____ = $ _____

6. (Appendix 10B) After making these calculations, Bullock Corporation would record the interest paid its bondholders and the discount amortized with the following journal entry:

DATE	ACCOUNT TITLES AND EXPLANATION	P.R.	DEBIT	CREDIT
20X8 June 30				
	Paid the semiannual interest on the bonds and			
	amortized a portion of the discount			

7. (Appendix 10A) To prove that the issue price equaled the present value of the rights received, the buyer of the bonds should discount the rights at the _____ % (semiannual) market rate for bond interest prevailing on the day of the purchase.

8. (Appendix 10A) The calculations for determining the present value of the bond buyer's two rights, using the tables in Appendix B in the text are:

Present value of $100,000 to be received _____ periods hence,
discounted at _____% per period ($100,000 x _____) $ _____
Present value of $ _____ to be received periodically
for _____ periods, discounted at _____ %
($_____ x _____) ....
Price to pay for the bonds.. $ _____

Problem VII

On December 31, 20X7, HX Company borrowed $60,000 by signing a 14% installment note that is to be repaid with six annual payments, the first of which is due on December 31, 20X8.

a. Prepare the journal entry to record the borrowing of the money.

DATE	ACCOUNT TITLES AND EXPLANATION	P.R.	DEBIT	CREDIT

b. Assume that the payments are to consist of accrued interest plus equal amounts of principal. Prepare the journal entries to record the first and second installment payments.

DATE	ACCOUNT TITLES AND EXPLANATION	P.R.	DEBIT	CREDIT

c. Contrary to the assumption in (b) above, assume now that the note requires each installment payment to be $15,464. Prepare journal entries to record the first and second installment payments. (Round all amounts to the nearest whole dollar.)

DATE	ACCOUNT TITLES AND EXPLANATION	P.R.	DEBIT	CREDIT

Problem VIII (Appendix 10A)

1. Use the present value tables in the text (Appendix B) to calculate the following present values:

    a. $1 to be received 9 years hence, at 10%. $ _____

    b. $2,000 to be received 6 years hence, at 8%. $ _____

    c. $1 to be received at the end of each year for 10 years, at 4%. _____

    d. $1,000 to be received at the end of each year for 7 years, at 6%. _____

2. When the rate of interest on an investment is 8% compounded annually, the present value of $1,000 to be received three years hence is the amount of money that must be invested today that together with the 8% compound interest earned on the investment will equal $ _____ at end of three years. The amount is $1,000 x _____ = $ _____.

3. If the interest rate is changed from 8% to 5%, will the present value of $1 to be received in one year be increased or decreased? _____

Solutions for Chapter 10

Problem I

1. T
2. T
3. T
4. T
5. F
6. F
7. F
8. T
9. F
10. F
11. T
12. F
13. T
14. F
15. F
16. T
17. T
18. F
19. T
20. T

Problem II

1. D
2. E
3. E
4. C
5. D
6. C
7. B

Problem III

16	Annuity	3	Market rate
6	Bearer bonds	8	Mortgage
21	Bond	28	Off-balance-sheet financing**
25	Bond certificate	27	Operating leases**
1	Bond indenture	15	Par value of a bond
13	Callable bonds	29	Pension plan**
30	Capital leases**	17	Pledged assets to secured liabilities
7	Carrying value of bonds	9	Premium on bonds payable
14	Contract rate	20	Registered bonds
5	Convertible bonds	24	Secured bonds
12	Coupon bonds	11	Serial bonds
17	Debt-to-equity ratio	10	Sinking fund bonds
2	Discount on bonds payable	18	Straight-line method
4	Effective interest method*	23	Term bonds
19	Installment note	22	Unsecured bonds
26	Lease**		

* *Key term discussed in Appendix 10B.*
** *Key term discussed in Appendix 10D.*

Problem IV

1. a. the right to receive periodic interest payments, and
   b. the right to receive the face amount of the bond when it matures
2. mortgage
3. contract; par
4. discount; premium
5. $45
6. callable
7. refunded
8. amortizing the bond discount
9. a. payments of accrued interest plus equal amounts of principal, or
   b. payments that are equal in total amount, consisting of changing amounts of interest and principal
10. carrying value of the bonds
11. a. Transfer title of leased asset to lessee.
    b. Contain a bargain purchase option.
    c. Have lease term of 75% or more of leased asset's useful life.
    d. Have present value of leased payments of 90% or more of leased asset's market value

Problem V

1.

Feb. 1	Cash..	1,008,500.00		
	Bond Interest Payable		8,500.00	
	Bonds Payable.................................		1,000,000.00	
	($1,000,000 x 0.102)/12 = $8,500			
June 30	Bond Interest Payable	8,500.00		
	Bond Interest Expense	42,500.00		
	Cash..		51,000.00	
	($1,000,000 x 0.102)/2 = $51,000			
Dec. 31	Bond Interest Expense.............................	51,000.00		
	Cash..		51,000.00	

2.

Bond Interest Expense	
June 30	42,500.00
Dec. 31	51,000.00

$93,500; $102,000

Problem VI

1. (a) $4,500, (b) $100,000
2.

Jan. 1	Cash..	96,138.00		
	Discount on Bonds Payable	3,862.00		
	Bonds Payable.................................		100,000.00	

3. $100,000 x 0.045 = $4,500
4. $96,138 x 0.05 = $4,807 (rounded to the nearest whole dollar)
5. $4,807 - $4,500 = $307
6.

June 30	Bond Interest Expense.............................	4,807.00		
	Discount on Bonds Payable...................		307.00	
	Cash..		4,500.00	

7. 5
8.

Present value of $100,000 to be received 10 periods hence, discounted at 5% per period ($100,000 x 0.6139)..	$61,390
Present value of $4,500 to be received periodically for 10 periods, discounted at 5% ($4,500 x 7.7217)..	34,748
Price to pay for the bonds (rounded to the nearest whole dollar)	$96,138

Problem VII

a. 20X7
   Dec. 31   Cash 60,000.00
            Notes Payable 60,000.00

b. 20X8
   Dec. 31   Interest Expense ($60,000 x 0.14) 8,400.00
            Notes Payable 10,000.00
               Cash 18,400.00

   20X9
   Dec. 31   Interest Expense ($60,000 - $10,000) x 0.14) 7,000.00
            Notes Payable 10,000.00
               Cash 17,000.00

c. 20X8
   Dec. 31   Interest Expense ($60,000 x 0.14) 8,400.00
            Notes Payable 7,064.00
               Cash 15,464.00

   20X9
   Dec. 31   Interest Expense ($60,000 - $7,064) x 0.14 .... 7,411.00
            Notes Payable 8,053.00
               Cash 15,464.00

Problem VIII

1.   a. $0.4241
       b. $2,000 x 0.6302 = $1,260.40
       c. $8.1109
       d. $1,000 x 5.5824 = $5,582.40
2. $1,000, $1,000 x 0.7938 = $793.80
3.   increased

CHAPTER 11
REPORTING AND ANALYZING EQUITY

Learning Objective C1:

Identify characteristics of corporations and their organization.

Corporations are legal entities whose stockholders are not liable for its debts. Stock is easily transferred, and the life of a corporation does not end with the incapacity of a stockholder. A corporation acts through its agents, who are its officers and managers. Corporations are regulated and subject to income taxes.

Learning Objective C2:

Describe the components of stockholders' equity.

Authorized stock is the stock that a corporation's charter authorizes it to sell. Issued stock is the portion of authorized shares sold. Par value stock is a value per share assigned by the charter. No-par value stock is stock *not* assigned a value per share by the charter. Stated value stock is no-par stock to which the directors assign a value per share. Stockholders' equity is made up of (1) contributed capital and (2) retained earnings. Paid-in capital consists of funds raised by stock issuances. Retained earnings consists of cumulative net income (losses) not distributed.

Learning Objective C3:

Explain characteristics of common and preferred stock.

Preferred stock has a priority (or senior status) relative to common stock in one or more areas, usually (1) dividends and (2) assets in case of liquidation. Preferred stock usually does not carry voting rights and can be convertible or callable. Convertibility permits the holder to convert preferred to common. Callability permits the issuer to buy back preferred stock under specified conditions.

Learning Objective C4:

Explain the items reported in retained earnings.

Many companies face statutory and contractual restrictions on retained earnings. Corporations can voluntarily appropriate retained earnings to inform others about their disposition. Prior period adjustments are corrections of errors in prior financial statements.

Learning Objective A1:

Compute earnings per share and describe its use.

A company with a simple capital structure computes basic EPS by dividing net income less any preferred dividends by the weighted-average number of outstanding common shares. A company with a complex capital structure must usually report both basic and diluted EPS.

Learning Objective A2:

Compute price-earnings ratio and describe its use in analysis.

A common stock's price-earnings (PE) ratio is computed by dividing the stock's market value (price) per share by its EPS. A stock's PE is based on expectations that can prove to be better or worse than eventual performance.

Learning Objective A3:

Compute dividend yield and explain its use in analysis.

Dividend yield is the ratio of a stock's annual cash dividends per share to its market value (price) per share. Dividend yield can be compared with the yield of other companies to determine whether the stock is expected to be an income or growth stock.

Learning Objective A4:

Compute book value and explain its use in analysis.

Book value per common share is equity applicable to common shares divided by the number of outstanding common shares. Book value per preferred share is equity applicable to preferred shares divided by the number of outstanding preferred shares.

Learning Objective P1:

Record the issuance of corporate stock.

When stock is issued, its par or stated value is credited to the stock account and any excess is credited to a separate contributed capital account. If a stock has neither par nor stated value, the entire proceeds are credited to the stock account. Stockholders must contribute assets equal to minimum legal capital or be potentially liable for the deficiency.

Learning Objective P2:

Record transactions involving cash dividends.

Preferred stockholders usually hold the right to dividend distributions before common stockholders. When preferred stock is cumulative and in arrears, the amount in arrears must be distributed to preferred before any dividends are distributed to common.

Financial Accounting, 4e

Learning Objective P3:

Account for stock dividends and stock splits.

Neither a stock dividend nor a stock split alters the value of the company. However, the value of each share is less due to the distribution of additional shares. The distribution of additional shares is according to individual stockholders' ownership percent. Small stock dividends (<=25%) are recorded by capitalizing retained earnings equal to the market value of distributed shares. Large stock dividends (>25%) are recorded by capitalizing retained earnings equal to the par or stated value of distributed shares. Stock splits do not yield journal entries but do yield changes in the description of stock.

Learning Objective P4:

Distribute dividends between common stock and preferred stock.

Cash dividends involve three events. On the date of declaration, the directors bind the company to pay the dividend. A dividend declaration reduces retained earnings and creates a current liability. On the date of record, recipients of the dividend are identified. On the date of payment, cash is paid to stockholders and the current liability is removed.

Learning Objective P5:

Record purchases and sales of treasury stock and the retirement of stock.

When a corporation purchases its own previously issued stock, it debits the cost of these shares to Treasury Stock. Treasury stock is subtracted from equity in the balance sheet. If treasury stock is reissued, any proceeds in excess of cost are credited to Paid-in Capital, Treasury Stock. If the proceeds are less than cost, they are debited to Paid-in Capital, Treasury Stock to the extent a credit balance exists. Any remaining amount is debited to Retained Earnings. When stock is retired, all accounts related to the stock are removed.

I.   **Corporate Form of Organization**—An entity created by law that is separate from its owners. Owners are called *stockholders*. A *publicly held* corporation offers its stock for public sale (organized stock market) whereas a *privately held* corporation does not.

A. Characteristics of **Corporations**

Advantages of Corporate Characteristics:

1. **Separate legal entity**—a corporation, through its agents (officers and managers), conducts business affairs with the same rights, duties, and responsibilities of a person.

2. **Limited liability of stockholders**—generally limited to investment. Stockholders are not liable for corporate acts or corporate debt.

3. **Transferable ownership rights**—through stock sale has no effect on the corporation.

4. **Continuous life**—perpetual life as long as it continues to be successful.

5. **Lack of mutual agency for stockholders**—stockholders do not have the power to bind the corporation to contracts.

6. **Ease of capital accumulation**—enables a corporation to accumulate large amounts of capital from the combined investments of many stockholders.

Disadvantages of Corporate Characteristics:

7. **Governmental regulation**—must meet requirements of a state's incorporation laws.

8. **Corporate taxation**—corporate income is taxed; and when income is distributed to shareholders as dividends, it is taxed a second time as personal income (*double taxation*).

B. Corporate Organization and Management

1. **Incorporation**—a charter application must be filed with the state. Upon payment of fees and issuance of the charter, the corporation is formed.

2. **Organizational Expenses** are the costs to organize a corporation and include legal fees, promoters' fees, and amounts paid to obtain a charter; these costs are expensed as incurred because it is difficult to determine the amount and timing of future benefits.

3. Management of a Corporation

a. Stockholders have ultimate control through vote to elect board of directors.

b. Board of directors has final managing authority, but it usually limits its actions to establishing broad policy.

c. Day-to-day direction of corporate business is delegated to executive officers appointed by the board.

    C. Stockholders of Corporations

        1. Rights of stockholders

Specific rights are granted by the charter and *general* rights by state laws. Common stockholders rights include right to:

            a. Vote at stockholders' meeting.

            b. Sell or otherwise dispose of their stock.

            c. Purchase their proportional share of any common stock later issued; this **preemptive right** protects stockholders' proportionate interest in the corporation.

            d. Share with other common stockholders in any dividends.

            e. Share equally in any assets remaining after creditors are paid when, and if the corporation is liquidated.

            f. Receive timely financial reports.

        2. Stock Certificates and Transfer—a stock certificate is sometimes received as proof of share ownership.

        3. Registrar and Transfer Agents—if stock is traded on a major exchange, the corporation must have:

            a. *Registrar* who keeps stockholder records and prepares official lists of stockholders for stockholders' meetings and dividend payments.

            b. *Transfer agent* who assists purchases and sales of shares by receiving and issuing certificates as necessary.

    D. Basics of Capital Stock

Capital stock refers to any shares issued to obtain capital (owner financing).

        1. **Authorized stock**—the total amount of stock that charter authorizes for sale.

            a. *Outstanding stock* refers to issued stock held by stockholders.

            b. No formal journal entry is required for stock authorization; the number of shares authorized is disclosed in the financial statements.

        2. Selling (Issuing) Stock—can be sold directly or indirectly to stockholders

            a. To sell *directly*, the corporation advertises its stock issuance to potential buyers.

            b. To sell *indirectly*, a corporation pays a brokerage house (investment banker) to issue its stock.

            c. A brokerage house may *underwrite* issuance (buy the stock from the corporation and take all gains or losses from its resale).

3. Market Value of Stock—**market value per share** is the price at which a stock is bought or sold.

   a. Influenced by expected future earnings, dividends, growth, and other company and economic events.

   b. Current market value of previously issued shares does not impact that corporation's stockholders' equity accounts.

4. Classes of Stock

   a. Common—stock is called **common stock** when all classes have the same rights and privileges.

   b. Additional classes—corporation is sometimes authorized to issue more than one class of stock.

5. **Par Value Stock**—assigned a value per share by the corporation in its charter. No minimum legal capital.

   a. Printed on the stock certificate.

   b. Establishes the **minimum legal capital** which is the least amount that the buyers of stock must contribute to the corporation or be subject to paying at a future date. Creditor's claims are limited to the corporation's assets and any minimum legal capital.

6. **No-Par Value Stock**—*not* assigned a value per share by the corporate charter.

7. **Stated Value Stock**—no-par stock that is assigned a "stated" value per share by the directors; becomes the minimum legal capital per share.

8. Stockholders' Equity—has two parts

   a. **Paid-in** (or contributed) **capital**—the total amount of cash and other assets received by the corporation from its stockholders in exchange for stock.

   b. **Retained earnings**—the cumulative net income (and loss) retained by a corporation.

II.   **Common Stock**—Issuance of stock affects only paid-in capital accounts, not retained earnings accounts.

   Note: When the corporation issues par value stock, it can only credit the stock account for the par value of shares issued.

   A. Issuing Par Value Stock

   1. Entry to record issuance at par for cash—debit Cash, credit Common Stock (both for the amount received which is the total *par value* of the shares issued).

2. Issuing Par Value Stock at a Premium

   a. A **premium on stock** is an amount paid in excess of par by the purchasers of newly issued stock.

   b. Entry to record issuance of par value stock at a premium: debit Cash (for amount received or issue price), credit Common Stock (for par value), credit Paid-in capital in Excess of Par Value, Common Stock (for the amount of the premium).

3. Issuing Par Value Stock at a Discount

   a. A **discount on stock** occurs when stock corporation sells its stock for less than its par (or stated) value.

   b. Entry to record issuance of par value stock at a discount: debit Cash (for amount received or issue price), debit Discount on Common Stock, a contra to the common stock account (for the amount of the discount), credit Common Stock (for par value).

   c. Issuance of par value stock at a discount is prohibited in most states since investment is below the minimum legal capital. When allowed, the purchasers usually become contingently liable to the corporation's creditors for the amount of the discount.

B. Issuing No-Par Value Stock

   1. When no-par stock is issued and is not assigned a stated value, the entire amount received becomes legal capital and is recorded as Common Stock.

   2. Entry to record issuance of no-par value stock: debit Cash, credit Common Stock (for the entire proceeds).

C. Issuing Stated Value Stock

   1. Stated value becomes legal capital and is credited to a stated value stock account. If stock is issued at an amount in excess of stated value, this excess is credited to Paid-in Capital in Excess of Stated Value, Common Stock.

   2. Entry to record issuance of no-par value stock: debit Cash, credit Common Stock, credit Contributed Capital in Excess of Stated Value, Common Stock (for the excess).

  D. Issuing Stock for Noncash Assets

  1. Issuing par value stock for other assets

Entry to record: debit the accounts relating to the asset(s) received (at market value(s) as of the date of the transaction), credit Common Stock, credit Paid-in Capital in Excess of Par Value, Common Stock (for the amount of the premium, if any).

  2. Issuing par value stock for organizational expenses

Entry to record: debit Organization Expenses, credit Common Stock , credit Paid-in Capital in Excess of Par Value, Common Stock (for the amount of the premium, if any).

III. Dividends

  A. Cash Dividends

Many corporations pay cash dividends to their stockholders at regular dates. Cash dividends reduce, in equal amounts, both cash and the retained earnings component of stockholders' equity.

  1. Accounting for Cash Dividends

Generally a cash dividend requires:

  a. Retained earnings (requirement of many states).

  b. Sufficient cash.

  c. Decision by the board of directors.

  2. Dividend dates

  a. **Date of Declaration**—date the directors vote to declare and pay a dividend (legal liability created). Journal entry required.

  b. **Date of Record**—date specified for identifying stockholders (owners on this date) who will receive the dividend. No journal entry required.

  c. **Date of Payment**—date stockholders receive payment. Journal entry required.

  3. Cash Dividend Entries

  a. Entry at declaration date: debit Retained Earnings, credit Dividends Payable.

  b. Entry at distribution date: debit Dividends Payable, credit Cash

  4. Deficits and Cash Dividends

A corporation with a debit (abnormal) balance in its Retained Earnings account has a **retained earnings deficit**.

  a. Arises when cumulative losses and/or dividends are greater than total earnings from current and prior years; reported as a deduction on the balance sheet.

      b. Most states prohibit a corporation with a deficit from paying cash dividends.

      c. Some states allow a **liquidating cash dividend** where capital contributed by stockholders is returned to the investors.

B. Stock Dividends

A **stock dividend** is a distribution of additional shares of the corporation's own stock to its stockholders without receipt of any payment in return.

  1. Reasons for Stock Dividends

      a. Keep the market price of stock affordable.

      b. Provide evidence of management's confidence that the company is doing well.

  2. Accounting for Stock Dividends—A stock dividend affects the components of equity by transferring part of retained earnings to contributed capital accounts.

      a. A **small stock dividend** is a distribution of 25% or less of the previously outstanding shares.

          i. The market value of the shares to be distributed is capitalized.

          ii. Entry to record a small stock dividend upon declaration: debit Retained Earnings (for the current market value of the stock to be distributed), credit Common Stock Dividend Distributable (for the par value of the stock to be distributed), credit Paid-in Capital in Excess of Par Value, Common Stock (for the excess).

          iii. Entry to record a small stock dividend at date of payment: debit Common Stock Dividend Distributable, credit Common Stock.

      b. A **large stock dividend** is a distribution of more than 25% of the shares outstanding before the dividend.

          i. Only the legally required minimum amount (par or stated value of shares) must be capitalized.

          ii. Entry to record a large stock dividend upon declaration: debit Retained Earnings, credit Common Stock Dividend Distributable (for the par value of the stock to be distributed).

          iii. Entry to record a large stock dividend at date of payment: debit Common Stock Dividend Distributable, credit Common Stock.

C. Stock Splits

A **stock split** is the distribution of additional shares of stock to stockholders according to their percent ownership. The corporation "calls in" the outstanding shares of stock and issues more than one share in exchange for each old share. A stock split reduces the par or stated value per share.

1. No journal entry is made - only a memorandum entry is required.

2. Total par value of outstanding shares does not change; retained earnings is not capitalized.

IV. **Preferred Stock**—Has special rights that give it priority over common stock in one or more areas such as preference for receiving dividends and for the distribution of assets if the corporation is liquidated. Usually does not have right to vote.

A. Issuance of Preferred Stock

Usually has a par value; can be sold at a price different from par.

1. Separate capital accounts are used to record preferred stock.

2. Preferred Stock account is used to record the par value of shares issued; Paid-in Capital in Excess of Par Value, Preferred Stock is used to record any value received above the par value.

3. Entry to record issuance of preferred stock: debit Cash, credit Preferred Stock account (for the par value of shares issued), credit Paid-in Capital in Excess of Par Value, Preferred Stock (for the value received above the par value).

B. Dividend Preference of Preferred Stock

Preferred stockholders are allocated their dividends before any dividends are allocated to common stockholders.

1. Cumulative or Noncumulative Dividend

a. **Cumulative preferred stock** has a right to be paid both current and all prior periods' unpaid dividends before any dividend is paid to common stockholders. Unpaid dividends are referred to as **dividends in arrears**.

b. **Noncumulative preferred stock** confers no right to prior periods' unpaid dividends if they were not declared in those prior periods.

c. *Full-disclosure principle* requires that the amount of preferred dividends in arrears be reported as of the balance sheet date, normally in a note to the financial statements.

      2. Participating or Nonparticipating Dividend

        a. **Nonparticipating preferred stock**—dividends are limited each year to a maximum amount determined by applying either the stated percentage or the stated specific dollar amount per share to the par value.

        b. **Participating preferred stock**—allows its owners the right to share with common stockholders in any dividends paid in excess of the stated percentage or dollar amount.

  C. Convertible Preferred Stock

      1. **Convertible preferred stock** gives holders the option of exchanging their preferred shares into common shares at a specified rate.

      2. If a company's common stock increases in value, the convertible preferred stockholders can share in this success by converting their stock into more valuable common stock.

  D. Callable Preferred Stock

      1. **Callable preferred stock** gives the issuing corporation the right to purchase (retire) this stock from its holders at specified future prices and dates.

      2. Amount paid to call and retire a preferred share is its **call price**, or *redemption value*, and is set when the stock is issued.

      3. Any dividends in arrears must also be paid when stock is called.

  E. Reasons for Issuing Preferred Stock

      1. Raise capital without sacrificing control of the corporation.

      2. Boost the return earned by common stockholders; called **financial leverage** or *trading on equity*.

V. **Treasury Stock**—A corporation acquires its own shares for several reasons such as to acquire another company, to avoid a hostile takeover, or to use for employee compensation. A corporation's treasury stock does not receive any cash or stock dividends, nor do they allow the corporation voting rights.

  A. Purchasing Treasury Stock—reduces the corporation's assets and stockholders' equity by equal amounts.

      1. Debit Treasury Stock (contra equity) and credit Cash for full cost (reduces total assets and total equity).

      2. Treasury Stock is a contra equity account; the equity reduction is reported by deducting the cost of treasury stock in the equity section of the balance sheet.

      3. The resulting restriction on retained earnings must be disclosed.

B. Reissuing Treasury Stock

1. Entry to record sale of treasury stock at cost: debit Cash, credit Treasury Stock, Common.

2. Entry to record sale of treasury stock above cost: debit Cash, credit Treasury Stock, Common, credit Paid-in Capital, Treasury Stock (for the amount received in excess of cost).

3. When sold below cost, entry depends on whether the Paid-in Capital, Treasury Stock account has a balance.

    i. If the Paid-in Capital, Treasury Stock account has no balance, the excess of cost over sales price is debited to Retained Earnings.

    ii. If the Paid-in Capital, Treasury Stock account has a balance, then it is debited for the excess of the cost over the sales price, not to exceed the balance in the account.

C. Retiring Stock—Retiring stock reduces the number of shares issued and results in a reduction in assets and equity equal to the amount paid for the retired stock.

1. When stock is purchased for retirement, all paid-in capital amounts that relate to the retired shares are removed from the accounts.

2. Any excess of original issuance price over cost from the transaction should be credited to Paid-in Capital from Retirement of Stock.

3. Any excess of cost over original issuance price from the transaction should be debited to Retained Earnings.

VI. **Reporting of Equity**

A. **Statement of Retained Earnings** – generally consist of a company's cumulative net income less any net losses and dividends declared since its inception.

1. Restricted and Appropriations

    a. **Restricted retained earnings**—Amount of retained earnings that are not available for dividends and refers to both statutory and contractual restrictions.

    b. **Appropriated retained earnings**—amount that the corporation *voluntarily restricts* from retained earnings which are available for dividends.

2. **Prior Period Adjustments - c**orrections of material errors made in prior periods.

    a. Include arithmetic mistakes, using unacceptable accounting principles, and ignoring relevant facts.

    b. Reported in *statement of retained earnings* as corrections to the beginning retained earnings balance.

      3. **Changes in Accounting Estimates** - Adjustments to previously made assumptions.

         a. No adjustment is made for prior periods.

         b. Revised estimate is applied in calculating the appropriate revenue or expense of the current and future periods.

   B. Statement of Stockholders' Equity – lists the beginning and ending balances of each equity account and describes the changes that occurred during the period.

      1. Provided by most companies rather than a separate statement of retained earnings.

      2. Statement of changes in stockholders' equity includes changes in retained earnings.

   C. Reporting Stock Options

      1. **Stock options** are rights to purchase common stock at a fixed price over a specified period of time.

      2. Stock options are said to motivate managers and employees to focus on company performance, take a long-run perspective, and remain with the company.

VII. Decision Analysis—Earnings per Share, Price-Earnings Ratio, Dividend Yield, and Book Value per Share

   A. Earnings per Share (EPS)—reported in final section of income statement. **Earnings per share** is the amount of income earned by each share of outstanding common stock (one of the most widely cited items of accounting information).

      1. **Basic earnings per share** is calculated as net income – preferred dividends (the numerator) divided by the weighted-average common shares outstanding.

         a. If preferred stock is *non*cumulativ*e*, the income available to common stockholders (the numerator) is the current period net income less any preferred dividends *declared* in that same period.

         b. If preferred stock is *cumulative*, the income available (numerator) is the current period net income less the preferred dividends, whether declared or not.

   B. Price-Earnings Ratio (PE ratio)

      1. The **price earnings ratio** is used to gain understanding of the market's expected earnings for the stockholders.

      2. It is calculated as market value per share divided by earnings per share.

      3. It can be based on current or *expected* EPS.

    C. Dividend Yield

        1. The **dividend yield** shows the annual amount of cash dividends distributed to common shares relative to their market value.

        2. It is used to determine whether a company's stock is an income stock (pays large and regular dividends) or a growth stock (pays little or no cash dividends).

        3. It is calculated as annual cash dividends per share divided by market value per share.

    D. Book Value per Share

        1. **Book value per common share**

           a. If only one class outstanding, equals total stockholders' equity divided by the number of common shares outstanding.

           b. If two classes of stock outstanding, equals stockholders' equity applicable to common shares (total stockholders' equity less *equity applicable to preferred stock*—see section below) divided by the number of common shares outstanding.

        2. **Book value per preferred share**

           a. The stockholders' *equity applicable to preferred* shares equals the preferred share's call price (or par value if the preferred is not callable) plus any cumulative dividends in arrears. The remaining stockholders' equity is the portion applicable to common shares.

           b. Book value per preferred share equals *equity applicable to preferred* shares divided by number of preferred shares outstanding.

Uzi Company received a charter granting the right to issue 200,000 shares of $1 par value common stock and 10,000 shares of 8% cumulative and nonparticipating, $50 par value preferred stock that is callable at $80 per share. Selected transactions are presented below.

20X7

Feb.   19   Issued 45,000 shares of common stock at par for cash.

       22   Gave the corporation's promoters 30,000 shares of common stock for their services in getting the corporation organized. The directors valued the services at $50,000.

Mar   30   Exchanged 100,000 shares of common stock for the following assets at fair market values: land, $25,000; building, $100,000; and machinery, $125,000.

Dec.   31   Closed the Income Summary account. A $25,000 loss was incurred.

20X8

Jan.   12   Issued 1,000 shares of preferred stock at $75 per share.

Dec.   15   The board of directors declared an 8% dividend on preferred shares and $0.10 per share on outstanding common shares, payable on January 31 to the January 17 stockholders of record.

       31   Closed the Income Summary and Dividend Declared accounts. A $69,000 net income was earned.

20X9

Jan.   31   Paid the previously declared dividends.

Required:

1. Prepare general journal entries to record the selected transactions.
2. Prepare a stockholders' equity section as of the close of business on December 31, 20X8.
3. Determine the book value per preferred share and per common stock as of December 31, 20X8.

(If this alternative demonstration problem is not covered in class, see your instructor for the solution.)

Problem I

The following statements are either true or false. Place a (T) in the parentheses before each true statement and an (F) before each false statement.

1. (F) Par value has nothing to do with a stock's worth.

2. (F) Final authority in the management of corporation affairs rests with its board of directors.

3. (T) The life of a corporation may be unlimited.

4. (F) To transfer and sell his or her interest in a corporation, a stockholder must secure permission from the corporation's secretary.

5. (T) The chief executive officer of a corporation is usually elected by the stockholders at one of their annual meetings.

6. (T) The president of a corporation is responsible to its board of directors for management of the corporation's affairs.

7. (T) A discount on stock is the difference between market value and the amount at which stock is issued when the stock is issued at a price below its par value.

8. (F) A small stock dividend should be recorded by capitalizing retained earnings equal to the book value of the stock to be distributed.

9. (F) In most states, a corporation must have current net income in order to pay a cash dividend.

10. ( ) Since a stock dividend is payable in stock rather than in assets, it is not a liability of its issuing corporation.

11. ( ) A stock split has no effect on total stockholders' equity, the equities of the individual stockholders, or on the balances of any of the contributed or retained capital accounts.

12. ( ) Dividend yield is an estimate of how much one share of stock will yield in cash dividends per year.

13. ( ) A company with common stock having a market value of $45 per share and earnings of $5 per share has a price-earnings ratio of 9.

14. ( ) A cash dividend reduces a corporation's cash and its stockholders' equity, but a stock dividend does not affect either cash or total stockholders' equity.

15. ( ) For companies with simple capital structures, earnings per share is calculated by dividing net income minus preferred dividends, if any, by the weighted-average number of common shares outstanding.

16. ( ) Hadley Corporation stock has a current market value of $16 and is expected to pay cash dividends of $1.20 during the next year. The expected dividend yield of Hadley stock is 7.5%.

Problem II

You are given several words, phrases, or numbers to choose from in completing each of the following statements or in answering the following questions. In each case select the one that best completes the statement or answers the question and place its letter in the answer space provided.

_____ 1. The difference between the par value of stock and its issue price when it is issued at a price above par value is the:

    a. Paid-in capital.

    b. Stock dividend.

    c. Minimum legal capital.

    d. Premium on stock.

    e. Discount on stock.

_____ 2. Vector Corporation has outstanding 3,000 shares of $100 par value, 7% cumulative and nonparticipating preferred stock and 10,000 shares of $10 par value common stock. Dividends have not been paid on the preferred stock for the current and one prior year. The corporation has recently prospered, and the board of directors has voted to pay out $49,000 of the corporation's retained earnings in dividends. If the $49,000 is paid out, how much should the preferred and common stockholders receive per share?

    a. $14.00 per share preferred, $0.70 per share common.

    b. $ 7.00 per share preferred, $2.80 per share common.

    c. $12.25 per share preferred, $1.23 per share common.

    d. $ 1.14 per share preferred, $4.56 per share common.

    e. $16.33 per share preferred, $ -0- per share common.

_____ 3. Vector Corporation has outstanding 3,000 shares of $100 par value, 7% noncumulative and nonparticipating preferred stock and 10,000 shares of $10 par value common stock. Dividends have not been paid on the preferred stock for the current and one prior year. The corporation has recently prospered, and the board of directors has voted to pay out $49,000 of the corporation's retained earnings in dividends. If the $49,000 is paid out, how much should the preferred and common stockholders receive per share?

    a. $ 1.14 per share preferred, $4.56 per share common.

    b. $9.33 per share preferred, $2.10 per share common.

    c. $ 7.00 per share preferred, $2.80 per share common.

    d. $14.00 per share preferred, $0.70 per share common.

    e. $12.25 per share preferred, $0.23 per share common.

_____4. Participating preferred stock is:

a. Preferred stock that can be exchanged for shares of the issuing corporation's common stock at the option of the preferred stockholder.

b. Preferred stock on which undeclared dividends accumulate annually until they are paid.

c. Preferred stock on which the right to receive dividends is forfeited for any year that the dividends are not declared.

d. Preferred stock that the issuing corporation, at its option, may retire by paying a specified amount to the preferred stockholders plus any dividends in arrears.

e. Preferred stock that gives its owners the right to share in dividends in excess of the stated percentage or amount.

_____5. Stated value of stock is:

a. One share's portion of the issuing corporation's net assets as recorded in the corporation's accounts.

b. An arbitrary amount assigned to stock by the corporation's board of directors which is credited to the stock account when the stock is issued.

c. The difference between the par value of stock and its issue price when it is issued at a price below or above par value.

d. The market value of the stock on the date of issuance.

e. The price at which a share of stock can be bought or sold.

_____6. Bartlett Company had 20,000 shares of common stock outstanding at the beginning of 20X8. On April 1, the company sold 20,000 additional shares of its common stock, and on November 1 the company declared a 2-for-1 stock split. For the purpose of determining earnings per share, calculate the weighted-average number of common shares outstanding during the year.

a. 60,000.00
b. 80,000.00
c. 70,000.00
d. 41,666.66
e. 83,333.33

_____ 7. The Poseidon Corporation issued $10 par value common stock for $15, with the premium being credited to Paid-in Capital in Excess of Par Value; Common Stock. Later, 500 shares of this stock was repurchased and retired at a cost of $17. The entry to record the retirement is as follows:

a. Common Stock   5,000
    Paid-in Capital in Excess of Par Value, Common Stock   2,500
    Retained Earnings   1,000
        Cash   8,500
b. Common Stock   5,000
    Paid-in Capital in Excess of Par Value, Common Stock   2,500
    Paid-in Capital from the Retirement of Common Stock   1,000
        Cash   8,500
c. Common Stock   5,000
    Paid-in Capital in Excess of Par Value, Common Stock   3,500
        Cash   6,500
d. Common Stock   5,000
    Paid-in Capital in Excess of Par Value, Common Stock   2,500
        Cash   6,500
        Paid-in Capital from the Retirement of Common Stock   1.000
e. Treasury Stock   8,500
        Cash   8,500

_____ 8. The statement of stockholders' equity is:

a. A financial statement that discloses the inflows and outflows of cash during the period.

b. A financial report showing the assets, liabilities, and equity of an enterprise on a specific date.

c. A financial statement showing revenues earned by a business, the expenses incurred in earning the revenues, and the resulting net income or net loss.

d. A financial statement that lists the beginning and ending balances of each equity account and describes all the changes that occurred during the year.

e. None of the above.

_____ 9. On December 15, RTA Corporation declares a $.75 per share cash dividend on its 4,000 outstanding shares. Payment date is January 15. On December 15, RTA should make the following entry related to the cash dividend:

a. Cash Dividends Declared   3,000
        Retained Earnings   3,000
b. Common Dividend Payable   3,000
        Cash Dividends Declared   3,000
c. Retained Earnings   3,000
        Cash Dividends Declared   3,000
d. Retained Earnings   3,000
        Common Dividend Payable   3,000
e. No entry should be made on December 15 related to the cash dividend.

Problem III

Many of the important ideas and concepts discussed in Chapter 11 are reflected in the following list of key terms. Test your understanding of these terms by matching the appropriate definitions with the terms. Record the number identifying the most appropriate definition in the blank space next to each term.

_____ Appropriated retained earnings

_____ Authorized stock

_____ Basic earnings per share

_____ Book value per common share

_____ Book value per preferred share

_____ Callable preferred stock

_____ Call price

_____ Capital stock

_____ Changes in accounting estimates

_____ Common stock

_____ Complex capital structure

_____ Convertible preferred stock

_____ Corporation

_____ Cumulative preferred stock

_____ Date of declaration

_____ Date of payment

_____ Date of record

_____ Diluted earnings per share

_____ Dilutive securities

_____ Discount on stock

_____ Dividend in arrears

_____ Dividend yield

_____ Earnings per share

_____ Financial leverage

_____ Large stock dividend

_____ Liquidating cash dividend

_____ Market value per share

_____ Minimum legal capital

_____ Noncumulative preferred stock

_____ Nonparticipating preferred stock

_____ No-par value stock

_____ Organization expenses

_____ Paid-in capital

_____ Paid-in capital in excess of par

_____ Participating preferred stock

_____ Par value

_____ Par value stock

_____ Preemptive right

_____ Preferred stock

_____ Premium on stock

_____ Price-earnings (PE) ratio

_____ Prior period adjustment

_____ Proxy

_____ Restricted retained earnings

_____ Retained earnings

_____ Retained earnings deficit

_____ Reverse stock split

_____ Simple capital structure

_____ Small stock dividend

_____ Stated value of stock

_____ Statement of stockholders' equity

_____ Stock dividend

_____ Stockholders' equity

_____ Stock options

_____ Stock split

_____ Treasury stock

1. Total amount of cash and other assets received from stockholders in exchange for stock.

2. Unpaid dividend on cumulative preferred stock; must be paid before any regular dividends on preferred stock and before any dividends on common stock.

3. Preferred stock on which the right to receive dividends is lost for any period when dividends are not declared.

4. Total amount of stock that a corporation's charter authorizes it to sell.

5. Preferred stock that the issuing corporation, at its option, may retire by paying the call price plus any dividends in arrears.

6. Preferred stock on which undeclared dividends accumulate until paid; common stockholders cannot receive dividends until cumulative dividends are paid.

7. Earning a higher return on equity by paying dividends on preferred stock or interest on debt at a rate lower than the return earned with the assets from issuing preferred stock or debt.

8. Stock dividend that is more than 25% of the previously outstanding shares.

9. Ratio of a company's market value per share to its earnings per share.

10. Occurs when a corporation calls in its stock and replaces each share with less than one new share; increases both the market value per share and any par or stated value per share.

11. Equity applicable to preferred shares (equals its call price [or par value if not callable] plus any cumulative dividends in arrears) divided by the number of preferred shares outstanding.

12. Amount that must be paid to call and retire a preferred share.

13. Amount of assets defined by law that stockholders must invest (potentially) and leave invested in a corporation; usually defined as par value of the stock; intended to protect creditors.

14. Corporation's own stock that it reacquired and still holds.

15. Price at which stock is bought or sold.

16. Capital structure that consists of only common stock and non-convertible preferred stock; consists of no dilutive securities.

17. Preferred stock on which dividends are limited to a maximum amount each year.

18. Stock dividend that is 25% or less of a corporation's previously outstanding shares.

19. Cumulative income less cumulative losses and dividends.

20. A corporation's basic stock; usually carries voting rights for controlling the corporation.

21. Debit (abnormal) balance in Retained Earnings; occurs when cumulative losses and dividends exceed cumulative income.

22. Rights to purchase common stock at a fixed price over a specified period of time.

23. Financial statement that lists the beginning and ending balances of each equity account and describes all changes in those accounts.

24. Retained earnings not available for dividends because of legal or contractual limitations.

25. Corporation's distribution of its own stock to its stockholders without the receipt of any payment.

26. Correction of an error in a prior year that is reported in the statement of retained earnings (or statement of changes in stockholders' equity) net of any income tax effects.

27. Difference between the par value of stock and its issue price when issued at a price below par value.

28. Preferred stock with an option to exchange it for common stock at a specified rate.

29. Stock class that has not been assigned a par value by the corporate charter.

30. Distribution of assets that returns part of the original investment to the stockholders; charged to contributed capital accounts.

31. Legal document giving a stockholder's agent the power to exercise the stockholder's voting rights.

32. Retained earnings reported separately as a way of informing stockholders of funding needs.

33. Date the directors vote to pay a dividend.

©The McGraw-Hill Companies, Inc., 2008

34. Ratio of the annual amount of cash dividends distributed to common shareholders relative to the common stock's market value (price).

35. Class of stock assigned a par value by the corporate charter.

36. Recorded amount of equity applicable to common shares divided by the number of common shares outstanding.

37. Date specified by the directors for identifying stockholders to receive dividends.

38. Amount of income earned by each share of a company's outstanding common stock; also called *net income per share*.

39. Stock with a priority status over common stockholders in one or more ways, such as paying of dividends or distributing assets.

40. Preferred stock that shares with common stockholders any dividends paid in excess of the percent stated on preferred stock.

41. Occurs when a corporation calls in its stock and replaces each share with more than one new share; decreases both the market value per share and the par or stated value per share.

42. No-par stock assigned a stated value per share; this amount is recorded in the stock account when the stock is issued.

43. Occurs when a corporation sells its stock for more than par value.

44. Revisions to previous estimates of future events and outcomes; accounted for in current and future periods.

45. Earnings per share calculation that requires dilutive securities be added to the denominator of the basic EPS calculation.

46. Stockholders' right to maintain their proportionate interest in a corporation with any additional shares issued.

47. Corporation's equity; also called *shareholders' equity* or *corporate capital*.

48. Value assigned a share of stock by the corporate charter when the stock is authorized.

49. Securities having the potential to increase common shares outstanding; examples are options, rights, convertible bonds and convertible preferred stock.

50. Net income less preferred dividends divided by the weighted-average common shares outstanding.

51. Capital structure that includes outstanding rights or options to purchase common stock, or securities that are convertible into common stock.

52. Date the corporation makes the dividend payment.

53. Costs such as legal fees and promoter fees to bring an entity into existence.

54. General term referring to a corporation's stock used in obtaining capital (owner financing).

55. Entity created by law and separate from its owners.

56. Account credited for the difference between the par value of stock and its issue price when issued at a price above par.

Problem IV

Complete the following by filling in the blanks.

1. Laws establishing minimum legal capital requirements were written to protect _____ with the protection resulting from making illegal the payment of any dividends that reduce stockholders' equity below _____.

2. When stock is issued at a price above its par value, the difference between par and the price at which the stock is issued is called a _____.

3. Advantages claimed for no-par stock are: (a) It may be issued at any price without _____, (b) Uninformed persons buying such stock are not misled as to the stock's worth by a _____ printed on the certificates.

4. Laws setting minimum legal capital requirements normally require stockholders to invest, in a corporation, assets equal in value to minimum legal capital or be contingently liable to _____ for the deficiency.

5. A preferred stock is so called because of the preferences granted its owners. The two most common preferences are a preference as to _____, and a preference _____.

6. In many jurisdictions when a corporation issues par value stock, it establishes for itself a _____ equal to the par value of the issued stock.

7. In addition to its separate legal existence, other characteristics of a corporation as a form of business organization are _____.

8. A corporation is said to be a separate legal entity; this phrase means that in a legal sense a corporation is _____.

9. When a corporation purchases treasury stock, a portion of its retained earnings equal to the cost of the treasury stock becomes _____ and unavailable for _____.

10. If treasury stock is reissued at a price above cost, the amount received in excess of cost is credited to _____. If treasury stock is sold below cost the difference between cost and the sale price is debited to either _____ or _____.

11. A stock dividend enables a corporation to give its shareholders some evidence of their interest in its retained earnings without reducing the corporation's _____.

12. Issued stock that has been reacquired by the issuing corporation is called _____.

13. If the book value of a share of common stock before the declaration and distribution of a 20% stock dividend was $90, the declaration and distribution of the dividend changed the book value to $_____.

14. If a corporation has sufficient cash to pay a dividend, it must also have sufficient _____ before it pays that dividend.

15. A small stock dividend contains a number of shares amounting to _____% or less of the previously outstanding shares.

16. Changes in accounting estimates _____ (are, are not) prior period adjustments.

17. Earnings per share calculated as if all dilutive securities had already been converted are called _____.

Problem V

The stockholders' equity section from Sonar Corporation's balance sheet shows the following:

Capital Stock And Retained Earnings

Preferred stock, $100 par value, 8% cumulative and nonparticipating, issued and outstanding 2,000 shares..	$200,000	
Common stock, $10 par value, issued and outstanding 25,000 shares.......	250,000	
Total contributed capital...		$450,000
Retained earnings		230,000
Total stockholders' equity...		$680,000

1. If there are no dividends in arrears, the book value per share of the corporation's preferred stock is $_____ and the book value per share of its common stock is $_____.

2. If a total of two years' dividends are in arrears on the preferred stock, the book value per share of the preferred stock is $_____, and the book value per share of the common stock is $_____.

Problem VI

On August 10 Mainline Corporation purchased for cash 2,000 shares of its own $25 par value common stock at $27 per share. On October 3 it sold 1,000 of the shares at $30 per share. Prepare the journal entries below to record the purchase and sale of the stock.

DATE	ACCOUNT TITLES AND EXPLANATION	P.R.	DEBIT		CREDIT	
Aug. 10						
	Purchased 2,000 shares of treasury stock.					
Oct. 3						
	Sold 1,000 shares of treasury stock.					

Problem VII

The May 31 balance sheet of Eastwood Corporation carried the following stockholders' equity section:

Stockholders' Equity

Common stock, $10 par value, 25,000 shares authorized, 20,000 shares issued........	$200,000
Retained earnings..	44,000
Total stockholders' equity	$244,000

On the balance sheet date, with the common stock selling at $12 per share, the corporation's board of directors voted a 2,000-share stock dividend distributable on June 30 to the June 20 stockholders of record.

Required:

1. Prepare the journal entries to record the declaration and distribution of the dividend.

DATE	ACCOUNT TITLES AND EXPLANATION	P.R.	DEBIT	CREDIT

2. Harold Jax owned 2,000 shares of the corporation's common stock before the declaration and distribution of the stock dividend; as a result, his portion of the dividend was _____ shares. The total book value of Jax's 2,000 shares before the dividend was $_____, the total book value of his shares after the dividend was $_____; consequently, Jax gained $_____ in the book value of his interest in the corporation.

Problem VIII

Retained earnings and shares issued and outstanding for Endel, Incorporated, are as follows:

	Retained Earnings	Shares Issued and Outstanding
December 31, 20X8	$475,000	35,000
December 31, 20X9	$447,000	38,500

On April 3, 20X9, the board of directors declared a $0.775 per share dividend on the outstanding stock. On August 7, while the stock was selling for $17.50 per share, the corporation declared a 10% stock dividend on the outstanding shares to be issued on November 7.

Under the assumption that there were no transactions affecting retained earnings other than the ones given, determine the 20X9 net income of Endel, Incorporated.

©The McGraw-Hill Companies, Inc., 2008

Solutions for Chapter 11

Problem I

1. T
2. T
3. T
4. F
5. F
6. T
7. F
8. F
9. F
10. T
11. T
12. F
13. T
14. T
15. T
16. T

Problem II

1. D
2. A
3. C
4. E
5. B
6. D
7. A
8. D
9. D

Problem III

32	Appropriated retained earnings		3	Noncumulative preferred stock
4	Authorized stock		17	Nonparticipating preferred stock
50	Basic earnings per share		29	No-par value stock
36	Book value per common share		53	Organization expenses
11	Book value per preferred share		1	Paid-in capital
5	Callable preferred stock		56	Paid-in capital in excess of par
12	Call price		40	Participating preferred stock
54	Capital stock		48	Par value
44	Changes in accounting estimates		35	Par value stock
20	Common stock		46	Preemptive right
51	Complex capital structure		39	Preferred stock
28	Convertible preferred stock		43	Premium on stock
55	Corporation		9	Price-earnings (PE) ratio
6	Cumulative preferred stock		26	Prior period adjustment
33	Date of declaration		31	Proxy
52	Date of payment		24	Restricted retained earnings
37	Date of record		19	Retained earnings
45	Diluted earnings per share		21	Retained earnings deficit
49	Dilutive securities		10	Reverse stock split
27	Discount on stock		16	Simple capital structure
2	Dividend in arrears		18	Small stock dividend
34	Dividend yield		42	Stated value of stock
38	Earnings per share		23	Statement of stockholders' equity
7	Financial leverage		25	Stock dividend
8	Large stock dividend		47	Stockholders' equity
30	Liquidating cash dividend		22	Stock options
15	Market value per share		41	Stock split
13	Minimum legal capital		14	Treasury stock

Problem IV

1. corporation creditors, minimum legal capital
2. premium
3. (a) discount liability, (b) par value
4. corporation creditors
5. the payment of dividends, in the distribution of assets if the corporation is liquidated
6. minimum legal capital
7. lack of stockholder liability, ease of transferring ownership rights, continuity of life, stockholders are not agents, ease of capital assembly, increased governmental regulation, and double taxation
8. an individual body, separate and distinct from its stockholders
9. restricted, dividends
10. Paid-in Capital, Treasury Stock; Paid-in capital, Treasury Stock; Retained Earnings
11. cash or other assets

12. treasury stock
13. $75
14. retained earnings
15. 25
16. are not
17. diluted earnings per share

Problem V

1. $100; $19.20

2. $116; $17.92

Problem VI

Aug. 10	Treasury Stock, Common	54,000	
	Cash		54,000
Oct. 3	Cash	30,000	
	Treasury Stock, Common		27,000
	Paid-in Capital, Treasury Stock		3,000

Problem VII

1.

May 31	Retained Earnings	24,000	
	Common Stock Dividend Distributable.....................................		20,000
	Paid-in Capital in Excess of Par Value, Common Stock		4,000
June 30	Common Stock Distributable..	20,000	
	Common Stock		20,000

2. 200; $24,400; $24,400; $0

Problem VIII

Retained earnings as of December 31, 20X8		$475,000
Reductions in retained earnings due to transactions:		
Dividends declared:		
April 3, on 35,000 shares	$27,125	
Retained earnings capitalized in stock dividend	61,250	
Total reductions..		88,375
Retained earnings balance before transfer of net income from Income Summary account		$386,625
Retained earnings, December 31, 20X9, after transfer of net income from Income Summary account		$447,000
Deduct retained earnings balance before transfer of net income from Income Summary account		386,625
Net income		$ 60,375

CHAPTER 12
REPORTING AND ANALYZING CASH FLOWS

Learning Objective C1:

Explain the purpose and importance of cash flow information.

The main purpose of the statement of cash flows is to report the major cash receipts and cash payments for a period. This includes identifying cash flows as relating to either operating, investing, or financing activities. Most business decisions involve evaluating activities that provide or use cash.

Learning Objective C2:

Distinguish between operating, investing, and financing activities.

Operating activities include the transactions and events that determine net income. Investing activities include transactions and events that mainly affect long-term assets. Financing activities include transactions and events that mainly affect long-term liabilities and equity.

Learning Objective C3:

Identify and disclose noncash investing and financing activities.

Noncash investing and financing activities must be disclosed in either a note or in a separate schedule to the statement of cash flows. Examples are the retirement of debt by issuing equity and the exchange of a note payable for plant assets.

Learning Objective C4:

Describe the format of the statement of cash flows.

The statement of cash flows separates cash receipts and payments into operating, investing, or financing activities.

Learning Objective A1:

Analyze the statement of cash flows.

To understand and predict cash flows, users stress identification of the sources and uses of cash flows by operating, investing, and financing activities. Emphasis is on operating cash flows since they derive from continuing operations.

Learning Objective A2:

Compute and apply the cash flow on total assets ratio.

The cash flow on total assets ratio is defined as operating cash flows divided by average total assets. Analysis of current and past values for this ratio can reflect a company's ability to yield regular and positive cash flows. It is also viewed as a measure of earnings quality.

Learning Objective P1:

Prepare a statement of cash flows.

Preparation of a statement of cash flows involves five steps: (1) Compute the net increase or decrease in cash, (2) compute net cash provided (used) by operating activities (using either the direct or indirect method), (3) compute net cash provided (used) by investing activities, (4) compute net cash provided (used) by financing activities, and (5) report the beginning and ending cash balance and prove that it is explained by net cash flows. Noncash investing and financing activities are also disclosed.

Learning Objective P2:

Compute cash flows from operating activities using the indirect method.

The indirect method for reporting net cash provided (used) by operating activities starts with net income and then adjusts it for three items: (1) changes in noncash current assets and current liabilities related to operating activities, (2) revenues and expenses not providing (using) cash, and (3) gains and losses from investing and financing activities.

Learning Objective P3:

Determine cash flows from both investing and financing activities.

Cash flows from both investing and financing activities are determined by identifying the cash flow effects of transactions and events affecting each balance sheet account related to these activities. All cash flows from these activities are identified when we can explain changes in these accounts from the beginning to the end of the period.

Learning Objective P4 (Appendix 12A):

Illustrate use of a spreadsheet to prepare a statement of cash flows.

A spreadsheet is a useful tool in preparing a statement of cash flows. Six steps (described in the appendix) are applied when using the spreadsheet to prepare a statement of cash flows.

Learning Objective P5 (Appendix 12B):

Compute cash flows from operating activities using the direct method.

The direct method for reporting net cash provided (used) by operating activities lists major classes of operating cash inflows less cash outflows to yield net cash inflow or outflow from operations.

Chapter Outline

I.   **Basics of Cash Flow Reporting**

A. Purpose of the **Statement of Cash Flows**

To report all major cash receipts (inflows) and cash payments (outflows) during a period. This report classifies cash flows into operating, investing, and financing activities. It answers important questions such as:

1. How does a company obtain its cash?

2. Where does a company spend its cash?

3. What is the change in the cash balance?

B. Importance of Cash Flows

Information about cash flows, and its sources and uses, can influence decision makers in important ways. This information helps users decide whether a company can pay its debts and other obligations, and its ability to take advantage of new business opportunities.

C. Measurement of Cash Flows

The phrase, *cash flows* refers to *both* cash and cash equivalents. A *cash equivalent* must satisfy two criteria:

1. Be readily convertible to a known amount of cash.

2. Be sufficiently close to its maturity date so its market value is unaffected by interest rate changes.

D. Classification of Cash Flows

Cash receipts and cash payments are classified and reported in one of three categories:

1. **Operating activities** include transactions and events that determine net income (with some exceptions such as unusual gains and losses). Specific examples:

   a. Cash inflows from cash sales, collections on credit sales, receipts of dividends and interest, sale of trading securities, and settlements of lawsuits.

   b. Cash outflows for payments to suppliers for goods and services, employees for wages, lenders for interest, government for taxes, charities, and purchase of trading securities.

2. **Investing activities** include transactions and events that affect long-term assets. Specific examples:

   a. Cash inflows from selling long-term assets, selling short-term investments other than cash equivalents, and collecting money the company has loaned to others.

   b. Cash outflows from purchasing long-term assets, purchasing short-term investments other than cash equivalents, and lending money to others.

3. **Financing activities** include transactions and events that affect long-term liabilities and equity:

   a. Cash inflows from issuing debt and obtaining cash from owners.

   b. Cash outflows from repaying amounts borrowed and distributing cash to owners.

E. Noncash Investing and Financing Activities

   Noncash investing and financing activities do not affect cash receipts or payments; however, they are disclosed at the bottom of the statement of cash flows or in a note to the statement because of their importance and the *full disclosure* principle.

F. Format of the Statement of Cash Flows

1. Lists cash flows by categories (operating, financing and investing) and identifies the net cash inflow or outflow in each category.

2. Combines the net cash flow in each of the three categories and identifies the net change (increase or decrease) in cash for the period.

3. Combines the net change in cash with the beginning cash to prove the ending cash.

4. Contains a separate schedule at bottom (or notes) to report the noncash financing and investing activities.

G. Preparing the Statement of Cash Flows

1. Five steps:

   a. Compute the net increase or decrease in cash.

   b. Compute net cash provided (used) by operating activities (using either the direct or indirect method).

   c. Compute net cash provided (used) by investing activities.

   d. Compute net cash provided (used) by financing activities.

   e. Compute net cash flows by combining the net cash provided (used) by operating, investing, and financing activities and then *prove it* by adding it to the beginning cash to show that it equals the ending cash.

2. Alternative approaches to preparing the statement:

   a. Analyzing the cash account.

   b. Analyzing noncash accounts.

3. Information to Prepare the Statement

    a. Comparative balance sheets.

    b. The current income statement.

    c. Other information—generally derived from analyzing noncash balance sheet accounts.

II. **Cash Flows from Operating** – cash flows from operating activities are reported in one of two ways—the direct method or the indirect method. Amount is *identical* under both methods.

A. Indirect and Direct Methods of Reporting

    1. The **direct method** separately lists each major item of operating cash receipts and each major item of operating cash payments. (See illustration in Exhibit 12.7.)

    2. The **indirect method** reports net income and then adjusts it for items necessary to obtain net cash provided (used) by operating activities. Reports the necessary adjustments to reconcile net income to net cash provided (used) by operating activities. (See illustration in Exhibit 12.9). This method is the most widely used.

B. Application of the Indirect Method of Reporting

    a. *Add,* as adjustments to net income: noncash expenses (e.g., depreciation), decreases in current assets, increases in current liabilities, and losses.

    b. *Subtract,* as adjustments to net income: increases in current assets, decreases in current liabilities, and gains.

    c. Does *not* report individual items of cash inflows and cash outflows from operating activities.

    d. Exhibit 12-12 summarizes the adjustments for the indirect method.

III. **Cash Flows from Investing**

Three-stage process is used to determine cash provided (used) by investing activities: (1) Identify changes in investing-related accounts, (2) explain these changes using reconstruction method, and (3) report their cash flow effects.

A. Analysis of Noncurrent Assets

    1. Determine changes in all noncurrent asset accounts (plant assets, intangible assets, investments)

    2. Analyze changes in these accounts using available information to determine their effect, if any, on cash.

B. Analysis of Other Assets

1. Certain other asset transactions such as those involving current notes receivable and investments in debt and equity securities (excluding trading) are considered investing activities.

2. Analyze using same process used for noncurrent asset accounts.

IV. **Cash Flows from Financing**

Three-stage process is used to determine cash provided (used) by investing activities: (1) Identify changes in financing-related accounts, (2) explain these changes using reconstruction method, and (3) report their cash flow effects.

A. Analysis of Noncurrent Liabilities

1. Determine changes in noncurrent liability accounts (e.g., long-term debt, notes payable, bonds payable).

2. Analyze changes in these accounts using available information to determine their effect, if any, on cash.

B. Analysis of Equity

1. Determine changes in equity accounts (e.g., owner's capital, all stock accounts, and retained earnings).

2. Analyze changes in these accounts using available information to determine their effect, if any, on cash.

C. Proving Cash Balances – the last step in preparing the statement is to report the beginning and ending cash balances and prove that the *net change in cash* is explained by operating, investing, and financing cash flows.

V. **Decision Analysis—Cash Flow Analysis**

A. Analyzing Cash Sources and Uses

1. Managers stress understanding and predicting cash flows for business decisions.

2. Creditor and investor decisions are also based on a company's cash flow evaluations.

3. Operating cash flows are generally considered to be most significant because they represent results of ongoing operations.

B. Cash Flow on Total Assets

1. The **cash flow on total assets** ratio is similar to return on total assets except the return is analyzed based on operating cash flows rather than net income.

2. It is calculated by dividing cash flow from operations by average total assets.

VI. **Spreadsheet Preparation of the Statement of Cash Flows (Appendix 12A)**

A spreadsheet approach may be used to organize and analyze the information to prepare a statement of cash flows by the indirect method, including the supplemental disclosures of noncash investing and financing activities.

A. The spreadsheet has four columns containing dollar amounts.

1. Columns one and four contain the beginning and ending balances of each balance sheet account.

2. Columns two and three are for reconciling the changes in each balance sheet account.

B. Separate sections on the working paper present (a) balance sheet items with debit balances; (b) balance sheet items with credit balances; (c) cash flows from operating activities, starting with net income; (d) cash flows from investing activities; (e) cash flows from financing activities; and (f) noncash investing and financing activities.

C. Information for sections (c) - (f) is developed in four steps in the Analysis of Changes columns:

1. By adjusting net income for the changes in all noncash current asset and current liability account balances. This reconciles the changes in these accounts.

2. By eliminating from net income the effects of all noncash revenues and expenses. This begins the reconciliation of noncurrent assets.

3. By eliminating from net income any gains or losses from investing and financing activities. This involves the reconciliation of noncurrent assets and noncurrent liabilities and perhaps the recording of disclosures.

4. By entering any remaining items, such as dividend payments, which are necessary to reconcile the changes in all balance sheet accounts.

VII. **Direct Method of Reporting Operating Cash Flows (Appendix 12B)**

The direct method adjusts accrual-based income statement items to the cash basis. Usual approach is to adjust income statement accounts related to operating activities for changes in their related balance sheet accounts. Separately list each major item or class of operating cash receipts and cash payments.

A. Operating Cash Receipts—include cash received from sales, rent, interest, and dividends.

B. Operating Cash Payments—include cash paid suppliers, for wages and other operating expense, interest, and income taxes.

C. Summary of Adjustments for the Direct Method

Exhibit 12B.6 summarizes the common adjustments for the items making up net income to arrive at net cash provided (used) by operating activities under the direct method.

D. Direct Method Format of Operating Activities

1. Major items of cash inflows and cash outflows are listed separately in the operating activities section.

2. The items to be listed are determined by adjusting individual accrual basis income statement items to cash basis items. This is done by determining the impact from changes in their related balance sheet accounts.

3. The operating cash outflows are subtracted from the operating cash inflows to determine the net cash provided (used) by operating activities.

4. This is the method recommended (but not required) by the FASB.

5. When the direct method is used, the FASB requires a reconciliation of net income to net cash provided (used) by operating activities. This is operating cash flows computed using the indirect method.

CLASSIFYING ACTIVITIES IN THE STATEMENT OF CASH FLOWS

OPERATING ACTIVITIES

Cash inflows from
- Sale of goods or services
- Interest
- Dividends
- Sale of trading securities
- Other operating receipts

Cash outflows to
- Suppliers of goods and services
- Salaries and wages
- Government for taxes
- Lenders for interest
- Purchase trading securities
- Others for expenses

INVESTING ACTIVITIES

Cash inflows from
- Sale of property plant, and equipment
- Sale of debt or equity securities of other entities
- Collection of principal on loans to other entities
- Selling (discounting) of loans

Cash outflows to
- Purchase property, plant, and equipment
- Purchase debt or equity securities of other entities
- Make loans to another entity

FINANCING ACTIVITIES

Cash inflows from
- Sale of capital stock (or owner investment)
- Issuance of debt (bonds and notes)
- Issuing short-term liabilities

Cash outflows to
- Shareholders as dividends (or owner's withdrawal)
- Repay debts
- Purchase treasury stock

NONCASH INVESTING AND FINANCING ACTIVITIES

- Retirement of debt by issuing stock
- Conversion of preferred stock to common stock
- Purchase of a long-term asset by issuing a note payable
- Leasing of assets classified as a capital lease

STEPS TO DETERMINE INFORMATION
STATEMENT OF CASH FLOWS

1. Find <u>change</u> in Cash—This is the target number.

2. Find cash flow from operations
   (Using direct or indirect method)

3. Find Cash Flow from   A. Financing <u>and</u>
                                 B. Investing
   Procedure:

   In real life: Using data from comparative balance sheets, trace changes through ledgers and journals probably using a worksheet to organize, analyze, and prove data disclosed.

   In the classroom: Determine the changes in noncurrent accounts and notes from comparative balance sheets. Use the relevant data the text provides that comes from the ledgers and the journals to systematically analyze the data using chart and/or reconstructing journal entries.

4. Combine cash flows from all three activities (from 2 and 3) to find net cash flow and prove change in cash. (Target number determined in Step 1).

Note: Once the above information has been gathered, the statement can be prepared following the required format. If the direct method was used, GAAP requires a reconciliation of net income to cash provided from operations.

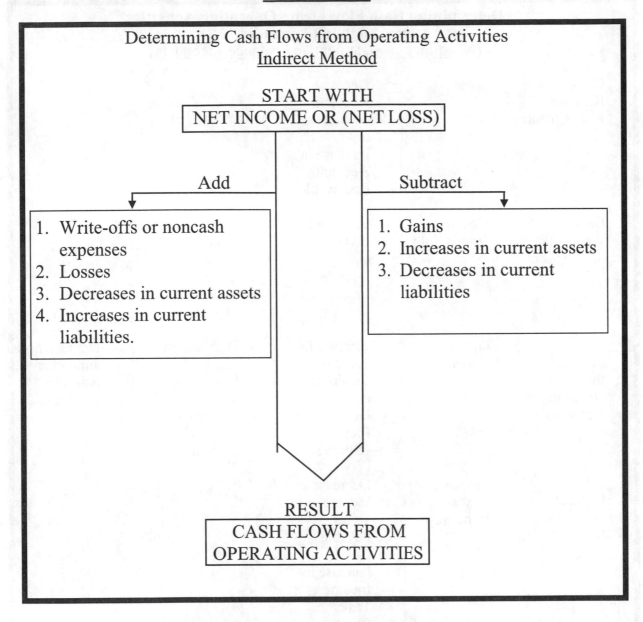

Determining Cash Flows from Operating Activities
Indirect Method

START WITH
NET INCOME OR (NET LOSS)

Add

1. Write-offs or noncash expenses
2. Losses
3. Decreases in current assets
4. Increases in current liabilities.

Subtract

1. Gains
2. Increases in current assets
3. Decreases in current liabilities

RESULT
CASH FLOWS FROM
OPERATING ACTIVITIES

Determining Cash Flows from Operating Activities
Direct Method (Appendix 12B)
(Need income statement and balance sheet data)

1. Cash = Sales
    Receipts
    from Customers*

    ⌐ + Decrease in
    │   Accounts
    │   Receivable
    │   or
    │ - Increase in
    │   Accounts
    └   Receivable

2. Cash = Cost of
    Payments   Goods Sold
    to Suppliers

    ⌐ + Increase in
    │   Inventory
    │   or
    │ - Decrease in
    └   Inventory

    ⌐ + Decrease in
    │   Accounts
    │   Payable
    │ - Increase in
    │   Accounts
    └   Payable

3. Cash = Operating
    Payments   Expenses
    for
    Operating**
    Expenses

    ⌐ + Increase in
    │   Prepaid
    │   Expenses
    │   or
    │ - Decrease in
    │   Prepaid
    └   Expenses

    ⌐ + Decrease in
    │   Accrued
    │   Liabilities
    │   or
    │ - Increase in
    │   Accrued
    └   Liabilities

    ⌐ - Depreciation
    │   and Other
    │   Noncash
    └   Expenses

4. Cash = Income
    Payments   Taxes
    for   Expense
    Income
    Taxes

    ⌐ + Decrease in
    │   Income
    │   Taxes
    │   Payable
    │   or
    │ - Increase in
    │   Income
    │   Taxes
    └   Payable

5. Cash = Interest
    Payments   Expense
    for
    Interest

    ⌐ + Decreases in
    │   Interest Payable
    │ - Increase in
    └   Interest Payable

*use similar computations for
CR from Interest
CR from Dividends

**Wage expense would be
taken out if CP for wages was
to be reported separately.
The related prepaids and
payables would be considered
in the computation.

The Carpet Company's 20X9 and 20X8 balance sheets:

	December 31	
	20X9	20X8
Debits		
Cash	$10,500	$ 4,000
Accounts receivable	8,000	9,000
Merchandise inventory	21,000	18,000
Equipment..	18,000	15,000
Totals..	$57,500	$46,000
Credits		
Accumulated depreciation, equipment......................	$ 4,000	$ 3,000
Accounts payable...	7,000	5,000
Taxes payable..	1,000	2,000
Dividends payable..	1,500	0
Common stock, $10 pay value...............................	27,000	25,000
Contributed capital in excess of par, common stock	6,000	5,000
Retained earnings	11,000	6,000
Totals..	$57,500	$46,000

The Carpet Company's income statement:

For the Year Ended December 31, 20X9

Sales		$61,000
Cost of goods sold...	$40,000	
Wages and other operating expenses	6,300	
Income taxes expense	4,200	
Depreciation expense	1,500	52,000
Net income		$ 9,000

Additional information includes the following:

  a. Equipment costing $3,500 was purchased during the year.

  b. Fully depreciated equipment that cost $500 was discarded and its cost and accumulated depreciation were removed from the accounts.

  c. Two hundred shares of stock were sold and issued at $15 per share.

  d. The company declared $4,000 of cash dividends and paid $2,500.

Required:

Prepare the statement of cash flows for the year ended December 31, 20X9 using the:

1. Indirect method.

2. Direct method (Appendix 12B).

(If this alternative demonstration problem is not covered in class, see your instructor for the solution.)

Problem I

The following statements are either true or false. Place a (T) in the parentheses before each true statement and an (F) before each false statement.

1. (   ) The FASB encourages companies to use the direct method of presenting cash flows from operating activities.

2. (   ) A statement of cash flows should explain the differences between the beginning and ending balances of cash and cash equivalents.

3. (   ) Cash outflows to purchase items classified as cash equivalents are not shown on a statement of cash flows.

4. (   ) A payment by a company in the form of a loan is an example of a financing activity.

5. (   ) The Cash account provides all of the information necessary to prepare a statement of cash flows.

6. (   ) If a company purchases all merchandise for cash and the ending balance of Merchandise Inventory is unchanged from the beginning balance, then cost of goods sold equals the total cash payments for merchandise.

Problem II

You are given several words, phrases, or numbers to choose from in completing each of the following statements or in answering the following questions. In each case select the one that best completes the statement or answers the question and place its letter in the answer space provided.

_____ 1.   Bat Company purchased a plant asset that cost $30,000 by paying $5,000 in cash and paying for the balance owed on a Note Payable. What would be reported on the statement of cash flows?

     a. Cash outflow from investing activities: $5,000.

     b. Cash inflow from financing activities: $25,000.

     c. Cash outflow from investing activities: $30,000.

     d. The transaction would only be reported on the schedule of noncash investing and financing activities.

     e. Both a and b.

_____ 2.   (Appendix 12B) If a company purchases merchandise on account and there are some changes in the Merchandise Inventory balance during a period, what calculations are necessary to calculate cash payments for merchandise?

     a. Purchases + Decrease (- Increase) in Merchandise Inventory.

     b. Cost of Goods Sold + Increase (- Decrease) in Merchandise Inventory.

     c. Purchases + Decrease (- Increase) in Accounts Payable.

     d. Both a and b.

     e. Both b and c.

_____3. (Appendix 12B) Given the following T-account (partially completed) , determine the cash payment for interest.

Interest Payable		
	12/31/X7 Bal.	12,000
	Interest expense	8,000
	12/31/X8 Bal.	13,000

a. $ 7,000.

b. $ 4,000.

c. $ 8,000.

d. $12,000.

e. $20,000.

Problem III

Many of the important ideas and concepts discussed in Chapter 12 are reflected in the following list of key terms. Test your understanding of these terms by matching the appropriate definitions with the terms. Record the number identifying the most appropriate definition in the blank space next to each term.

_____ Cash flow on total assets   _____ Investing activities

_____ Direct method   _____ Operating activities

_____ Financing activities   _____ Statement of cash flows

_____ Indirect method

1. Transactions with owners or creditors that include obtaining cash from issuing debt, repaying amounts borrowed, and obtaining cash from or distributing cash to owners.

2. Activities that involve the production or purchase of merchandise and the sale of goods and services to customers, including expenditures related to administering the business.

3. Presentation of the net cash from operating activities that lists major operating cash receipts, less the major operating cash payments.

4. Financial statement that reports cash inflows and outflows for an accounting period and classifies them as operating, investing, or financing activities.

5. Presentation that reports net income and then adjusts it by adding and subtracting items necessary to yield net cash from operating activities.

6. Transactions that involve purchasing and selling long-term assets, including making and collecting notes receivable and investments in other than cash equivalents.

7. Ratio of operating cash flows to average total assets; not affected by income recognition and measurement rules, reflects earnings quality.

Problem IV

Opposite each transaction, place an "X" in the box below the caption that best describes its disclosure category on a statement of cash flows or supplemental schedule in the case of noncash investing and financing activities.

Transaction	Operating Activity	Investing Activity	Financing Activity	Noncash Investing & Financing Activity
1. Paid wages and salaries.				
2. Cash sale of used equipment.				
3. Received a cash dividend.				
4. Issued a long-term bond payable for cash.				
5. Cash sale of merchandise.				
6. Purchased land in exchange for common stock.				
7. Paid a cash dividend.				
8. Paid interest expense.				
9. Purchased stock in another company for cash.				
10. Repaid a six-month note payable.				

Problem V (Appendix 12B)

Analyze the information presented in each question below and determine the missing amounts.

1. Accounts receivable decreased from $25,000 at the beginning of the period to $18,000 at the end of the period. Sales revenue was $280,000. Assume all sales were on account. There were no uncollectible accounts written off during the period. How much cash was collected from customers during the period? $_____

2. Merchandise inventory increased from $90,000 at the beginning of the period to $100,000 at the end of the period. Cost of goods sold was $160,000. How much merchandise inventory was purchased during the period? $_____

3. The accounts payable balance decreased during the period from $30,000 to $26,000. Disregard your answer to question 2 and assume purchases of merchandise during the period totaled $120,000. Assume all purchases were on account. How much cash was paid to merchandise suppliers during the period? $_____

4. The balance of accumulated depreciation increased during the period from $200,000 to $220,000. Also, machinery originally costing $10,000 with accumulated depreciation of $8,000 was sold during the period. What was the amount of the period's depreciation expense? $_____

5. Refer back to question 1. Instead of assuming all sales revenues of $280,000 were on account, assume cash sales totaled $100,000 and credit sales totaled $180,000. How much cash was collected from customers during the period? $_____

©The McGraw-Hill Companies, Inc., 2008

Problem VI

Iker Company's 20X9 and 20X8 balance sheets are presented below along with its 20x9 income statement.

IKER COMPANY
Balance Sheet
December 31, 20X9, and 20X8
Assets

	20X9		20X8	
Cash		$ 8,000		$ 5,000
Accounts receivable		15,000		12,000
Merchandise inventory		30,000		33,000
Equipment	$40,000		$38,000	
Less accumulated depreciation	16,000	24,000	18,000	20,000
Total assets		$77,000		$70,000
Liabilities and Stockholders' Equity				
Accounts payable		$21,000		$17,000
Accrued liabilities		4,000		5,000
Common stock, $5 par value		35,000		30,000
Retained earnings		17,000		18,000
Total liabilities and stockholders' equity		$77,000		$70,000

IKER COMPANY
Income Statement
For Year Ended December 31, 20X9

Sales		$80,000
Cost of goods sold		30,000
Gross profit on sales		50,000
Operating expenses	$20,000	
Depreciation expense	10,000	
Loss from sale of plant assets	5,000	35,000
Net income		$15,000

Additional information about the company's activities in 20X9:

1. Sold used equipment costing $20,000 with accumulated depreciation of $12,000 for $3,000 cash.
2. Purchased equipment costing $22,000 by paying $17,000 cash and issuing 1,000 shares of common stock.
3. Paid cash dividends of $16,000.

Required:

Note: If you are responsible for Appendix 12A, complete part (a) and then (b). If you are not responsible for the appendix, skip part (a) and complete only part (b).

a. A partially completed spreadsheet for Iker Company's statement of cash flows (assuming the indirect method is used) for the year ended December 31, 20X9 appears below. Complete the spreadsheet.
b. Prepare the Iker Company's statement of cash flows for the year ended December 31, 20X9 using the indirect method.

a.

IKER COMPANY
Spreadsheet for Statement of Cash Flows (Indirect Method)
For Year Ended December 31, 20X9

	December 31, 20X8	Analysis of Changes Debit	Analysis of Changes Credit	December 31, 20X9
Balance sheet—Debits:				
Cash	5,000			8,000
Accounts receivable	12,000			15,000
Merchandise inventory	33,000			30,000
Equipment	38,000			40,000
	88,000			93,000
Balance sheet—Credits:				
Accumulated depreciation	18,000			16,000
Accounts payable	17,000			21,000
Accrued liabilities	5,000			4,000
Common stock, $5 par value	30,000			35,000
Retained earnings	18,000			17,000
	88,000			93,000
Statement of Cash Flows				

b.

IKER COMPANY		
Statement of Cash Flows		
For Year Ended December 31, 20X9		

Solutions for Chapter 12

Problem I

1. T
2. T
3. T
4. T
5. F
6. T

Problem II

1. A
2. C
3. A

Problem III

7	Cash flow on total assets	6	Investing activities
3	Direct method	2	Operating activities
1	Financing activities	4	Statement of cash flows
5	Indirect method		

Problem IV

	Transaction	*Classification*
1.	Paid wages and salaries.	Operating activity
2.	Cash sale of used equipment.	Investing activity
3.	Received a cash dividend.	Operating activity
4.	Issued a long-term bond payable for cash.	Financing activity
5.	Cash sale of merchandise.	Operating activity
6.	Purchased land in exchange for common stock.	Noncash investing and financing activity
7.	Paid a cash dividend.	Financing activity
8.	Paid interest expense.	Operating activity
9.	Purchased stock in another company for cash.	Investing activity
10.	Repaid a six-month note payable.	Financing activity

Problem V (Appendix 12B)

1.	Cash collections from customers	$280,000	+	$ 25,000	-	$18,000	=	$287,000		
2.	Merchandise purchases	$160,000	+	$100,000	-	$90,000	=	$170,000		
3.	Cash payments for merchandise	$120,000	+	$ 30,000	-	$26,000	=	$124,000		
4.	Depreciation expense	$220,000	-	$200,000	+	$ 8,000	=	$ 28,000		
5.	Cash collections from customers	$100,000	+	$180,000	+	$25,000	-	$18,000	=	$287,000

Problem VI

a.

IKER COMPANY
Spreadsheet for Statement of Cash Flows (Indirect Method)
For Year Ended December 31, 20X9

	December 31, 20X8	Analysis of Changes Debit	Analysis of Changes Credit	December 31, 20X9
Balance sheet—Debits:				
Cash	5,000			8,000
Accounts receivable	12,000	3,000 (b)		15,000
Merchandise inventory	33,000		3,000 (c)	30,000
Equipment	38,000	22,000 (h)	20,000 (g)	40,000
	88,000			93,000
Balance sheet—Credits:				
Accumulated depreciation	18,000	12,000 (g)	10,000 (f)	16,000
Accounts payable	17,000		4,000 (d)	21,000
Accrued liabilities	5,000	1,000 (e)		4,000
Common stock, $5 par value	30,000		5,000 (h)	35,000
Retained earnings	18,000	16,000 (i)	15,000 (f)	17,000
	88,000			93,000
Statement of Cash Flows				
Operating activities:				
Net Income		15,000 (a)		
Increase in accounts receivable			3,000 (b)	
Decrease in merchandise inventory		3,000 (c)		
Increase in accounts payable		4,000 (d)		
Decrease in accrued liabilities			1,000 (e)	
Depreciation expense		10,000 (f)		
Loss on sale of equipment		5,000 (g)		
Investing activities				
Proceeds from sale of equipment		3,000 (g)		
Payment for purchase of equipment			17,000 (h)	
Financing activities				
Payment of cash dividends			16,000 (i)	
Noncash investing and financing activities				
Issued stock to purchase equipment		5,000 (h)	5,000 (h)	
		99,000	99,000	

b.

IKER COMPANY

Statement of Cash Flows

For Year Ended December 31, 20X9

Cash flows from operating activities
   Net income .... $ 15,000
   Adjustments to reconcile net income to net cash provided by operating
activities
      Increase in accounts receivable .... (3,000)
      Decrease in merchandise inventory 3,000
      Increase in accounts payable 4,000
      Decrease in accrued liabilities... (1,000)
      Depreciation expense 10,000
      Loss on sale of equipment 5,000
   Net cash provided by operating activities... $ 33,000

Cash flows from investing activities
   Cash received from sale of equipment.. 3,000
   Cash paid for purchase of equipment .... (17,000)
   Net cash used in investing activities.. (14,000)

Cash flows from financing activities ....
   Cash paid for dividends .... (16,000)
   Net cash used in financing activities... (16,000)

Net increase in cash 3,000
Cash balance at beginning of 20X9 5,000
Cash balance at end of 20X9 .... $ 8,000

CHAPTER 13
ANALYZING AND INTERPRETING FINANCIAL STATEMENTS

Learning Objective C1:

Explain the purpose of analysis.

The purpose of financial statement analysis is to help users make better business decisions. Internal users want information to improve company efficiency and effectiveness in providing products or services. External users want information to make better and more informed decisions in pursuing their goals. The common goals of all users are to evaluate a company's (1) past and current performance, (2) current financial position, and (3) future performance and risk.

Learning Objective C2:

Identify the building blocks of analysis.

Financial statement analysis focuses on four "building blocks" of analysis: (1) liquidity and efficiency—ability to meet short-term obligations and efficiently generate revenues; (2) solvency—ability to generate future revenues and meet long-term obligations; (3) profitability—ability to provide financial rewards sufficient to attract and retain financing; and (4) market prospects—ability to generate positive market expectations.

Learning Objective C3:

Describe standards for comparisons in analysis.

Standards for comparisons include (1) intracompany—prior performance and relations between financial items for the company under analysis; (2) competitor—one or more direct competitors of the company; (3) industry—industry statistics; and (4) guidelines (rules-of-thumb)—general standards developed from past experiences and personal judgments.

Learning Objective C4:

Identify the tools of analysis.

The three most common tools of financial statement analysis are: (1) horizontal analysis—comparing a company's financial condition and performance across time; (2) vertical analysis—comparing a company's financial condition and performance to a base amount such as revenues or total assets; and (3) ratio analysis—using and quantifying key relations among financial statement items.

Learning Objective A1:

Summarize and report results of analysis.

A financial statement analysis report is often organized around the building blocks of analysis. A good report separates interpretations and conclusions of analysis from the information underlying them. An analysis report often consists of six sections: (1) executive summary; (2) analysis overview; (3) evidential matter; (4) assumptions; (5) key factors; and (6) inferences.

Learning Objective A2: (Appendix 13A)

Explain the form and assess the content of a complete income statement.

An income statement has four *potential* sections: (1) continuing operations, (2) discontinued segments, (3) extraordinary items, and (4) earnings per share.

Learning Objective P1:

Explain and apply methods of horizontal analysis.

Horizontal analysis is a tool to evaluate changes in data across time. Two important tools of horizontal analysis are comparative statements and trend analysis. Comparative statements show amounts for two or more successive periods, often with changes disclosed in both absolute and percent terms. Trend analysis is used to reveal important changes occurring from one period to the next.

Learning Objective P2:

Describe and apply methods of vertical analysis.

Vertical analysis is a tool to evaluate each financial statement item or group of items in terms of a base amount. Two tools of vertical analysis are common-size statements and graphical analyses. Each item in common-size statements is expressed as a percent of a base amount. For the balance sheet, the base amount is usually total assets, and for the income statement, it is usually sales.

Learning Objective P3:

Define and apply ratio analysis.

Ratio analysis provides clues to and symptoms of underlying conditions. Ratios, properly interpreted, identify areas requiring further investigation. A ratio expresses a mathematical relation between two quantities such as a percent, rate, or proportion. Ratios can be organized into the building blocks of analysis: (1) liquidity and efficiency, (2) solvency, (3) profitability, and (4) market prospects.

Chapter Outline

I. **Basics of Analysis**—Transforming data into useful information for decision making.

    A. Purpose of Analysis

    To help users (both internal and external) make better business decisions.

        1. Internal users (managers, officers, internal auditors, consultants, budget officers, and market researchers) make the strategic and operating decisions of a company.

        2. External users (shareholders, lenders, directors, customers, suppliers, regulators, lawyers, brokers, and the press) rely on financial statement analysis to make decisions in pursuing their own goals.

        3. The common goal of all users is to evaluate:

            a. Past and current performance.

            b. Current financial position.

            c. Future performance and risk.

    B. Building Blocks of Analysis

    The four areas of inquiry or building blocks are:

        1. Liquidity and efficiency—ability to meet short-term obligations and to efficiently generate revenues.

        2. Solvency—ability to generate future revenues and meet long-term obligations.

        3. Profitability—ability to provide financial rewards sufficient to attract and retain financing.

        4. Market Prospects—ability to generate positive market expectations.

    C. Information for Analysis

        1. Most users rely on **general purpose financial statements** that include:

            a. Income statement

            b. Balance sheet

            c. Statement of changes in stockholders' equity (or statement of retained earnings)

            d. Statement of cash flows

            e. Notes related to the statements

        2. **Financial reporting**—is the communication of financial information useful for making investment, credit, and other business decisions. Includes information from SCE 10-K or other filings, press releases, shareholders' meetings, forecasts, management letters, auditor's reports, and Webcasts.

    D. Standards for Comparisons

Used to determine if analysis measures suggest good, bad, or average performance. Standards can include the following types of comparisons:

1. *Intracompany*—based on prior performance and relationships between its financial items.

2. *Competitor*—compared to one or more direct competitors (often best).

3. *Industry*—published industry statistics (available from services like Dun & Bradstreet, Standard and Poor's, and Moody's).

4. *Guidelines (rules-of-thumb)*—general standards developed from past experiences.

    E. Tools of Analysis – includes horizontal, vertical and ratio analysis.

II.   **Horizontal Analysis**—Tool to evaluate changes in financial statement data *across time*. This analysis utilizes:

    A. Comparative Statements—reports financial amounts for more than one period placed side by side in columns on a single statement.

1. Computation of Dollar Changes and Percentage Changes—usually shown in line items.

    a. Dollar change = Analysis period amount minus Base period amount.

    b. Percent change = Analysis period amount minus Base period amount divided by Base period amount times 100.

Notes:

(1) When a negative amount appears in the base period and a positive amount in the analysis period (or vice versa) — a meaningful percentage change cannot be computed. (2) When there is no value in the base period—percentage change is not computable.

(3) When an item has a value in the base period and zero in the next period—the decrease is 100 percent.

2. Comparative balance sheets

    a. Consist of balance sheet amounts from two or more balance sheet dates arranged side by side.

    b. Usefulness is improved by showing each item's dollar change and percent change to highlight large changes.

3. Comparative income statements

    a. Amounts for two or more period are placed side by side.

    b. Additional columns are included for dollar and percent changes.

    B. Trend Analysis—used to reveal patterns in data across successive periods. Involves computing trend percents (or *index number*) as follows:

        1. Select a *base period* and assign each item in the base period a weight of 100%.

        2. Express financial numbers as a percent of their base period number.

        3. Trend percent equals analysis period amount divided by base period amount times 100.

III.   **Vertical Analysis**—Comparing financial condition and performance to a *base amount*. The analysis tools include:

    A. **Common-Size Financial Statements**—reveal changes in the relative importance of each financial statement item. All amounts are redefined in terms *of common-size percents.*

        1. Common-size percentage equals analysis amount divided by base amounts multiplied by 100.

        2. Common-size balance sheets—base amount is usually total assets.

        3. Common-size income statements—base amount is usually revenues.

    B. Common-Size Graphics

    Graphical analysis (e.g., pie charts and bar charts) of common-size statements that visually highlight comparison information.

IV.   **Ratio Analysis**—Using key relationships among financial statement items. Ratios organized into the four (items A through D below) building blocks of analysis:

    A. Liquidity and Efficiency

        1. *Liquidity* refers to the availability of resources to meet short-term cash requirement.

        2. *Efficiency* refers to how productive a company is in using its assets. Efficiency is usually measured relative to how much revenue is generated for a certain level of assets.

        3. Ratios in this block:

            a. Working capital—the excess of current assets over current liabilities.

            b. Current ratio—current assets divided by current liabilities; describes a company's ability to pay its short-term obligations.

            c. Acid-test ratio—similar to current ratio but focuses on quick assets (i.e., cash, short-term investments and current receivables) rather than current assets. Calculated as quick assets divided by current liabilities.

   d. Accounts receivable turnover—net sales or credit sales divided by average accounts receivable; a measure of how long it takes a company to collect its accounts.

   e. Inventory turnover—cost of goods sold divided by average inventory; the number of times a company's average inventory is sold during an accounting period.

   f. Days' sales uncollected—accounts receivable divided by net credit sales multiplied by 365 days; measures how frequently a company collects its accounts receivable.

   g. Days' sales in inventory—ending inventory divided by cost of goods sold multiplied by 365; measures how many days it will take to convert the inventory on hand at the end of the period into accounts receivable or cash.

   h. Total asset turnover—net sales divided by average total assets; describes the ability to use assets to generate sales.

B. Solvency

   1. *Solvency* refers to a company's long-run financial viability and its ability to cover long-term obligations. *Capital structure* is one of the most important components of solvency analysis.

   2. *Capital structure* refers to a company's sources of financing.

   3. Ratios in this block:

      a. Debt ratio—total liabilities divided by total assets.

      b. Equity ratio—total stockholders' equity divided by total assets.

         Note: A company is considered less risky if its capital structure (equity and long-term debt) is composed more of equity.

      c. Debt-to-Equity Ratio – total liabilities divided by total equity; measure of solvency. A larger debt-to-equity ratio implies greater risk.

      d. Times interest earned—income before interest expense and income taxes divided by interest expense; reflects the risk of loan repayments with interest to creditors.

C. Profitability

   1. *Profitability* refers to a company's ability to generate an adequate return on invested capital.

   2. *Return* is judged by assessing earnings relative to the level and sources of financing.

3. Ratios in this block:

 a. Profit margin—net income divided by net sales; describes the ability to earn net income from sales.

 b. Return on total assets—net income divided by average total assets; a summary measure of operating efficiency; comprises profit margin (net income divided by net sales) and total asset turnover (net sales divided by average total assets).

 c. Return on common stockholders' equity—net income less preferred dividends divided by average common stockholders' equity; measures the success of a company in earning net income for its owners.

D. Market Prospects

 1. Market measures are useful for analyzing corporations with publicly traded stock.

 2. Market measures use stock price in their computation.

 3. Ratios in this block:

 a. Price-earnings ratio—market price per common stock divided by earnings per share; used to evaluate the profitability of alternative common stock investments.

 b. Dividend yield—annual cash dividends paid per share of stock divided by market price per share; used to compare the dividend-paying performance of different investment alternatives.

E. Summary of Ratios

 Exhibit 13.16 sets forth the names of each of the common ratios by category, and includes the formula and a description of what is measured by each ratio.

V. **Decision Analysis—Analysis Reporting**

 Goal of financial statement analysis report is to reduce uncertainty through rigorous and sound evaluation. A good analysis report usually consists of six sections:

 1. Executive summary.
 2. Analysis overview.
 3. Evidential matter.
 4. Assumptions.
 5. Key factors.
 6. Inferences.

VI. **Sustainable Income – Appendix 13A**

 When a company's activities involve income-related events that are not part of its normal, continuing operations, it often separates the income statement into different sections as follows:

A. Continuing Operations

Reports the revenues, expenses, and income generated by the company's continuing operations.

B. Discontinued Segments

1. A **business segment** is a part of a company's operations that serves a particular line of business or class of customers.

2. A company's gain or loss from selling or closing down a segment is separately reported as follows:

   a. Income from operating the discontinued segment for the current period prior to its disposal.

   b. The gain or loss from disposing of the segment's net assets.

C. Extraordinary Items

1. **Extraordinary gains and losses** are those that are *both unusual* and *infrequent*.

   a. An **unusual gain or loss** is abnormal or otherwise unrelated to the company's regular activities and environment.

   b. An **infrequent gain or loss** is not expected to recur given the company's operating environment.

2. Reporting extraordinary items in a separate category helps users predict future performance, absent the effects of the extraordinary items.

3. Items that are either unusual or infrequent, but *not* both, are reported in the income statement but after the normal revenues and expenses.

D. Earnings per Share (EPS) — is the amount of income earned by each share of outstanding common stock and is reported in the final section of income statement. One of the most widely cited items of accounting information.

E. Changes in Accounting Principles

1. The *consistency principle* requires a company apply the same accounting principles across periods (examples in this context: (include inventory or depreciation methods). Changes in accounting principles are acceptable if justified as improvements in financial reporting.

2. Cumulative effect of the change on prior periods' incomes should be reported on the income statement (net of taxes) below extraordinary items.

3. A footnote should describe and justify the change and report what income would have been under the old method.

F. Comprehensive Income is net income plus certain gains and losses that bypass the income statement. The change in equity for the period, excluding investments from and distributions to its stockholders.

Following are data from the statements of two companies selling similar products:

Current Year-End Balance Sheets

	Sled Company	Zip Company
Cash	$ 11,900	$ 20,000
Notes receivable	7,700	3,200
Accounts receivable, net	42,000	64,000
Inventory..	58,800	87,680
Prepaid expenses	1,680	3,520
Plant and equipment, net.................................	232,120	274,400
Total assets	$354,200	$452,800
Current liabilities	$ 56,000	$ 80,800
Mortgage payable	70,000	80,000
Common stock, $10 par value..........................	140,000	160,000
Retained earnings..	88,200	132,000
Total liabilities and stockholders' equity	$354,200	$452,800

Beginning-of-Year Data

	Sled Company	Zip Company
Inventory..	$ 53,200	$ 85,120
Total assets	345,800	443,200
Stockholders' equity	217,000	285,120

Data from the Current Year's Income Statement

	Sled Company	Zip Company
Sales	$672,000	$880,000
Cost of goods sold	528,080	699,840
Interest expense	4,200	5,600
Net income	23,373	28,896

Required:

1. Calculate current ratios, acid-test ratios, inventory turnovers, and days' sales uncollected for the two companies. Then state which company you think is the better short-term credit risk and why.

2. Calculate return on total assets employed and return on stockholders' equity. Then, under the assumption that each company's stock can be purchased at book value, state which company's stock you think is the better investment and why.

(If this alternative demonstration problem is not covered in class, see your instructor for the solution.)

©The McGraw-Hill Companies, Inc., 2008

Problem I

The following statements are ether true or false. Place a (T) in the parentheses before each true statement and an (F) before each false statement.

1. ( ) A current ratio of 2 to 1 always indicates that a company can easily meet it's current debts.

2. ( ) Accounts receivable turnover of 6.4 times in 20X8 and 8.2 times in 20X7 indicates that a company is collecting its accounts receivable more rapidly in 20x8 than in 20X7.

3. ( ) If accounts receivable is $150,000, and net credit sales is $1,000,000, days' sales uncollected is 15.

4. ( ) On a common-size income statement, the amount of net sales is assigned a value of 100%.

5. ( ) To calculate inventory turnover, cost of goods sold is divided by gross sales.

6. ( ) The ratios and turnovers of a selected group of competitive companies normally are the best bases of comparison for analyzing financial statements.

7. ( ) Return on total assets summarizes the two components of operating efficiency—profit margin and total asset turnover.

8. ( ) Current ratio, acid-test ratio, accounts receivable turnover, and inventory turnover are tools for evaluating short-term liquidity.

9. ( ) The cumulative effect on prior years' incomes of a change in accounting principle is reported on the statement of retained earnings. (Appendix 13A).

Problem II

You are given several words, phrases, or numbers to choose from in completing each of the following statements or in answering the following questions. In each case select the one that best completes the statement or answers the question and place its letter in the answer space provided.

_____1. To analyze long-term risk and capital structure, the following ratios and statistics for analysis would be used:

    a. Debt ratio.
    b. Equity ratio.
    c. Times fixed interest charges earned.
    d. Pledged assets to secured liabilities.
    e. All of the above.

_____2. During 20X7, a company's sales were $360,000. In 20X8 they were $334,800 and in 20X9 they were $374,400. Express the sales in trend percentages, using 20X7 as the base year.

    a. 20X7—96%; 20X8—89%; 20X9—100%,
    b. 20X7—100%; 20X8—108%; 20X9—96%.
    c. 20X7—100%; 20X8—100%; 20X9—100%.
    d. 20X7—104%; 20X8—112%; 20X9—100%.
    e. 20X7—100%; 20X8—93%; 20X9—104%.

_____ 3. Information from the 20X7 income statement of Becker Company follows:

Sales	$320,000
Gross profit on sales.................................	138,000
Operating income.....................................	32,000
Income before taxes	22,000
Net income	16,800

If the company's 20X7, accounts receivable were $23,200 and $28,000 at January 1 and December 31, 20X7, respectively, what was the company's accounts receivable turnover?

a. 7.1 times.

b. 5.4 times.

c. 12.5 times.

d. 3.9 times.

e. 10.1 times.

_____ 4. Use the following information from the 20X7 income statement of Sumner Company to calculate the company's inventory turnover:

Sales	$300,000
Cost of goods sold:...................................	
Inventory, January 1, 20X7.................................	28,480
Purchases, net..	171,040
Goods available for sale	199,520
Inventory, December 31, 20X7	19,520
Cost of goods sold..................................	180,000
Gross profit on sales.................................	120,000
Operating expenses	34,000
Income from operations	$ 86,000

a. 7.5 times.

b. 9.2 times.

c. 12.5 times.

d. 8.3 times.

e. 17.9 times.

_____ 5. The Keyes Company had the following comparative income statements for 20X8 and 20X7:

	20X8	20X7
Net sales	$630,000	$552,000
Cost of goods sold...................................	428,400	389,160
Gross profit from sales.............................	201,600	162,840
Operating expenses	97,500	78,600
Net income	$104,100	$ 84,240

What are the cost of goods sold in common-size percentages for 20X8 and 20X7?

a. 110.1% in 20X8; 100.0% in 20X7.

b. 24.3% in 20X8; 21.6% in 20X7.

c. 41.2% in 20X8; 46.2% in 20X7.

d. 68.0% in 20X8; 70.5% in 20X7.

e. 147.0% in 20X8; 141.8% in 20X7.

_____ **6.** Captan, Inc., has a depreciable asset that cost $500,000 (no salvage value) and has decided to switch from straight-line depreciation to declining-balance depreciation at twice the straight-line rate. The company depreciated the asset for 1 year based on straight-line depreciation and a 5-year life. The company is subject to a 30% income tax rate. Calculate the amount of depreciation expense to be reported in the current year (year 2).

    a. $200,000.

    b. $100,000.

    c. $120,000.

    d. $180,000.

    e. $20,000.

Problem III

Many of the important ideas and concepts discussed in Chapter 13 are reflected in the following list of key terms. Test your understanding of these terms by matching the appropriate definitions with the terms. Record the number identifying the most appropriate definition in the blank space next to each term.

_____ Business segment		_____ Infrequent gain or loss
_____ Common-size financial statement		_____ Liquidity
_____ Comparative financial statement		_____ Market prospects
_____ Efficiency		_____ Profitability
_____ Equity ratio		_____ Ratio analysis
_____ Extraordinary gains and losses		_____ Solvency
_____ Financial reporting		_____ Unusual gain or loss
_____ Financial statement analysis		_____ Vertical analysis
_____ General-purpose financial statements		_____ Working capital
_____ Horizontal analysis		

1. Process of communicating information relevant to investors, creditors, and others in making investment, credit, and other decisions.

2. Statements published periodically for use by a variety of interested parties; includes the income statement, balance sheet, statement of changes in equity (or statement of retained earnings), statement of cash flows, and notes to these statements.

3. Statement with data for two or more successive periods placed in side-by-side columns, often with changes shown in dollar amounts and percents.

4. Current assets minus current liabilities.

5. Statement that expresses each amount as a percentage of a base amount. In the balance sheet, total assets is usually the base amount and is expressed as 100%. In the income statement, net sales is usually the base.

6. Portion of total assets provided by equity, calculated as total equity divided by total assets.

7. Evaluation of each financial statement item or group of items in terms of a specific base amount.

8. Availability of resources to meet short-term cash requirements.

9. Company's productivity in using its assets; usually measured relative to how much revenue a certain level of assets generates.

10. Company's long-run financial viability and its ability to cover long-term obligations.

11. Application of analytical tools to general-purpose financial statements and related data for making business decisions.

12. Company's ability to generate an adequate return on invested capital.

13. Comparison of a company's financial condition and performance across time.

14. Expectations (both good and bad) about a company's future performance as assessed by users and other interested parties.

15. Determination of key relationships between financial statement items.

16. Gain or loss that is abnormal or unrelated to the ordinary activities and environment.

17. Gains or losses reported separately from continuing operations because they are both unusual and infrequent.

18. Part of operations that serves a line of business or class of customers and that has assets, liabilities, and operating results distinguishable from other parts.

19. Gain or loss is not expected to recur, given the operating environment of the business.

Problem IV

The sales, cost of goods sold, and gross profits from sales of the Laker Company for a five-year period are shown below:

	20X5	20X6	20X7	20X8	20X9
Sales	$350,000	$385,000	$413,000	$455,000	$497,000
Cost of goods sold	250,000	280,000	305,000	345,000	375,000
Gross profit	100,000	105,000	108,000	110,000	122,000

Laker Company's sales are expressed in trend percentages below. Express its cost of goods sold and gross profit in trend percentages in the spaces provided.

	20X5	20X6	20X7	20X8	20X9
Sales	100	110	118	130	142
Cost of goods sold					
Gross profit					

Comment on the situation shown by the data: _____

_____

_____

_____

Problem V

Complete the following by filling in the blanks.

1. When calculating accounts receivable turnover, the preferable sales number to use is _____ (cash, credit, total) sales.

2. The acid-test ratio is calculated by dividing _____ by _____.

3. Inventory turnover is calculated by dividing _____ by _____.

4. A slower turnover of inventory _____ (will, will not) tend to increase working capital requirements.

5. The current ratio is calculated by dividing _____ by _____. It is an indication of a company's _____ to meet its current obligations.

6. Return on total assets is calculated by dividing _____ by the amount of _____.

7. Times fixed interest charges earned is calculated by dividing income before deducting _____ and _____ by the amount of _____.

8. Days' sales uncollected is calculated by dividing _____ by _____ and multiplying the resulting quotient by _____. Days' sales uncollected is an indication of _____.

9. The price-earnings ratio for a company's common stock is calculated by dividing the _____ per share of the common stock by _____.

10. Return on common stockholders' equity is calculated by dividing _____
_____ by _____ stockholders' equity.

11. Compared to companies with an average growth rate, companies in a growth industry would be expected to have a _____ (higher, lower) price-earnings ratio.

12. Days' stock on hand is calculated by dividing _____ by _____ and multiplying by 365.

13. The results of discontinued segments are separated from the results of other activities on the income statement in order to _____
_____.

Problem VI

Following are the condensed income statements of two companies of unequal size. Common-size percents are often used in comparing the statements of companies of unequal size. The income statement amounts of Company A have already been expressed in common-size percents in the condensed income statements presented below. Express the income statement amounts of Company Z in common-size percents in the spaces provided.

COMPANIES A AND Z

Income Statements

For Year Ended December 31, 20—

	Dollar Amounts		Common-Size Percentages	
	Company A	Company Z	Company A	Company Z
Sales...	$325,000	$265,000	100.0	_____
Cost of goods sold	204,750	164,300	63.0	_____
Gross profit on sales	120,250	100,700	37.0	_____
Selling expenses	61,750	49,025	19.0	_____
Administrative expenses...............	42,250	34,450	13.0	_____
Total operating expenses..............	104,000	83,475	32.0	_____
Net income	$ 16,250	$ 17,225	5.0	_____

Based on a review of the income statement amounts expressed in common-sized percents, which company appeared to operate more efficiently during the year? _____

Problem VII

Explain where each of the following items should appear in the financial statements of Odyssey Corporation.

1. The company maintains a stock investment portfolio as part of its business activities to enhance earnings. This year, for the first time in seven years, it sold stock for a gain of $27,000.

2. After depreciating equipment for three years based on an expected six-year life, the company decided this year that the value of the equipment would last five more years. As a result, the depreciation for the current year is $18,000 instead of $30,000.

Solutions for Chapter 13

Problem I

1. F
2. F
3. F
4. T
5. F
6. T
7. T
8. T
9. F

Problem II

1. E
2. E
3. C
4. A
5. D
6. A

Problem III

18	Business segment	19	Infrequent gain or loss
5	Common-size financial statement	8	Liquidity
3	Comparative financial statement	14	Market prospects
9	Efficiency	12	Profitability
6	Equity ratio	15	Ratio analysis
17	Extraordinary gains and losses	10	Solvency
1	Financial reporting	16	Unusual gain or loss
11	Financial statement analysis	7	Vertical analysis
2	General-purpose financial statements	4	Working capital
13	Horizontal analysis		

Problem IV

	20X5	20X6	20X7	20X8	20X9
Sales	100	110	118	130	142
Cost of goods sold	100	112	122	138	150
Gross profit...................................	100	105	108	110	122

Laker Company's sales increased each year throughout the five-year period, but its cost of goods sold increased more rapidly. This slowed the rate of increase in its gross profit.

Problem V

1. credit

2. quick assets; current liabilities

3. cost of goods sold; average inventory

4. will

5. current assets; current liabilities; ability

6. net income; average total assets

7. income taxes; fixed interest charges; fixed interest charges

8. accounts receivable; credit sales; the number of days in a year; collection efficiency (how frequently a company collects its accounts)

9. market price; earnings per share

10. net income less any preferred dividends; average common

11. higher

12. ending inventory; cost of goods sold

13. more clearly present the results of continuing operations

Problem VI

COMPANIES A AND Z
Income Statements
For Year Ended December 31, 20—

	Dollar Amounts		Common-Size Percentages	
	Company A	Company Z	Company A	Company Z
Sales...	$325,000	$265,000	100.0	100.0
Cost of goods sold.........................	204,750	164,300	63.0	62.0
Gross profit on sales.....................	120,250	100,700	37.0	38.0
Selling expenses	61,750	49,025	19.0	18.5
Administrative expenses...............	42,250	34,450	13.0	13.0
Total operating expenses..............	104,000	83,475	32.0	31.5
Net income	$ 16,250	$ 17,225	5.0	6.5

Company Z appeared to operate more efficiently during the year.

Problem VII

1. This gain is neither unusual nor infrequent. As a result, it should be reported in the income statement as part of income from continuing operations.
2. This change from an expected useful life of six to eight years is a change in an accounting estimate. The $18,000 should be reported in the income statement as part of income from continuing operations.

APPENDIX B
TIME VALUE OF MONEY

Learning Objective C1:

Describe the earning of interest and the concepts of present and future values.

Summary

Interest is the payment by a borrower to the owner of an asset for its use. Present and future value computations are a way for us to estimate the interest component of holding assets or liabilities over a period of time.

Learning Objective P1:

Apply present value concepts to a single amount by using interest tables.

Summary

The present value of a single amount received at a future date is the amount that can be invested now at the specified interest rate to yield that future value.

Learning Objective P2:

Apply future value concepts to a single amount by using interest tables.

Summary

The future value of a single amount invested at a specified rate of interest is the amount that would accumulate by the future date.

Learning Objective P3:

Apply present value concepts to an annuity by using interest tables.

Summary

The present value of an annuity is the amount that can be invested now at the specified interest rate to yield that series of equal periodic payments.

Learning Objective P4:

Apply future value concepts to an annuity by using interest tables.

Summary

The future value of an annuity invested at a specified rate of interest is the amount that would accumulate by the date of the final payment.

Appendix Outline

I.   Present Value and Future Value Concepts

    A. As time passes, certain assets and liabilities that are held grow.

    B. Growth is due to interest.

    C. Present and future value computations are a way for us to measure or estimate the interest component of holding assets or liabilities over time.

II.   Present Value of a Single Amount

    A. The present value of a single amount received at a future date is the amount that can be invested now at the specified interest rate to yield that future value.

    B. A table of present values for a single amount shows the present values of $1 for a variety of interest rates and a variety of time periods that will pass before the $1 is received.

II.   Future Value of a Single Amount

    A. The future value of a single amount invested at a specified rate of interest is the amount that would accumulate by the future date.

    B. A table of future values of a single amount shows the future values of $1 invested now at a variety of interest rates for a variety of time periods.

III.   Present Value of an Annuity

    A. An *ordinary annuity* is defined as equal end-of-period payments at equal intervals.

    B. The present value of an annuity is the amount that can be invested now at the specified interest rate to yield that series of equal periodic payments.

    C. A table of present values for an annuity shows the present values of annuities where the amount of each payment is $1 for different numbers of periods and a variety of interest rates.

IV.   Future Value of an Annuity

    A. The future value of an annuity invested at a specified rate of interest is the amount that would accumulate by the date of the final payment.

    B. A table of future values for an annuity shows the future values of annuities where the amount of each payment is $1 for different numbers of periods and a variety of interest rates.

Problem I

The following statements are either true or false. Place a (T) in the parentheses before each true statement and an (F) before each false statement.

1. ( ) In discounting, the number of periods must be expressed in terms of 6-month periods if interest is compounded semiannually.

2. ( ) One way to calculate the present value of an annuity is to find the present value of each payment and add them together.

3. ( ) A table for the future values of 1 can be used to solve all problems that can be solved using a table for the present values of 1.

4. ( ) Erlich Enterprises should be willing to pay $100,000 for an investment that will return $20,000 annually for 8 years if the company requires a 12% return. (Use the tables to get your answer.)

Problem II

You are given several words, phrases, or numbers to choose from in completing each of the following statements or in answering the following questions. In each case select the one that best completes the statement or answers the question and place its letter in the answer space provided. Use the tables in your text as necessary to answer the questions.

_____ 1. Ralph Norton has $300 deducted from his monthly paycheck and deposited in a retirement fund that earns an annual interest rate of 12%. If Norton follows this plan for 1 year, how much will be accumulated in the account on the date of the last deposit? (Round to the nearest whole dollar.)

   a. $3,600.
   b. $4,032.
   c. $3,805.
   d. $7,240.
   e. $4,056.

_____ 2. Maxine Hansen is setting up a fund for a future business. She makes an initial investment of $15,000 and plans to make semiannual contributions of $2,500 to the fund. The fund is expected to earn an annual interest rate of 8%, compounded semiannually. How much will be in the fund after five years?

   a. $52,218.
   b. $36,706.
   c. $68,600.
   d. $45,332.
   e. $51,373.

_____ 3. Tricorp Company is considering an investment that is expected to return $320,000 after four years. If Tricorp demands a 15% return, what is the most that it will be willing to pay for this investment?

   a. $320,000.
   b. $177,696.
   c. $182,976.
   d. $ 45,216.
   e. $278,272.

_____ 4. Tom Snap can invest $6.05 for 17 years, after which he will be paid $10. What annual rate of interest will he earn?

 a. 15%.

 b. 9%.

 c. 7%.

 d. 5%.

 e. 3%.

Problem III

Complete the following by filling in the blanks. Use the tables in Appendix C to find the answers.

1. Leila Turner expects to invest $0.83 at a 7% annual rate of interest and receive $2 at the end of the investment. Turner must wait _____ years before she receives payment.

2. Jim Ables expects to invest $5 for 35 years and receive $102.07 at the end of that time. He will earn interest at a rate of _____% on this investment.

Solutions for Appendix B

Problem I

 1. T

 2. T

 3. T

 4. F

Problem II

 1. C

 2. A

 3. C

 4. E

Problem III

1. Table E-1 show that when the interest rate = 7% and the present value of 1 = 0.4150 ($0.83/$2), the number of periods = 13.

2. Table E-2 shows that when the number of periods = 35 and the future value of 1 = 20.4140 ($102.07/$5), the interest rate = 9%.

APPENDIX C
REPORTING AND ANALYZING INVESTMENTS AND INTERNATIONAL OPERATIONS

Learning Objective C1:

Distinguish between debt and equity securities and between short-term and long-term investments.

Debt securities reflect a creditor relationship and include investments in notes, bonds, and certificates of deposit. *Equity securities* reflect an owner relationship and include shares of stock issued by other companies. Short-term investments in securities are current assets that meet two criteria: (1) They are expected to be converted into cash within one year or the current operating cycle of the business, whichever is longer and (2) they are readily convertible to cash, or *marketable*. All other investments in securities are long-term. Long-term investments also include assets not used in operations and those held for special purposes, such as land for expansion.

Learning Objective C2:

Identify and describe the different classes of investments in securities.

Investments in securities are classified into one of five groups: (1) trading securities, which are always short-term, (2) debt securities held-to-maturity, (3) debt and equity securities available-for-sale, (4) equity securities in which an investor has a significant influence over the investee, and (5) equity securities in which an investor has a controlling influence over the investee.

Learning Objective C3:

Describe how to report equity securities with controlling influence.

If an investor owns more than 50% of another company's voting stock and controls the investee, the investor's financial reports are prepared on a consolidated basis. These reports are prepared as if the company were organized as one entity.

Learning Objective C4 (Appendix C-A):

Explain foreign exchange rates between currencies.

A foreign exchange rate is the price of one currency stated in terms of another. An entity with transactions in a foreign currency when the exchange rate changes between the transaction dates and their settlement will experience exchange gains or losses.

Learning Objective A1:

Compute and analyze the components of return on total assets.

Return on total assets has two components: profit margin and total asset turnover. A decline in one component must be met with an increase in another if return on assets is to be maintained. Component analysis is helpful in assessing company performance compared to that of competitors and its own past.

Learning objective P1:

Account for trading securities.

Investments are initially recorded at cost, and any dividend or interest from these investments is recorded in the income statement. Investments classified as trading securities are reported at market value. Unrealized gains and losses on trading securities are reported in income. When investments are sold, the difference between the net proceeds from the sale and the cost of the securities is recognized as a gain or loss.

Learning objective P2:

Account for held-to-maturity securities.

Debt securities held-to-maturity are reported at cost when purchased. Interest revenue is recorded as it accrues. The cost of long-term held-to-maturity securities is adjusted for the amortization of any difference between cost and maturity value.

Learning objective P3:

Account for available-for-sale securities.

Debt and equity securities available-for-sale are recorded at cost when purchased. Available-for-sale securities are reported at their market values on the balance sheet with unrealized gains or losses shown in the equity section. Gains and losses realized on the sale of these investments are reported in the income statement.

Learning Objective P4:

Account for equity securities with significant influence.

The equity method is used when an investor has a significant influence over an investee. This usually exists when an investor owns 20% or more of the investee's voting stock but not more than 50%. The equity method means an investor records its share of investee earnings with a debit to the investment account and a credit to a revenue account. Dividends received reduce the investment account balance.

Learning Objective P5 (Appendix C-A):

Record transactions listed in a foreign currency.

When a company makes a credit sale to a foreign customer and sales terms call for payment in a foreign currency, the company must translate the foreign currency into dollars to record the receivable. If the exchange rate changes before payment is received, exchange gains or losses are recognized in the year they occur. The same treatment is used when a company makes a credit purchase from a foreign supplier and is required to make payment in a foreign currency.

Appendix Outline

I. **Basics of Investments**

A. Motivation for Investments

1. Companies transfer *excess* cash into investments to produce higher income.

2. Some entities, such as mutual funds and pension funds, are set up to produce income from investments.

3. Companies make investments for strategic reasons. Examples: investments in competitors, suppliers, and even customers.

B. Short-Term versus Long-Term Investments

1. **Short-term investments** (temporary *investments* and *marketable securities*)—securities that must meet these two requirements:

a. Expected to be converted into cash within one year or the current operating cycle of the business, whichever is longer.

b. Readily convertible to cash.

2. **Long-term investments**—investments not meeting the two requirements for short-term investments.

C. Classes of and Reporting for Investments

1. Accounting for investments depends on three factors:

a. Security type, either debt or equity.

b. The company's intent to hold the security either short-term or long-term, and

c. The company's (investor's) percent ownership in the other company's (investee's) equity securities.

2. Using these three factors, investments are separated into five classes of securities:

a. **Trading -** Includes debt and noninfluential equity securities that are actively traded.

b. **Held-to-maturity -** Includes debt securities intended to be held-to-maturity.

      c. **Available-for-sale** - Includes debt and noninfluential equity securities.

      d. **Significant influence-** Includes equity securities with significant influence.

      e. **Controlling influence-** Includes equity securities with controlling influence.

D. Basics of Accounting for Investments

    1. Accounting Basics for Debt Securities

      a. Debt securities that will be held-to maturity are recorded at cost when purchased.

      b. Interest revenue for investments in debt securities is recorded when earned.

    2. Accounting Basics for Equity Securities

      a. Equity securities that are available-for-sale are recorded at cost when acquired, including commissions or brokerage fees paid.

      b. Any cash dividends received are credited to Dividend Revenue and reported in the income statement.

      c. When the securities are sold, the proceeds are compared with cost, and any gain or loss is recorded.

E. Accounting for Noninfluential Investments – companies must value and report at fair market value. Exact requirements depend on classification.

    1. Trading   securities
Trading securities are *debt and equity securities* that the company intends to actively manage and trade for profit. Frequent purchases and sales are expected and are made to earn profits on short-term price changes.

      a. Valuing and reporting trading securities

         i. The entire portfolio of trading securities is reported at its market value; this requires a "market adjustment" from the cost of the portfolio.

         ii. Any **unrealized gain (or loss)** from a change in the market value of the portfolio of trading securities is reported on the income statement.

      b. Selling trading securities

         i. When individual trading securities are sold, the difference between the net proceeds (sale price less fees) and the cost of the individual trading securities that are sold is recognized as a gain or a loss.

         ii. Any prior period market adjustment to the portfolio is *not* used to compute the gain or loss from sale of individually traded securities.

          iii. A gain is reported in the Other Revenues and Gains section of the income statement; a loss is reported in Other Expenses and Losses section.

  2. Held-to-maturity securities

  Held-to-maturity (HTM) securities are *debt securities* a company intends and is able to hold until maturity.

    a. HTM securities are reported in

       i. Current assets if their maturity dates are within one year or the operating cycle, whichever is longer.

       ii. Long-term assets when the maturity dates extend beyond one year or the operating cycle, whichever is longer.

    b. All HTM securities are recorded at cost when acquired.

    c. Interest revenue on HTM securities is recorded when earned.

    e. The portfolio of HTM securities is reported at (amortized) cost which is explained in advanced courses.

    f. There is no market adjustment to the portfolio of HTM securities.

  3. Available-for-sale securities

  Available-for-sale securities (AFS) are *debt and equity securities* not classified as trading or held-to-maturity securities. AFS securities are purchased to yield interest, dividends, or increases in market value.

    a. AFS securities are reported as short-term investments if the intent is to sell the AFS securities within the longer of one year or the operating cycle; otherwise, they are classified as long-term.

    b. Valuing and reporting AFS securities

       i. The cost of the AFS securities is adjusted to reflect changes in market value (as with trading securities).

       ii. However, any unrealized gain or loss for the portfolio of AFS securities is *not* reported on the income statement; instead, it is reported in the equity section of the balance sheet (and is part of *comprehensive income*—explained below).

    c. Selling AFS securities

       i. Accounting for the sale of AFS securities is identical to that described for the sale of trading securities. (See section E.1.b above.)

       ii. The difference between the cost of the individual securities sold and the net proceeds (sales price less fees) is recognized as a gain or loss.

II. **Accounting for Influential Investments**

A. Investment in Equity Securities with Significant Influence

A long-term investment classified as **equity securities with significant influence** implies that the investor can exert significant influence over the investee.

1. An investor that owns 20% or more (but not more than 50%) of a company's voting stock is usually presumed to have significant influence over the investee. (In some cases, the 20% test is overruled by other, more persuasive, evidence.)

2. The **equity method** of accounting and reporting is used for long-term investments in equity securities with significant influence.

   a. Long-term investments in equity securities with significant influence are recorded at cost in a Long-Term Investments account when acquired.

   b. When the investee reports its earnings, the investor records its share of those earnings in its investment account and credits the Earnings from Long-Term Investments account.

   c. The receipt of cash dividends is not revenue because the investor has already recorded its share of the investee's earnings; instead, the cash dividends received reduce the balance of the Long-Term Investments account.

   d. The book value of an investment under the equity method equals the cost of the investment plus (minus) the investor's equity in the *undistributed (distributed)* earnings of the investee.

   e. When the investment is sold, the gain or loss is computed by comparing the proceeds from the sale with the book value on the date of the sale.

B. Investment in Equity Securities with Controlling Influence

A long-term investment classified as **equity securities with controlling influence** implies that the investor can exert a controlling influence over the investee.

1. An investor who owns more than 50% of a company's voting stock has control over the investee. (In some cases, controlling influence can extend to situations of less than 50% ownership.)

2. The *equity method with consolidation* is used to account for long-term investments in equity securities with controlling influence.

   a. The investor reports *consolidated financial statements* when owning such securities. The controlling investor is called the **parent** and the investee is called the **subsidiary**.

      b. **Consolidated financial statements** show the financial position, results of operations, and cash flows of all entities under the parent's control, including all subsidiaries; these statements are prepared as if the business were organized as one entity.

      c. The parent uses the equity method in its accounts, but the investment account is *not* reported on the consolidated financial statements.

  C. Accounting Summary for Investments in Securities—See Exhibit C.8 for a summary of the accounting for investments in securities.

  D. Comprehensive Income

    1. The term **comprehensive income** refers to all changes in equity for a period except those due to investments and distributions to owners. This means that it includes:

      a. The revenues, gains, expenses, and losses reported in net income, and

      b. The gains and losses that bypass net income but affect equity.

    2. Most often this simply requires one additional column for Other Comprehensive Income in the statement of stockholders' equity.

III. Decision Analysis—Components of Return on Total Assets

  A. A company's **return on total assets** is used to assess financial performance.

  B. It can be separated into two components: profit margin and total asset turnover.

  C. Return on total assets is calculated as profit margin times total asset turnover.

  D. Profit margin is calculated as net income divided by net sales. It reflects the percent of net income in each dollar of net sales.

  E. Total asset turnover is calculated as net sales divided by average total assets. It reflects a company's ability to produce net sales from total assets.

  F. Generally, if a company is to maintain or improve its return on total assets, it must meet any decline in either profit margin or total asset turnover with an increase in the other. If not, return on assets will decline.

IV. Investments in International Operations (Appendix C-A)

Some entities' operations occur in so many different countries that the companies are called **multinationals**. Two major accounting challenges include accounting for sales and purchases listed in a foreign currency and preparing consolidated financial statements with international subsidiaries.

Appendix Outline

A. Exchange Rates between Currencies

The price of one currency stated in terms of another currency is called a **foreign exchange rate.**

B. Sales and Purchases Listed in a Foreign Currency

1. When a U.S. company makes a credit sale to an international customer, accounting for the sale and the account receivable is straightforward if sales terms require the international customer's payment in U.S. dollars.

2. If sale terms require (or allow) payment in a foreign currency, the U.S. company must account for the sale and the account receivable in a different manner.

    a. The sales price must be translated from the foreign currency to dollars by multiplying the sales price (stated in the foreign currency) by the exchange rate on the date of the sale; entry (for U.S. company) for sale of merchandise on credit: debit Accounts Receivable, credit Sales.

    b. If the receivable is still outstanding at the end of the end of the accounting period, the receivable must again be translated from the foreign currency to dollars by multiplying the sales price (stated in the foreign currency) by the exchange rate at the end of the accounting period. Entry assuming the amount of the receivable (when translated) is higher: debit Accounts Receivable, credit Foreign Exchange Gain.

3. When payment is received from the foreign customer, the U.S. company will immediately exchange the payment into dollars. Entry assuming the amount of the payment (when translated) is lower: debit Cash, debit Foreign Exchange Loss, credit Accounts Receivable.

4. The balance in the Foreign Exchange Gain (or Loss) account is reported on the income statement and closed to the Income Summary account at year-end.

C. Consolidated Statements with International Subsidiaries

Before preparing consolidated statements, the parent must translate financial statements of a foreign subsidiary into U.S. dollars. This topic is covered in advanced accounting courses.

20X7

Jan 1 Purchased 8,000 shares (20%) of Investee Company's outstanding stock at a cost of $150,000.

May 31 Investee Company declared and paid a cash dividend of $1.50 per share.

Dec 31 Investee Company announced that its net income for the year was $100,000.

20X8

Oct 1 Investee Company declared and paid a cash dividend of $1.00 per share.

Dec 31 Investee Company announced that its net income for the year was $80,000.

20X9

Jan 1 Investor Corporation sold all of its shares of Investee Company for $178,000 cash.

Required:

Prepare journal entries on Investor Corporation's books using the equity method, which assumes that Investor has significant influence over Investee Company.

(If this alternative demonstration problem is not covered in class, see your instructor for the solution.)

Problem I

The following statements are either true or false. Place a (T) in the parentheses before each true statement and an (F) before each false statement.

1. ( ) Trading securities are either debt or equity securities that the company intends to actively trade for profit.

2. ( ) An investor who owns 20% or more of a corporation's voting stock is presumed to have significant influence over the investee.

3. ( ) A short-term investment in a security available-for-sale is reported on the balance sheet at cost.

4. ( ) Unrealized holding gains and losses on investments in equity securities available-for-sale are reported in the stockholders' equity section of the balance sheet.

5. ( ) An unrealized gain on a short-term investment in a trading security is reported on the income statement.

6. ( ) The equity method is used to account for investments in equity securities available-for-sale.

7. ( ) At acquisition, the purchase of equity securities is recorded at cost regardless of which method is used to account for the investment.

8. ( ) A short-term investment in a security held-to-maturity is reported on the balance sheet at its fair (market) value.

9. ( ) The only difference between accounting for debt securities held-to-maturity and debt securities available-for-sale is that interest is not accrued on debt securities held-to-maturity.

10. ( ) Investments in equity securities available-for-sale are reported on the balance sheet at their market values.

Problem II

You are given several words, phrases, or numbers to choose from in completing each of the following statements or in answering the following questions. In each case select the one that best completes the statement or answers the question and place its letter in the answer space provided.

_____1. On January 1, 20X8, Allured Company purchased 12,000 shares of More Corporation's common stock at 60-1/4 plus a $6,000 commission. On July 1, 20X8, More Corporation declared and paid dividends of $0.85 per share, and on December 31, 20X8, it reported a net income of $156,000. Assuming More Corporation has 48,000 outstanding common shares and that the market value per share at December 31, 20X8, is $65, what is the carrying value of Alfred's investment in More at December 31?

    a. $729,000.

    b. $757,800.

    c. $751,800.

    d. $723,000.

    e. $780,000.

_____ 2. On January 1, 20x8, Allured Company purchased 12,000 shares of More Corporation's common stock at 60-1/4 plus a $6,000 commission. On July 1, 20X8, More Corporation declared and paid dividends of $0.85 per share, and on December 31, 20X8, it reported a net income of $156,000. Assuming More Corporation has 96,000 outstanding common shares and that the market value per share at December 31, 20X8, is $65, what is the carrying value of Allured's investment in More at December 31?

    a. $723,000.

    b. $742,500.

    c. $738,300.

    d. $780,000.

    e. $729,000.

_____ 3. The cost and market values of Company B's short-term investments on December 31, 20X8, follow:

	Cost	Market
Securities held-to-maturity	$30,000	$28,000
Trading securities	34,000	32,500
Securities available-for-sale...................................	28,000	31,000

What dollar amount should be reported on Company B's December 31, 20X8, balance sheet for each of the three types of short-term investments?

    a. $30,000; $34,000; $28,000.

    b. $30,000; $32,500; $31,000.

    c. $28,000; $32,500; $31,000.

    d. $28,000; $34,000; $28,000.

    e. $28,000; $32,500; $28,000.

Problem III

Many of the important ideas and concepts discussed in Appendix C are reflected in the following list of key terms. Test your understanding of these terms by matching the appropriate definitions with the terms. Record the number identifying the most appropriate definition in the blank space next to each term.

_____ Available-for-sale securities	_____ Held-to-maturity securities
_____ Comprehensive income	_____ Long-term investments
_____ Consolidated financial statements	_____ Multinational*
_____ Equity method	_____ Parent
_____ Equity securities with controlling influence	_____ Return on total assets
	_____ Short-term investment
_____ Equity securities with significant influence	_____ Subsidiary
	_____ Trading securities
_____ Foreign exchange rate*	_____ Unrealized gain

* Key term discussed in Appendix C-A.

1. Long-term investment when the investor is able to exert controlling influence over the investee; investors owning 50% or more of voting stock are presumed to exert controlling influence.

2. Long-term investment when the investor is able to exert significant influence over the investee; investors owning 20% or more (but less than 50%) of a voting stock are presumed to exert significant influence.

3. Long-term investments in securities held with the intent to sell them in the future.

4. Investments in debt and equity securities that are not marketable or, if marketable, are not intended to be converted into cash in the short-term; also special purpose funds and assets not used in operations.

5. Debt securities that the company has the intent and ability to hold until they mature.

6. Company that owns a controlling interest in another corporation (requires more than 50% of voting stock).

7. Accounting method used for long-term investments when the investor has "significant influence" over the investee.

8. Entity controlled by another entity (parent) when the parent owns more than 50% of the subsidiary's voting stock.

9. Financial statements that show all (combined) activities under the parent's control, including those of any subsidiaries.

10. Gain (loss) not yet realized by an actual transaction or event such as a sale.

11. Net change in equity for a period, excluding owner investments and distributions.

12. Price of one currency stated in terms of another currency.

13. Company that operates in several countries.

14. Ratio reflecting operating efficiency; defined as net income divided by average total assets for the period; also called *return on assets* or *return on investment*.

15. Debt and equity securities that management expects to convert to cash within the next 3 to 12 months (or the operating cycle if longer); also called *temporary securities* or *marketable securities*.

16. Investments in debt and equity securities that the company intends to actively trade for profit.

Problem IV

Hailey Company had no short-term investments prior to 20X8. The following transactions involving short-term investments in trading securities occurred during 20X8:

Mar. 1   Purchased 500 shares of Abco common stock at 40-3/4 plus a $200 brokerage fee.
June 20   Purchased 1,000 shares of Carr common stock at 10-1/2 plus a $100 brokerage fee.
Nov. 3   Purchased 600 shares of TCY common stock at 20-1/4 plus a $120 brokerage fee.

On December 31, 20X8, the fair market value of these trading securities held by Hailey were: Abco, 48-1/2; Carr, 9-3/4; and TCY, 22-1/2.

Prepare the journal entries to record the preceding transactions. Also prepare an adjusting entry, if necessary, to record the market adjustment of the short-term investments. Do not provide explanations. Skip a line between entries.

DATE	ACCOUNT TITLES AND EXPLANATION	P.R.	DEBIT	CREDIT

Problem V

On January 1, 20X8, Large Company paid $90,000 for 36,000 of Small Company's 90,000 outstanding common shares. Small Company paid a dividend of $20,000 on November 1, 20X8, and at the end of the year reported earnings of $40,000. The market value per share on December 31, 20X8, was $2.10. On January 3, 20X9, Large Company sold its interest in Small Company for $120,000.

1. Complete the following by filling in the blanks.

   The _____ method should be used in Large Company's books to account for the investment in Small Company since an investor that owns ____% or more, but not more than ____%, of a company's voting stock is normally presumed to have a _____ influence over the investor.

2. Prepare the journal entries for Large Company to record the facts presented above. Do not provide explanations. Skip a line between entries.

DATE	ACCOUNT TITLES AND EXPLANATION	P.R.	DEBIT			CREDIT		

Problem VI

On January 1, 20X8, Celestial Company paid $25,000 for 20,000 of Yardley Company's 120,000 outstanding common shares. Yardley Company paid a dividend of $.10 per share on June 1, 20X8, and at the end of the year reported earnings of $500,000. The market value per share on December 31, 20X8, was $1.90. Assume that Celestial did not own any investments prior to 20X8. On January 1, 20X9, Celestial Company sold its interest in Yardley Company for $37,900.

1. Complete the following by filling in the blanks.

   Celestial's long-term investment in Yardley would be considered as _____ because the company owns less than _____% of the outstanding voting stock of the investee.

2. Prepare the journal entries for Celestial Company to record the facts presented above. Also, prepare a journal entry, dated January 1, 20X9, to remove any balances related to the market value adjustment. Do not include explanations. Skip a line between entries.

DATE	ACCOUNT TITLES AND EXPLANATION	P.R.	DEBIT	CREDIT

Solutions for Appendix C

Problem I

1. T
2. T
3. F
4. T
5. T
6. F
7. T
8. F
9. F
10. T

Problem II

1. B
2. D
3. B

Problem III

3	Available-for-sale securities	5	Held-to-maturity securities
11	Comprehensive income	4	Long-term investments
9	Consolidated financial statements	13	Multinational*
7	Equity method	6	Parent
1	Equity securities with controlling Influence	14	Return on total assets
		15	Short-term investment
2	Equity securities with significant Influence	8	Subsidiary
		16	Trading securities
12	Foreign exchange rate*	10	Unrealized gain (loss)

* *Key term discussed in Appendix C-A.*

Financial Accounting, 4e

Problem IV

Mar. 1	Short-Term Investments—Trading	20,575	
	Cash [(500 x $40.75) + $200]		20,575
June 20	Short-Term Investments—Trading	10,600	
	Cash [(1,000 x $10.50) + $100]		10,600
Nov. 3	Short-Term Investments—Trading	12,270	
	Cash [(600 x $20.25) + $120]		12,270
Dec. 31	Market Adjustment—Trading	4,055	
	Unrealized Gain—Income		4,055
	(See calculation below.)		

Short-Term Investments in Trading Securities	Cost	Fair (Market) Value
Abco	$20,575	$24,250
Carr	10,600	9,750
TCY	12,270	13,500
Total	$43,445	$47,500

$47,500 - $43,445 = $4,055

Problem V

1. equity; 20; 50; significant

2.   20X8

Jan. 1	Long-Term Investments—Small Company	90,000	
	Cash		90,000
Nov. 1	Cash	8,000	
	Long-Term Investments—Small Company		8,000
Dec. 31	Long-Term Investments—Small Company	16,000	
	Earnings from Long-Term Investments		16,000

20X9

Jan. 3	Cash	120,000	
	Long-Term Investments—Small Company		98,000
	Gain on Sale of Investments		22,000

Problem VI

1. noninfluential; 20

2. 20X8

Jan. 1	Long-Term Investments—Yardley Company	25,000	
	Cash		25,000
June 1	Cash	2,000	
	Dividend Revenue		2,000
Dec. 31	Market Adjustment—Available-for-Sale (LT)	13,000	
	Unrealized Gain—Equity		13,000

20X9

Jan. 1	Cash	37,900	
	Long-Term Investments—Yardley Company		25,000
	Gain on Sale of Investments		12,900
1	Unrealized Gain—Equity	13,000	
	Market Adjustment—Available-for-Sale (LT)		13,000

APPENDIX D
REPORTING AND ANALYZING PARTNERSHIPS

Learning Objective C1:

Identify characteristics of partnerships and similar organizations.

Partnerships are voluntary associations, involve partnership agreements, have limited life, are not subject to income tax, include mutual agency, and have unlimited liability. Organizations that combine selected characteristics of partnerships and corporations include limited partnerships, limited liability partnerships, S corporations, and limited liability companies.

Learning Objective A1:

Compute partner return on equity and use it to evaluate partnership performance.

Partner return on equity provides each partner an assessment of his or her return on equity invested in the partnership.

Learning Objective P1:

Prepare entries for partnership formation.

A partner's initial investment is recorded at the market value of the assets contributed to the partnership.

Learning Objective P2:

Allocate and record income and loss among partners.

A partnership agreement should specify how to allocate partnership income or loss among partners. Allocation can be based on a stated ratio, capital balances, or salary and interest allowances to compensate partners for differences in their service and capital contributions.

Learning Objective P3:

Account for the admission and withdrawal of partners.

When a new partner buys a partnership interest directly from one or more existing partners, the amount of cash paid from one partner to another does not affect the partnership total recorded equity. When a new partner purchases equity by investing additional assets in the partnership, the new partner's investment can yield a bonus either to existing partners or to the new partner. The entry to record a withdrawal can involve payment from either (1) the existing partners' personal assets or (2) partnership assets. The latter can yield a bonus to either the withdrawing or remaining partners.

Learning Objective P4:

Prepare entries for partnership liquidation.

When a partnership is liquidated, losses and gains from selling partnership assets are allocated to the partners according to their income-and-loss-sharing ratio. If a partner's capital account has a deficiency that the partner cannot pay, the other partners share the deficit according to their relative income-and-loss-sharing ratio.

Appendix Outline

I. **Partnership Form of Organization**—An unincorporated association of two or more people to pursue a business for profit as co-owners.

    A. Characteristics of Partnerships

        1. Voluntary Association between partners.

        2. Partnership Agreement—**partnership contract** normally includes details of partners' (1) names and contributions, (2) right and duties, (3) sharing of income and losses, (4) withdrawal arrangement, (5) dispute procedures, (6) admission and withdrawal of partners, and (7) rights and duties in the event a partner dies. This agreement should be in writing but is binding even if only expressed orally.

        3. Limited Life—death, bankruptcy, or expiration of the contract period automatically ends a partnership.

        4. Taxation—partnerships are not subject to tax on income—partners report their share of income on their personal income tax return.

        5. **Mutual agency**—each partner is an agent of the partnership and can enter into and bind the partnership to any contract within the normal scope of its business.

        6. **Unlimited liability**—each general partner is responsible for payment of all the debts of the partnership if the other partners are unable to pay their share.

        7. Co-Ownership of Property—assets are owned jointly by all partners but claims on partnership assets are based on their capital account and the partnership contract.

    B. Organizations with Partnership Characteristics

        1. **Limited Partnership** (L.P. or Ltd.) has two classes of partners, general and limited. **General partners** assume unlimited liability for the debts of the partnership. The **limited partners** assume no personal liability beyond their invested amounts and cannot take an active role in managing the company.

        2. Limited liability partnership (L.L.P.) is designed to protect innocent partners from malpractice or negligence claims resulting from the acts of another partner. Generally, all partners are personally liable for other partnership debts.

        3. S Corporation has 75 or fewer stockholders, is treated as a partnership for income tax purposes but otherwise is accounted for as a "C" corporation.

        4. Limited Liability Company (L.L.C. or L.C) owners are called members, are protected with the limited liability feature as owners of corporations and can assume an active management role. L.L.C.'s have a limited life and are typically classified as a partnership for tax purposes.

C. Choosing a Business Form

Factors to be considered include: taxes, liability risk, tax and fiscal year-end, ownership structure, estate planning, business risks, and earnings and property distributions.

II. **Basic Partnership Accounting**—same as accounting for a proprietorship except for transactions directly affecting partners' equity. Use separate capital and withdrawal accounts for each partner.

A. Organizing a Partnership

Each partner's investment is recorded at an agreed upon value, normally the fair market value of the assets and liabilities at their date of contribution.

B. Dividing Income or Loss

1. Any agreed upon method of dividing income or loss is allowed. If there is no agreement, the net income or loss is divided equally.

2. Common methods of dividing partnership earnings use:

a. Allocation on stated ratios —partners must agree on the fractional share each receives.

b. Allocation on capital balances—based on the ratio of each partner's relative capital balance.

c. Allocation on service, capital, and stated ratios—salary and interest allowances, and a fixed ratio are specified.

i. When income exceeds allowances, the remainder is allocated to individual partners using a fixed ratio and added to their individual planned allowance.

ii. When allowances exceed the income, the negative amount or shortage is allocated using the ratio and applied *against* each partner's total allowance.

3. Salaries to partners and interest on partners' investments are not partnership expenses; they are allocations of net income.

4. Partners may agree to salary and interest allowances to reward unequal contributions of services or capital.

C. Partnership Financial Statements

Similar to those of other organizations except:

1. The **statement of partners' equity** shows changes for each partner's capital account, including the allocation of income.

2. The equity section of the balance sheet generally lists a separate capital account for each partner.

III. **Admission and Withdrawal of Partners**

   A. Admission of a Partner

      1. Purchase of Partnership Interest

         a. The purchase is a personal transaction between one or more current partners and the new partner.

         b. Purchaser does not become a partner until accepted by the current partners.

         c. Involves a reallocation of current partners' capital to reflect the transaction.

      2. Investing Assets in a Partnership

         a. The transaction is between the new partner and the partnership. Invested assets become partnership property.

         b. New partner's equity recorded for assets invested may be equal to, less than, or greater than the investment.

         c. When the new partner's equity differs from the investment, there is a bonus to new or old partner's equity.

         d. Bonuses to old partners are allocated based on their income and loss sharing agreement.

   B. Withdrawal of a Partner—two ways:

      1. Withdrawing partner sells his or her interest to another person who pays cash or other assets to the withdrawing partner.

      2. Cash or other assets of the partnership can be distributed to the withdrawing partner in settlement of his or her interest.

         a. Withdrawing partner may accept assets equal to, less than, or greater than his/her equity.

         b. When the withdrawing partner's equity differs from assets withdrawn, there is a bonus to remaining or withdrawing partner's equity.

         c. Bonuses to remaining partners are allocated based on their income and loss sharing agreement.

   C. Death of a Partner

      1. Dissolves a partnership.

      2. Deceased partner's estate is entitled to receive his or her equity. Contract usually calls for closing of the books and determining current value of assets and liabilities to update equity.

      3. Settlement of the deceased partner's equity can involve selling the equity to remaining partners or to an outsider, or it can involve withdrawing assets.

IV.   **Liquidation of a Partnership**

A.   Involves four steps:

1.   Noncash assets are sold for cash and a gain or loss on liquidation is recorded.

2.   Allocate gain or loss from liquidation of the assets to partners using their income-and-loss ratio.

3.   Pay or settle liabilities.

4.   Distribute any remaining cash to partners based on their capital balances.

B.   Allocating gains or losses on liquidation may result in:

1.   No Capital Deficiency—all partners' have a zero or credit balance in their capital accounts equivalent to final distribution of cash.

2.   Capital deficiency—when at least one partner has a debit balance in his/her capital account.

a.   Partners with a capital deficiency must, if possible, cover the deficit by paying cash into the partnership.

b.   When a partner is unable to pay the deficiency, the remaining partners with credit balances absorb the unpaid deficit according to their income-and-loss ratio. Inability to cover deficiency does not relieve partner of liability.

V.   **Decision Analysis—Partnership Return on Equity**

A.   The **partnership return on equity ratio** evaluates partnership success compared with other opportunities.

B.   It is calculated by dividing a partner's share of net income by that partner's average partner equity.

Sand, Mell, and Rand are partners who share income and losses in a 1:4:5 ratio. After lengthy disagreements among the partners and several unprofitable periods, the partners decided to liquidate the partnership. Before the liquidation, the partnership balance sheet showed Cash $10,000, total "other assets", $106,000; total liabilities, $88,000; Sand, Capital, $1,200; Mell, Capital, $11,700; and Rand, Capital, $15,100. The "other assets" were sold for $ 85,000.

Determine the following:

1.   The gain (or loss) realized on the sale of the assets.

2.   The balances in the partners' capital accounts after the distribution of this gain or loss to the capital accounts.

3.   Assume that if any capital deficits exist, they are not made-up. How much cash will each of the partners receive in the final liquidation?

(If this alternative demonstration problem is not covered in class, see your instructor for the solution.)

Problem I

The following statements are either true or false. Place a (T) in the parentheses before each true statement and an (F) before each false statement.

1. (   ) Partnership accounting is exactly like that of a single proprietorship except for transactions affecting the partners' equities.

2. (   ) Although a partner does not work for either a salary or interest, to be fair in the distribution of partnership earnings, it is often necessary to provide allowances for services and investments.

3. (   ) In the liquidation of a partnership, after selling all assets and paying all debts, the partners share any remaining cash equally.

4. (   ) When a partner withdraws from a partnership, that partner always withdraws assets equal to his equity.

5. (   ) Partners return on equity is computed by dividing a partner's average investment by that partner's share of net income.

Problem II

You are given several words, phrases, or numbers to choose from in completing each of the following statements or in answering the following questions. In each case select the one that best completes the statement or answers the question and place its letter in the answer space provided.

_____1. Reggie and Veronica began a partnership by investing $28,000 and $20,000, respectively, and during its first year the partnership earned a $42,000 net income. What would be the share of each partner in the net income if the partners had agreed to share by giving a $16,400 per year salary allowance to Reggie and an $18,000 per year salary allowance to Veronica, plus 10% interest on their beginning-of-year investments, and the remainder equally?

    a. Reggies' share, $20,600; Veronica's share, $21,400.

    b. Reggies' share, $22,200; Veronica's share, $19,800.

    c. Reggies' share, $21,400; Veronica's share, $20,600.

    d. Reggies' share, $24,500; Veronica's share, $17,500.

    e. Reggies' share, $21,000; Veronica's share, $21,000.

_____2. Red and White operate a partnership in which they have agreed to share profits and losses in a ratio of 3:2 respectively. They have agreed to accept Blue as a partner, offering him a 25% share for an $80,000 investment. Prior to his investment the combined equity of Red and White totals $120,000. The admission of Blue as a partner will result in

    a. a bonus of $30,000 to Blue.

    b. a bonus of $18,000 to Red and $12,000 to White.

    c. a bonus of $30,000 each to Red and Blue.

    d. a bonus of 15,000 each to Red and Blue.

    e. no bonus for any of the parties.

Problem III

Many of the important ideas and concepts discussed in Appendix D are reflected in the following list of key terms. Test your understanding of these terms by matching the appropriate definitions with the terms. Record the number identifying the most appropriate definition in the blank space next to each term.

_____ C corporation
_____ General partner
_____ General partnership
_____ Limited liability company
_____ Limited liability partnership
_____ Limited partners
_____ Limited partnership
_____ Mutual agency

_____ Partner return on equity
_____ Partnership
_____ Partnership contract
_____ Partnership liquidation
_____ S Corporation
_____ Statement of changes in partners'
  equity
_____ Unlimited liability

1. Partners who have no personal liability for partnership debts beyond the amounts they invested in the partnership.

2. Partnership in which all partners have mutual agency and unlimited liability for partnership debts.

3. Partnership that has two classes of partners, limited partners and general partners.

4. Partner who assumes unlimited liability for the debts of the partnership; responsible for its management.

5. Legal relationship among partners whereby each partner is an agent of the partnership and is able to bind the partnership to contracts within the scope of the partnership's business.

6. Agreement among partners that sets terms under which the affairs of the partnership are conducted.

7. Legal relationship among general partners that makes each of them responsible for partnership debts if the other partners are unable to pay their shares.

8. Unincorporated association of two or more persons to pursue a business for profit as co-owners.

9. Corporation that does not qualify for and elect to be treated as a partnership for income tax purposes and therefore is subject to income taxes.

10. Partnership in which partner is not personally liable for malpractice or negligence unless that partner is responsible for providing the service that resulted in the claim.

11. Dissolution of a business partnership by (1) selling noncash assets and allocating any gain or loss according to partners' income-and-loss ratio, (2) paying liabilities, and (3) distributing any remaining cash according to partners' capital balances.

12. Corporation that meets special tax qualifications so as to be treated as a partnership for income tax purposes.

13. Financial statement that shows the total capital balances at the beginning of the period, any additional investment by partners, the income or loss of the period, the partners' withdrawals, and the partners' ending capital balances; also called *statement of partners' capital.*

14. Form of organization that combines corporation and limited partnership features; provides limited liability to its members (owners), and allows members to actively participate in management.

15. Partner net income divided by average partner equity.

Problem IV

Complete the following by filling in the blanks.

1. A _____ (limited, general) partnership has two classes of partners.

2. Blake and Dillon are partners who have always shared incomes and losses equally. Hester has sued the partners on a partnership debt and obtained a $12,000 judgment. The partnership and Dillon have no assets; consequently, Hester is attempting to collect the entire $12,000 from Blake. Blake has sufficient assets to pay the judgment but refuses, claiming she is liable for only one half the $12,000. Hester _____ (can, cannot) collect the entire $12,000 from Blake because _____ .

3. Since a partnership is a voluntary association, an individual _____ (can, cannot) be forced against his will to become a partner; and since a partnership is based on a contract, its life is _____ .

4. Partners work for partnership _____ and not for a salary. Furthermore, when a partnership agreement calls for an interest and/or salary allowance, these allowances are only used to calculate the allocation of _____ .

5. The phrase mutual agency, when applied to a partnership, means _____ _____ .

6. The four steps in the liquidation of a partnership are:

   _____

   _____

   _____

   _____ .

7. If the allocation of loss from sale of the assets results in a deficit balance in a partner's capital account, that partner is responsible for making up the negative amount. If the partner fails to make up the negative then the other partners _____ _____ .

Problem V

Flip and Flop began a partnership by investing $14,000 and $10,000, respectively, and during its first year the partnership earned a $21,000 net income. Complete the tabulation below to show, under each of the three assumptions, the share of each partner in the $21,000 net income.

		Flip's Share	*Flop's Share*
1.	The partners failed to agree as to the method of sharing	_____	_____
2.	The partners had agreed to share in their beginning-of-year investment ratio..	_____	_____
3.	The partners had agreed to share by giving an $8,200 per year salary allowance to Flip and a $9,000 per year salary allowance to Flop, plus 10% interest on their beginning-of-year investments, and the remainder equally	_____	_____

Solutions for Appendix D

Problem I

1. T
2. T
3. F
4. F
5. F

Problem II

1. A
2. B

Problem III

9	C corporation	15	Partner return on equity
4	General partner	8	Partnership
2	General partnership	6	Partnership contract
14	Limited liability company	11	Partnership liquidation
10	Limited liability partnership	12	S Corporation
1	Limited partners	13	Statement of changes in partners'
3	Limited partnership		equity
5	Mutual agency	7	Unlimited liability

Problem IV

1. limited
2. can; each partner has unlimited liability for the debts of the partnership
3. cannot; limited
4. profits, or earnings; profits or earnings (net income also correct)
5. each partner is an agent of the partnership and can bind it to contracts
6. (1) Noncash assets are sold for cash and a gain or loss on liquidation is recorded; (2) gain or loss on liquidation is allocated to partners using their income-and-loss ratio; (3) liabilities are paid; and (4) remaining cash is distributed to partners based on their capital balances.
7. must absorb the negative according to their ratio for sharing income or loss.

Problem V

1. $10,500; $10,500

2. $12,250; $8,750

3. $10,300; $10,700

APPENDIX E
REPORTING AND PREPARING SPECIAL JOURNALS

Learning Objective C1:

Identify fundamental principles of accounting information systems.

Accounting information systems are governed by five fundamental principles: control, relevance, compatibility, flexibility, and cost-benefit.

Learning Objective C2:

Identify components of accounting information systems.

The five basic components of an accounting information system are source documents, input devices, information processors, information storage, and output devices.

Learning Objective C3:

Explain the goals and uses of special journals.

Special journals are used for recording transactions of similar type, each meant to cover one kind of transaction. Four of the most common special journals are the sales journal, cash receipts journal, purchases journal, and cash disbursements journal. Special journals are efficient and cost-effective tools in the journalizing and posting processes.

Learning Objective C4:

Describe the use of controlling accounts and subsidiary ledgers.

A general ledger keeps controlling accounts such as Accounts Receivable and Accounts Payable, but details on individual accounts making up the controlling account are kept in subsidiary ledgers (such as an accounts receivable ledger). The balance in a controlling account must equal the sum of its subsidiary account balances after posting is complete.

Learning Objective C5:

Explain how technology-based information systems impact accounting.

Technology-based information systems aim to increase the accuracy, speed, efficiency, and convenience of accounting procedures.

Learning Objective A1:

Compute segment return on assets and use it to evaluate segment performance.

A business segment is a part of a company that is separately identified by its products or services or by the geographic market it serves. Analysis of a company's segments is aided by the segment return on assets (segment operating income divided by segment average assets).

Learning Objective P1:

Journalize and post transactions using special journals.

Each special journal is devoted to similar kinds of transactions. Transactions are journalized on one line of a special journal, with columns devoted to specific accounts, dates, names, posting references, explanations, and other necessary information. Posting is threefold: (1) individual amounts in the Other Accounts column are posted to their general ledger accounts on a regular (daily) basis, (2) individual amounts in a column whose total is *not* posted to a controlling account at the end of a period (month) are posted regularly (daily) to their general ledger accounts, and (3) total amounts for all columns except the Other Accounts column are posted at the end of a period (month) to their column's account title in the general ledger.

Learning Objective P2:

Prepare and prove the accuracy of subsidiary ledgers.

Account balances in the general ledger and its subsidiary ledgers are tested for accuracy after posting is complete. This procedure is twofold: (1) prepare a trial balance of the general ledger to confirm that debits equal credits and (2) prepare a schedule to confirm that the controlling account's balance equals the subsidiary ledger's balance.

Learning Objective P3 (Appendix EA):

Journalize and post transactions using special journals in a periodic inventory system.

Transactions are journalized and posted using special journals in a periodic system. The methods are similar to those in a perpetual system; the primary difference is that both cost of goods sold and inventory are not adjusted at the time of each sale. This usually results in the deletion (or renaming) of one or more columns devoted to these accounts in each special journal.

Appendix Outline

I. **Fundamental System Principles**—Accounting information systems (AIS) collect, process, organize, and communicate information to decision makers. *The five fundamental principles* of accounting information systems are:

    A. **Control Principle**

    Requires that AIS include methods and procedures called **internal controls**. These controls allow managers to control and monitor activities.

    B. **Relevance Principle**

    Requires that AIS report useful, understandable, timely and pertinent information for effective decision making.

    C. **Compatibility Principle**

    Requires that AIS conform with a company's activities, personnel and structure. It must adapt to the unique characteristics of a company.

    D. **Flexibility Principle**

    Requires that AIS adapt to changes in the company, business environment, and needs of decisions makers.

    E. **Cost-Benefit Principle**

    Requires that the benefits from an activity in AIS outweigh the costs of that activity.

II. **Components of Accounting Systems**—AIS consist of people, records, methods and equipment. Five basic **components of AIS** are:

    A. Source Documents

    Documents (paper and electronic) that provide the basic information to be processed by an accounting system.

    B. Input Devices

    Capture information from source documents and enable its transfer to the information system's processing component.

    C. Information Processors

    Systems that interpret, transform, and summarize information for use in analysis and reporting.

    D. Information Storage

    System component that keeps data in a form accessible to information processors.

    E. Output Devices

    Means to take information out of the accounting system and make it available for use.

Appendix Outline

III. **Special Journals in Accounting**

   A. Basics of **Special Journals**

     Used to record and post transactions of similar type. Use reduces recording and posting labor by grouping similar transactions and periodically posting totals accumulated.

   B. **Subsidiary Ledgers**

     List of individual accounts with a common characteristic. Supports the general ledger by providing detailed information on specific general ledger accounts.

     1. Two common subsidiary ledgers are:

       a. Accounts receivable ledger--contains accounts for and stores transaction data of individual customers; controlled by Accounts Receivable in General Ledger.

       b. Accounts payable ledger-- contains accounts for and stores transaction data of individual suppliers; controlled by Accounts Payable in General Ledger.

     2. Subsidiary ledgers are common for other general ledger accounts such as equipment or investments.

   C. **Sales Journal** – used to record sales of inventory on credit.

     1. Generally contains two columns. The first column is used to record each sale and the *total* is posted to Accounts Receivable (debit) and to Sales (credit) in the General Ledger. It has a second column to record the tracking of the perpetual inventory cost. This column *total* is posted to Cost of Goods Sold (debit) and Inventory (credit).

     2. Debits to the accounts of particular customers are *individually* posted to the customer's account in the subsidiary accounts receivable ledger.

     3. A *schedule* (list) *of accounts receivable* is used to prove the accuracy of the subsidiary ledger. The total of this schedule must equal the balance of the Accounts Receivable controlling account in the general ledger.

   D. **Cash Receipts Journal** - multicolumn journal used to record all receipts of cash.

     1. Every transaction increases Cash and is recorded in a special Cash *debit* column. Only the *total* of this column is posted.

2. Special *credit* columns are usually established for Accounts Receivable and Sales. A special *debit* column may be used for Sales Discounts. A special column is established to record the tracking of the perpetual inventory cost. Amounts in this column are *debits* to Cost of Goods Sold and *credits* to Inventory. Only the *totals* of special columns are posted to the General Ledger.

3. A column titled "Other Accounts - Credit" is used to record all types of receipts that are not frequent enough to justify having special columns. Each credit in the Other Accounts column must be posted *individually*.

4. Credits to the accounts of particular customers are *individually* posted to the customer's account in the subsidiary Accounts Receivable Ledger.

E. **Purchases Journal** - multicolumn journal used to record all purchases on credit.

1. In addition to a special column for Inventory *debit* and Accounts Payable *credit,* separate columns may be established for frequent credit purchases, such as Store Supplies *debit* and Office Supplies *debit*.

2. Only the *totals* of special columns are posted to the General Ledger. Amounts in the "Other Accounts" columns are posted *individually*.

3. *Credits* to the accounts of particular creditors are *individually* posted to the subsidiary Accounts Payable Ledger.

4. A *schedule* (list) *of accounts payable* is used to prove the accuracy of the subsidiary ledger. The total of this schedule must equal the balance of the Accounts Payable controlling account in the general ledger.

F. **Cash Disbursements (Payments) Journal**

Used to record all payments of cash.

1. A Check Register is a cash disbursements journal that includes a column for entering the number of each check.

2. A special Cash *credit* column is established. Only the *total* of this column is posted to the general ledger.

3. Special columns are usually established for Accounts Payable *debit* and Inventory *credit* (for purchase discounts received). Only the *totals* of special columns are posted to the General Ledger.

4. A column titled "Other Accounts -Debit" is used to record all types of payments that are not frequent enough to justify having a special column. Each debit in the Other Accounts column must be posted *individually*.

5. Debits to the accounts of particular creditors are *individually* posted to the supplier's account in the subsidiary Accounts Payable Ledger.

G. General Journal Transactions - used to record transactions that do not fit in any of the special journals. Examples:

1. Adjusting entries.

2. Closing entries.

3. Correcting entries.

4. Other transactions may include sales returns, purchases returns, purchases of plant assets by issuing a note, and receipt of notes from customers.

IV. **Technology-Based Accounting Information Systems**—AIS are supported with technology ranging from simple calculators to state-of-the-art advanced electronic systems.

A. Computer Technology in Accounting--reduces time required for recordkeeping tasks and provides more time for accounting professionals to focus on analysis and managerial decision making.

Two broad components of computer technology:

1. Computer hardware—physical computer equipment.

2. Computer software—programs that direct the operations of computer hardware.

B. Data   Processing   in   Accounting
Two types of processing are:

1. **On-line processing**—enters and processes data as soon as source documents are available. Updates databases immediately. Examples: airline reservations, credit card records, and rapid mail-order processing.

2. **Batch processing** - accumulates source documents for a period of time and then processes them all at once such as daily, weekly, or monthly.

C. Computer Networks in Accounting - links among computers giving different users and different computers access to common databases, programs, and hardware.

D. Enterprise-Resource Planning Software - programs that manage a company's vital operations.

VI. **Decision Analysis—Segment Return on Assets**

A. A *business segment* is a part of a company that is separately identified by its products or services or by the geographic market it serves.

B. One measure of success for business segments is the **segment return on assets ratio**.

C. It is calculated as segment operating income divided by segment average assets.

VII. **Special Journals Under a Periodic System. (Appendix E-A)**

A. Transactions are journalized and posted using special journals in a periodic system using methods similar to those in a perpetual system.

B. Primary difference is that the periodic system does not record the increase in cost of goods sold and the decrease in inventory at the time of each sale. This results in the deletion of these columns in the sales and cash receipt journals. Also, in the purchases journal the Inventory debit column is replaced with a Purchases debit column and in the cash disbursements journal the Inventory credit column is replaced with a Purchases Discount credit column.

Bedrock Corporation completed these transactions during February of the current year:

Feb   1   F. Stone invested $100,000 cash in the business in exchange for common stock with a total par value of $100,000.

         1   Sent Flint Company check No. 413 for a cash purchase of inventory $ 75,000.

         2   Sold inventory costing $500 on credit to Dale Dent for $800, Invoice No. 711. (Terms of all credit sales are 2/10, n/60.)

         3   Received inventory and an invoice dated January 30, terms 2/10, n/60, from Able Company, $1,750.

         4   Sold inventory costing $850 on credit to Gary Glen for $1,250, Invoice No. 712.

         5   Purchased on credit from Best Company inventory, $1,855; store supplies, $75; and office supplies, $35. Invoice dated February 4, terms n/10, EOM.

         7   Borrowed $5,000 by giving First National Bank a promissory note payable.

         9   Purchased office equipment on credit from More Company, invoice dated February 6, terms n/10, EOM, $625.

         9   Sent Able Company Check No. 414 in payment of its January 30 invoice less the discount.

      11   Sold inventory costing $1,000 on credit to Carl Cole for $ 1,650, Invoice No. 713.

      12   Received payment from Dale Dent of the February 2 sale less the discount.

      14   Received payment from Gary Glen of the February 4 sale less the discount.

      14   Received inventory and an invoice dated February 11, terms 2/10, n/60, from Old Company, $1,985.

Feb. 14 Issued Check No. 415, payable to Payroll, in payment of sales salaries for the first half of the month, $855. Cashed the check and paid the employees.

14 Cash sales for the first half of the month, $18,460. Cost of this merchandise was $ 9,500. (Normally, cash sales are recorded daily; they are recorded only twice in this problem to reduce the number of repetitive entries.)

14 Post to the customer and creditor accounts and also post any amounts that should be posted as individual amounts to the general ledger accounts. (Normally, such items are posted daily; but you are asked to post them only twice in this problem.)

16 Purchased inventory on credit from Best Company, $410; store supplies, $45; and office supplies, $30. Invoice dated February 12, terms n/10, EOM.

17 Received a credit memorandum from Old Company for unsatisfactory inventory received on February 14 and returned for credit, $85.

18 Received a credit memorandum from More Company for office equipment received on February 9 and returned for credit, $130.

21 Received payment from Carl Cole for the sale of February 11 less the discount.

21 Issued Check No. 416 to Old Company in payment of its invoice of February 11 less the return and the discount.

24 Sold inventory costing $475 on credit to Carl Cole for $835, Invoice No. 714.

26 Sold inventory costing $375 on credit to Gary Glen for $775, Invoice No. 715.

Feb.   28   Issued Check No. 417, payable to Payroll, in payment of sales salaries for the last half of the month, $855. Cashed the check and paid the employees.

     28   Cash sales for the last half of the month, $20,215. Cost of this merchandise was $ 11,500.

     28   Post to the customer and creditor accounts and post any amounts that should be posted as individual amounts to general ledger accounts.

     28   Foot and crossfoot the journals and make the month-end postings.

Required:

1. Open the following general ledger accounts: Cash, Accounts Receivable, Inventory, Store Supplies, Office Supplies, Office Equipment, Notes Payable, Accounts Payable, F. Stone, Capital, Sales, Sales Discounts, Cost of Goods Sold, and Sales Salaries Expense.

2. Open the following accounts receivable ledger accounts: Carl Cole, Dale Dent, and Gary Glen.

3. Open the following accounts payable ledger accounts: Able Company, Best Company, More Company, and Old Company.

4. Enter the transactions in a Sales Journal, a Purchases Journal, a Cash Receipts Journal, a Cash Disbursements Journal, and a General Journal similar to the ones illustrated in this appendix. Post when instructed to do so.

5. Prepare a trial balance and prove the subsidiary ledgers by preparing schedules of accounts receivable and payable.

(If this alternative demonstration problem is not covered in class, see your instructor for the solution.)

Problem I

The following statements are either true or false. Place a (T) in the parentheses before each true statement and an (F) before each false statement.

1. ( ) A Purchases Journal is used to record all purchases.

2. ( ) At month-end, the total sales recorded in the Sales Journal is debited to Accounts Receivable and credited to Sales.

3. ( ) Sales is a General Ledger account.

4. ( ) Transactions recorded in journals do not necessarily result in equal debits and credits to General Ledger accounts.

5. ( ) If a general journal entry is used to record a charge sale, the credit of the entry must be posted twice.

6. ( ) A printer is one example of an input device for a computer system.

7. ( ) Business segment information is required of all U.S. companies.

Problem II

You are given several words, phrases or numbers to choose from in completing each of the following statements or in answering the following questions. In each case select the one that best completes the statement or answers the question and place its letter in the answer space provided.

_____ 1. A company that uses a sales journal, a purchases journal, a cash receipts journal, a cash disbursements journal, and a general journal borrowed $1,500 from the bank in exchange for a note payable to the bank. In which journal would the transaction be recorded?

    a. Sales journal

    b. Purchases journal

    c. Cash receipts journal

    d. Cash disbursements journal

    e. General journal

_____ 2. A company that uses a sales journal, a purchases journal, a cash receipts journal, a cash disbursements journal, and a general journal paid a creditor for office supplies purchased on account. In which journal would the transaction be recorded?

    a. Sales journal

    b. Purchases journal

    c. Cash receipts journal

    d. Cash disbursements journal

    e. General journal

_____ 3. A book of original entry that is designed and used for recording only a specified type of transaction is a:

    a. Check register

    b. Subsidiary ledger

    c. General ledger

    d. Special journal

    e. Schedule of accounts payable

_____ 4. A company that accumulates source documents for a period of time and then processes all at the same time:

    a. is most likely an airline company.

    b. must be using a manual accounting system.

    c. uses batch processing.

    d. uses on-line processing.

    e. always has an up-to-date data base.

Problem III

Many of the important ideas and concepts discussed in Appendix E are reflected in the following list of key terms. Test your understanding of these terms by matching the appropriate definitions with the terms. Record the number identifying the most appropriate definition in the blank space next to each term.

_____ Accounting information system	_____ Enterprise resource planning (ERP) software
_____ Accounts payable ledger	
_____ Accounts receivable ledger	_____ Flexibility principle
_____ Batch processing	_____ Information processor
_____ Business segment	_____ Information storage
_____ Cash disbursements journal	_____ Input device
_____ Cash receipts journal	_____ On-line processing
_____ Check register	_____ Output devices
_____ Columnar journal	_____ Purchases journal
_____ Compatibility principle	_____ Relevance principle
_____ Computer hardware	_____ Sales journal
_____ Computer network	_____ Schedule of accounts payable
_____ Computer software	_____ Schedule of accounts receivable
_____ Controlling account	_____ Segment contribution matrix
_____ Control principle	_____ Special journal
_____ Cost-benefit principle	_____ Subsidiary ledger

1. Means of capturing information from source documents that enables its transfer to information processors.
2. Another name for a cash disbursements journal when the journal has a column for check numbers.
3. Component of an accounting system that keeps data in a form accessible to information processors.
4. List of balances of all the accounts in the accounts receivable ledger and their total.
5. General ledger account, the balance of which (after posting) equals the sum of the balances in its related subsidiary ledger.

6. People, records and methods that collect and process data from transactions and events, organize them into useful forms, and communicate results to decision makers.

7. Special journal used to record all payments of cash; also called *cash payments journal*.

8. Any journal used for recording and posting transactions of a similar type.

9. Information system principle that requires an accounting system to be able to adapt to changes in the company, business, and needs of decision makers.

10. Subsidiary ledger listing individual creditor (supplier) accounts.

11. List of the balances of all accounts in the accounts payable ledger and their totals.

12. Component of an accounting system that interprets, transforms, and summarizes information for use in analyses and reporting.

13. Subsidiary ledger listing individual customer accounts.

14. Information system principle that requires an accounting information system to conform with a company's activities, personnel, and structure.

15. List of individual accounts with a common characteristic; linked to a controlling account in the general ledger.

16. Means by which information is taken out of the accounting system and made available for use.

17. Journal with more than one column.

18. Special journal used to record all receipts of cash.

19. Part of a company that can be separately identified by the products or services that it provides or by the geographic markets that it serves.

20. List of one or more measures (such as sales) by segment; usually in dollars and percents along with a growth rate.

21. Journal used to record sales of merchandise on credit.

22. Information system principle requiring its reports be useful, understandable, timely, and pertinent for decision making.

23. Journal used to record all purchases on credit.

24. Information system principle that requires the benefits from an activity in an accounting information system to outweigh the costs of that activity.

25. Information system principle that requires an accounting information system to aid managers in controlling and monitoring business activities.

26. Programs that direct the operations of computer hardware.

27. Physical equipment in a computerized accounting information system.

28. Linkage giving different users and different computers access to common databases and programs.

29. Programs that manage a company's vital operations, which range from order taking to manufacturing to accounting.

30. Approach to inputting data from source documents as soon as a document is available.

31. Approach that accumulates source documents for a period of time and then processes them all at once such as once a day, week, or month.

Problem IV

Complete the following by filling in the blanks.

1. The five basic components of an accounting system are: source documents, _____, the information processor, _____, and output devices.

2. When a company records sales returns with general journal entries, the credit of an entry recording such a return is posted to two different accounts. This does not cause the trial balance to be out of balance because _____
   _____.

3. Cash sales _____ (are, are not) normally recorded in the Sales Journal.

4. When special journals are used, credit purchases of store supplies or office supplies should be recorded in the _____.

5. The posting principle upon which a subsidiary ledger and its controlling account operate requires that the controlling account be debited for an amount or amounts equal to the sum of _____ to the subsidiary ledger and that the controlling account be credited for an amount or amounts equal to the sum of _____ to the subsidiary ledger.

6. Cash purchases of store supplies or office supplies should be recorded in a(n) _____.

7. When a subsidiary Accounts Receivable Ledger is maintained, the equality of the debits and credits posted to the General Ledger is proved by preparing _____. At the same time the balances of the customer accounts in the Accounts Receivable Ledger are proved by preparing _____.

8. Business _____ information is required of public companies with material operations in more than one industry. The categories of required reporting information include: revenues, _____ (before interest and taxes), capital expenditures, depreciation and amortization expense, and _____.

Problem V

The journals and ledgers of McGuff Company appear on the following pages. All transactions through September 29 have already been journalized and posted and, as such, are already entered into those journals and ledgers. The following is a list of the transactions completed on September 30.

Sept. 30   Received an $808.50 check from Ted Clark in full payment of the September 20, $825 sale, less the $16.50 discount.

30   Received a $550 check from a tenant in payment of his September rent.

30   Sold merchandise costing $840 to Inez Smythe for $1,675 on credit, Invoice No. 655.

30   Received merchandise and an invoice dated September 28, terms 2/10, n/60 from Johnson Company, $4,000.

30   Purchased store equipment on account from Olson Company, invoice dated September 30, terms n/10, EOM, $950.

30   Issued Check No. 525 to Kerry Meadows in payment of her $650 salary.

30   Issued Check No. 526 for $1,715 to Olson Company in full payment of its September 20 invoice, less–a $35 discount.

30   Received a credit memorandum from Olson Company for unsatisfactory merchandise received on September 24 and returned for credit, $625.

30   Cash sales for the last half of the month totaled $9,450.50. This merchandise cost $4,275.

Required:

1. Enter the nine transactions described above in the company's journals.

2. Make the necessary postings to the accounts receivable and accounts payable subsidiary ledgers.

3. Foot and crossfoot the journals and make the month-end postings to the general ledger.

4. Complete the trial balance and test the subsidiary ledgers by preparing schedules of accounts receivable and accounts payable.

GENERAL JOURNAL   Page 17

DATE	ACCOUNT TITLES AND EXPLANATION	P.R.	DEBIT	CREDIT

SALES JOURNAL   PAGE 8

DATE	ACCOUNT DEBITED	INVOICE NUMBER	P.R.	Accts Receivable Dr. Sales Cr.				Cost of Goods Sold Dr. Inventory Cr.			
20--- SEPT. 3	N.R. Boswell	651	√	1	8	7	5	00	9	5	0	00
15	Inez Smythe	652	√	1	5	0	0	00	8	0	0	00
20	Ted Clark	653	√		8	2	5	00	4	2	0	00
24	N.R. Boswell	654	√	2	2	5	0	00	1	2	5	00

PURCHASES JOURNAL   Page 8

DATE	ACCOUNT	DATE OF INVOICE	TERMS	P.R.	ACCOUNTS PAYABLE CREDIT				INVENTORY DEBIT				OTHER ACCOUNTS DEBIT
20--- Sept. 8	Johnson Company	9/6	2/10, n/60	√	3	7	5	0	00	3	7	5	0	00	
22	Olson Company	9/20	2/10, n/60	√	1	7	5	0	00	1	7	5	0	00	
24	Olson Company	9/22	2/10. n/60	√	5	6	2	5	00	5	6	2	5	00	

CASH RECEIPTS JOURNAL

DATE	ACCOUNT CREDITED	P.R.	CASH DEBIT	SALES DISCOUNT DEBIT	ACCOUNTS RECEIVABLE CREDIT	SALES CREDIT	OTHER ACCOUNTS CREDIT	Cost of Goods Sold Dr. Inventory Cr.
20—Sept. 1	Rent Earned	406	5 5 0 00				5 5 0 00	
13	N.R. Boswell	√	1 8 3 7 50	3 7 50	1 8 7 5 00			
15	Sales	√	9 0 0 0 00			9 0 0 0 00		4 6 0 0 00

CASH DISBURSEMENTS JOURNAL

DATE	CH. NO.	PAYEE	ACCOUNT DEBITED	P.R.	CASH CREDIT	INVENTORY CREDIT	OTHER ACCOUNTS DEBIT	ACCOUNTS PAYABLE DEBIT
20—Sept. 15	523	Kerry Meadows	Salaries Expense	622	6 5 0 00		6 5 0 00	
16	524	Johnson Company	Johnson Company	√	3 6 7 5 00	7 5 00		3 7 5 0 00

ACCOUNTS RECEIVABLE LEDGER

N.R. Boswell

2200 Falstaff Street

DATE	EXPLANATION	P.R.	DEBIT			CREDIT			BALANCE		
20--- Sept. 3		S-8	1	8 7 5	00				1	8 7 5	00
13		R-9				1	8 7 5	00			
24		S-8	2	2 5 0	00				2	2 5 0	00

Ted Clark

10765 Catonsville Avenue

DATE	EXPLANATION	P.R.	DEBIT			CREDIT			BALANCE		
20--- Sept. 20		S-8		8 2 5	00					8 2 5	00

Inez Smythe

785 Violette Circle

DATE	EXPLANATION	P.R.	DEBIT			CREDIT			BALANCE		
20--- Sept. 15		S-8	1	5 0 0	00				1	5 0 0	00

ACCOUNTS PAYABLE LEDGER

Johnson Company

118 E. Seventh Street

DATE	EXPLANATION	P.R.	DEBIT			CREDIT			BALANCE		
20--- Sept. 8		P-8				3	7 5 0	00	3	7 5 0	00
16		D-7	3	7 5 0	00					- 0 -	

Olson Company

788 Hazelwood Avenue

DATE	EXPLANATION	P.R.	DEBIT	CREDIT	BALANCE
20--- Sept. 22		P-8		1 7 5 0 00	1 7 5 0 00
24		p-8		5 6 2 5 00	7 3 7 5 00

GENERAL LEDGER

Cash   Account No. 101

DATE	EXPLANATION	P.R.	DEBIT	CREDIT	BALANCE

Accounts Receivable   Account No. 106

DATE	EXPLANATION	P.R.	DEBIT	CREDIT	BALANCE

Inventory   Account No.107

DATE	EXPLANATION	P.R.	DEBIT	CREDIT	BALANCE

Store Equipment   Account No. 165

DATE	EXPLANATION	P.R.	DEBIT	CREDIT	BALANCE

Accounts Payable   Account No.201

DATE	EXPLANATION	P.R.	DEBIT	CREDIT	BALANCE

Rent Earned   Account No. 406

DATE	EXPLANATION	P.R.	DEBIT	CREDIT	BALANCE
20--- Sept. 1		R-9		5 5 0 00	5 5 0 00

Sales   Account No. 413

DATE	EXPLANATION	P.R.	DEBIT	CREDIT	BALANCE

Sales Discounts   Account No. 415

DATE	EXPLANATION	P.R.	DEBIT	CREDIT	BALANCE

Cost of Goods Sold   Account No. 613

DATE	EXPLANATION	P.R.	DEBIT	CREDIT	BALANCE

Salaries Expense   Account No. 622

DATE	EXPLANATION	P.R.	DEBIT	CREDIT	BALANCE
20--- Sept. 15		D-7	6 5 0 00		6 5 0 00

MCGUFF COMPANY

Trial Balance

September 30, 20--

	Cash							
	Accounts receivable							
	Inventory							
	Store equipment							
	Accounts payable							
	Rent earned							
	Sales							
	Sales discounts							
	Cost of goods sold							
	Salaries expense							

MCGUFF COMPANY

Schedule of Accounts Receivable

September 30, 20--

MCGUFF COMPANY

Schedule of Accounts Payable

September 30, 20--

Solutions for Appendix E

Problem I

1. F
2. T
3. T
4. F
5. F
6. F
7. F

Problem II

1. C
2. D
3. D
4. C

Problem III

6	Accounting information system	29	Enterprise resource planning (erp) software
10	Accounts payable ledger		
13	Accounts receivable ledger	9	Flexibility principle
31	Batch processing	12	Information processor
19	Business segment	3	Information storage
7	Cash disbursements journal	1	Input device
18	Cash receipts journal	30	On-line processing
2	Check register	16	Output devices
17	Columnar journal	23	Purchases journal
14	Compatibility principle	22	Relevance principle
27	Computer hardware	21	Sales journal
28	Computer network	11	Schedule of accounts payable
26	Computer software	4	Schedule of accounts receivable
5	Controlling account	20	Segment contribution matrix
25	Control principle	8	Special journal
24	Cost-benefit principle	15	Subsidiary ledger

Problem IV

1. input devices; information storage
2. only the balance of one of the accounts, the Accounts Receivable account, appears on the trial balance.
3. are not
4. Purchases journal
5. the debits posted; the credits posted
6. cash disbursements journal
7. a trial balance; a schedule of accounts receivable
8. segment; operating profits; identifiable assets

Problem V

DATE		ACCOUNT TITLES AND EXPLANATION	P.R.	DEBIT				CREDIT			
Sept	30	Accounts Payable-Olson Company	201/√	6	2	5	00				
		Inventory	107					6	2	5	00

DATE	ACCOUNT DEBITED	INVOICE NUMBER	P.R.	Accts Receivable Dr. Sales Cr.					Cost of Goods Sold Dr. Inventory Cr.				
20--- SEPT. 3	N.R. Boswell	651	√		1	8	7	5	00		9	5	0	00
15	Inez Smythe	652	√		1	5	0	0	00		8	0	0	00
20	Ted Clark	653	√			8	2	5	00		4	2	0	00
24	N.R. Boswell	654	√		2	2	5	0	00		1	2	5	00
30	Inez Smythe	655	√		1	6	7	5	00		8	4	0	00
30	Totals.				8	1	2	5	00	3	1	3	5	00
						(106/413)					(501/107)			

DATE	ACCOUNT	DATE OF INVOICE	TERMS	P.R.	ACCOUNTS PAYABLE CREDIT				INVENTORY DEBIT				OTHER ACCOUNTS DEBIT			
20--- Sept. 8	Johnson Company	9/6	2/10, n/60	√	3	7 5 0		00	3	7 5 0		00				
22	Olson Company	9/20	2/10, n/60	√	1	7 5 0		00	1	7 5 0		00				
24	Olson Company	9/22	2/10. n/60	√	5	6 2 5		00	5	6 2 5		00				
30	Johnson Company	9/28	2/10, n/60	√	4	0 0 0		00	4	0 0 0		00				
30	Str Equip/Olsn Co.	9/30	n/10 EOM	165√		9 5 0		00						9 5 0		00
30	Totals				16	0 7 5		00	15	1 2 5		00		9 5 0		00
						(201)				(107)				(√)		

CASH RECEIPTS JOURNAL

DATE	ACCOUNT CREDITED	P.R.	CASH DEBIT	SALES DISCOUNT DEBIT	ACCOUNTS RECEIVABLE CREDIT	SALES CREDIT	OTHER ACCOUNTS CREDIT	Cost of Goods Sold Debit Inventory Cr.
20--								
Sept. 1	Rent Earned	406	5 5 0 00				5 5 0 00	
13	N.R. Boswell	√	1 8 3 7 50	3 7 50	1 8 7 5 00			
15	Sales	√	9 0 0 0 00			9 0 0 0 00		
30	Ted Clark	√	8 0 8 50	1 6 50	8 2 5 00			4 6 0 0 00
30	Rent Earned	406	5 5 0 00				5 5 0 00	
30	Sales	√	9 4 5 0 50			9 4 5 0 50		4 2 7 5 00
30	Totals		22 1 9 6 50	5 4 00	2 7 0 0 00	18 4 5 0 50	1 1 0 0 00	8 8 7 5 00
			(101)	(415)	(106)	(413)	(√)	(501/107)

CASH DISBURSEMENTS JOURNAL

DATE	CH. NO.	PAYEE	ACCOUNT DEBITED	P.R.	CASH CREDIT	INVENTORY CREDIT	OTHER ACCOUNTS DEBIT	ACCOUNTS PAYABLE DEBIT
20--								
Sept. 15	523	Kerry Meadows	Salaries Expense	622	6 5 0 00		6 5 0 00	
16	524	Johnson Company		√	3 6 7 5 00	7 5 00		3 7 5 0 00
30	525	Kerry Meadows	Salaries Expense	622	6 5 0 00		6 5 0 00	
30	526	Olson Company		√	1 7 1 5 00	3 5 00		1 7 5 0 00
30		Totals			6 6 9 0 00	1 1 0 00	1 3 0 0 00	5 5 0 0 00
					(101)	(107)	(√)	(201)

GENERAL LEDGER

Cash   No. 101

Date	Debit	Credit	Balance
Sept. 30	22,196.50		22,196.50
30		6,690.00	15,506.50

Accounts Receivable   No. 106

Date	Debit	Credit	Balance
Sept. 30	8,125.00		8,125.00
30		2,700.00	5,425.00

Inventory   No. 107

Date	Debit	Credit	Balance
Sept. 30	15,125.00		15,125.00
30		625.00	14,500.00
30		110.00	14,390.00
30		3,135.00	11,255.00
30		8,875.00	2,380.00

Store Equipment   No. 165

Date	Debit	Credit	Balance
Sept. 30	950.00		950.00

Accounts Payable   No. 201

Date	Debit	Credit	Balance
Sept 30		16,075.00	16,075.00
30	5,500.00		10,575.00
30	625.00		9,950.00

Rent Earned   No. 406

Date	Debit	Credit	Balance
Sept. 1		550.00	550.00
30		550.00	1,100.00

Sales   No. 413

Date	Debit	Credit	Balance
Sept. 30		8,125.00	8,125.00
30		18,450.50	26,575.50

Sales Discounts   No. 415

Date	Debit	Credit	Balance
Sept. 30	54.00		54.00

Cost of Goods Sold   No. 501

Date	Debit	Credit	Balance
Sept. 30	3,135.00		3,135.00
30	8,875.00		12,010.00

Salaries Expense   No. 622

Date	Debit	Credit	Balance
Sept. 15	650.00		650.00
30	650.00		1,300.00

ACCOUNTS PAYABLE LEDGER

Johnson Company

Date	Debit	Credit	Balance
Sept. 8		3,750.00	3,750.00
16	3,750.00		-0-
30		4,000.00	4,000.00

Olson Company

Date	Debit	Credit	Balance
Sept. 22		1,750.00	1,750.00
24		5,625.00	7,375.00
30		950.00	8,325.00
30	1,750.00		6,575.00
30	625.00		5,950.00

ACCOUNTS RECEIVABLE LEDGER

N.R. Boswell

Date	Debit	Credit	Balance
Sept. 3	1,875.00		1,875.00
13		1,875.00	-0-
24	2,250.00		2,250.00

Inez Smythe

Date	Debit	Credit	Balance
Sept. 15	1,500.00		1,500.00
30	1,675.00	5,625.00	3,175.00

Ted Clark

Date	Debit	Credit	Balance
Sept. 20	825.00		825.00
30		825.00	-0-

MCGUFF COMPANY
Trial Balance
September 30, 20--

Cash	$15,506.50	
Accounts receivable	5,425.00	
Inventory	2,380.00	
Store equipment	950.00	
Accounts payable		$ 9,950.00
Rent earned		1,100.00
Sales		26,575.50
Sales discounts	54.00	
Cost of goods sold	12,010.00	
Salaries expense	1,300.00	
Totals	$37,625.50	$37,625.50

MCGUFF COMPANY
Schedule of Accounts Receivable
September 30, 20--

N.R. Boswell	$2,250.00
Inez Smythe	3,175.00
Total accounts receivable	$5,425.00

MCGUFF COMPANY
Schedule of Accounts Payable
September 30, 20--

Johnson Company	$4,000.00
Olson Company	5,950.00
Total accounts payable	$9,950.00